The 2005
Washington Nationals

# The 2005 Washington Nationals

*Major League Baseball Returns to the Capital*

TED LEAVENGOOD

McFarland & Company, Inc., Publishers
*Jefferson, North Carolina, and London*

Photographs by George R. Clark

LIBRARY OF CONGRESS CATALOGUING-IN-PUBLICATION DATA

Leavengood, Ted.
    The 2005 Washington Nationals : Major League baseball returns to the capital / Ted Leavengood.
       p.    cm.
    Includes index.

    ISBN-13: 978-0-7864-2678-2
    ISBN-10: 0-7864-2678-0
    (softcover : 50# alkaline paper) ∞

GV875.W27L43   2006
796.357/6409753—dc22                           2006025155

British Library cataloguing data are available

©2006 Ted Leavengood. All rights reserved

*No part of this book may be reproduced or transmitted in any form or by any means, electronic or mechanical, including photocopying or recording, or by any information storage and retrieval system, without permission in writing from the publisher.*

On the cover: Nick Johnson, Washington Nationals first baseman, at bat. (photograph courtesy of George R. Clark)

Manufactured in the United States of America

*McFarland & Company, Inc., Publishers*
  *Box 611, Jefferson, North Carolina 28640*
    *www.mcfarlandpub.com*

For Bill and Clara Leavengood

# Contents

*Introduction* .................................................. 1

———————— **PART ONE** ————————

1. Do You Believe in Magic? ........................... 11
2. In for the Long Haul ................................. 27
3. After the Thrill Is Gone ............................. 35
4. Playing in the Shadows ............................. 45
5. Cream at the Fillmore West ....................... 56
6. Seven Days in May ................................... 62
7. Oh, Canada ............................................. 75
8. Where's That Famous Golden Touch? ......... 82
9. There's No Place Like Home ..................... 97
10. Money Buys You Everything .................... 115
11. Won't Wipe Off Your Face, No Matter How Hard You Try ............................................ 127

———————— **PART TWO** ————————

12. That Little Something Extra ..................... 145
13. I Put a Spell on You ................................. 153

14. Head to Head at the Ted .............................. 167
15. It Takes a Worried Mind ............................. 174
16. Baby, I Always Take the Long Way Home .............. 185
17. Staying the Course .................................. 199
18. Cry Me a River ..................................... 213
19. Just Another Turner Classic Movie ................... 225
20. Trojan Horse ....................................... 237
21. Our Winning Season ................................ 244

*Epilogue* ................................................. 258
*Appendix* ................................................ 261
*Index* ................................................... 265

# Introduction

Like a friendly building superintendent—good with the gab but slow with the furnace—the Washington Senators were a dependable presence in the basement of the American League during much of the 20th century. During the last decade of the 19th century, Washington played in the National League, where they were often at the bottom of the standings. Financial concerns led the Senior Circuit to consolidate into eight teams in 1900, dropping the Washington franchise and three others. After only a single season without a professional team in Washington, the Senators became one of the eight original teams that formed the American League for its inaugural year of 1901.

An overflow throng of more than 10,000 fans gathered to watch their new team in the stadium that carpenters had finished only days before the season began. The now defunct *Washington Star* described the opening day crowd of late April 1901. "The commodious grandstand packed ... enthusiasm was rampant," the newspaper reported, going on to describe how Admiral Dewey, the hero of Manila Bay, received a standing ovation as he paraded to his seat during pre-game festivities. The Senators, playing in blue and gray uniforms, won that opener against the Baltimore Orioles, the ill-fated club that would give way to the New York Highlanders (Yankees) in 1903.

The Washington team started well in 1901, but they finished last. The Senators stayed at the bottom each year until Clark Griffith took over as manager of the team in 1911.

The herald of a new era in Washington baseball, Griffith was a superb player in his own right. A pitcher who won more than twenty games on seven different occasions during the 1890s for the Chicago clubs, he proved just as capable as manager, and with Walter Johnson on the mound his team began to compete seriously. Griffith bought the Senators outright in 1920 after failing to convince the team owners to spend money for the best talent.

By 1924 Griffith had put together his best team. With Goose Goslin in left field, manager Bucky Harris at second, and Walter Johnson pitching the best season of his career, the Senators won their first pennant that year, edging the Yankees and Babe Ruth. They went on to beat the Giants in an exciting seven-game World Series that was not decided until the twelfth inning of the last game. Griffith kept the team competitive and they came back to win the pennant again in 1925 (although they lost the series in seven games to Pittsburgh). With Walter Johnson as both pitcher and manager, the team stayed competitive throughout the 1920s, and when Griffith brought in a young shortstop named Joe Cronin to take over in 1933, the future looked rosy.

Cronin led the Senators to the pennant again that year, but they lost to the Giants in the series. It was the last pennant the Senators would win. The following year they finished seventh and attendance plummeted. With depression era financing difficult, Griffith sold Cronin to the Red Sox after the 1934 season to cover his losses on the team.

The sale of Joe Cronin to the Red Sox was as much a curse for the Senators as the more famous urban myth surrounding Babe Ruth's sale to the Yankees. The Senators after 1934 became a benchmark of futility, a cultural icon of haplessness. Clark Griffith died in 1955 and left the team to his adopted son, Calvin Griffith, who believed from the start that baseball was doomed in the nation's capital. Protests from President Eisenhower and Congress could not dissuade him from moving the team to Minneapolis in 1960, although a deal was worked out that Washington would get an expansion franchise to start the next season.

The futility continued for the new Senators, though such greats as Ted Williams tried to bail the team out during the late 1960s. By the end of that decade the nation was facing far more serious concerns than the demise of baseball in Washington, D.C. Race riots spread from major cities to small ones and a million angry Vietnam War protesters marched down Pennsylvania Avenue. At the end of the 1971 season, when baseball quietly slipped away from D.C., it was just another tear in a national fabric already rent in so many places.

During the three decades that the Senators' fans wandered the baseball wilderness, the Baltimore Orioles provided sustenance. From the posh green suburbs of Montgomery County in Maryland and the equally affluent Northern Virginia population centers of Alexandria and Arlington County, Washington baseball fans drove north to Baltimore, about an hour's trip.

Then, in the late 1980s, the State of Maryland and its governor decreed a new stadium should be built for their flagship sports franchise, the Orioles, a stadium located so that it could become a home for Washington, D.C.'s lost baseball fans. The resulting baseball complex was, at its birth, a masterpiece, so much so that other cities copied its style, often in considerable detail. The location near the I-95 interchange was intended to cut down on driving time for Washington fans as they made their way to the D.C. Beltway.

The long drive to the beautiful Baltimore ball field—Camden Yards—is dull, the landscape a suburban null set of low-flung office buildings and interchangeable condo tracts until the skyline of the old industrial city appears on the horizon. As you drive into Baltimore on I-95, you arc high above the city's sprawling industrial heartland on a spaghetti ribbon of pavement that leads west to the park. To the east of the highway the Baltimore port is visible, with its huge derricks that pluck containers from ships that can be seen coming and going in the distance. The sight of that skyline came to signify to children in the back seat that they had arrived at the home of baseball for D.C. fans.

Ultimately, Camden Yards is the house that Cal Ripken built. Cal Ripken is what everyone was paying to see in the early days of Camden Yards. He was the franchise player, the overly tall shortstop who used that size to add power to a position that was more known for speed and agility. Ripken was a smart baseball player and he positioned himself in the field just right, to counter his lack of speed, so that he could get to balls hit deep into the hole between second and third base or hit over the second base bag. He set fielding records for consistency. And he could hit, better than anyone who had played the position previously, before the onslaught of taller and more robust shortstops for whom he paved the way.

Fans came to see Ripken because he was always, always there, the Iron Man who did not bend or break. They came to see him best Lou Gehrig's record of consecutive games played, which stood at 2,130. The games when Ripken tied then broke the record in 1995 are part of Maryland lore shared with D.C. fans who rode the train or drove to see the spectacle as it unfolded over two glorious nights. Ripken ended his streak in 1998 and retired as an active player in 2001.

It seems long ago that those great teams the Orioles fielded in the mid-1990s played with Cal at short. Kids revered him, read primary school books about his life, made posters to bring to class and proudly read their reports on those books and his legend. Yet, even at its zenith, when the arc of baseball legend was high above the cities of Baltimore and Washington, even when the fans were in love with the experience, baseball games had gotten longer, like the distance to Baltimore.

Old Senators hats could be seen there at Camden Yards, a rare item to be certain; but still refusing to go into that good night, they remained a symbol of hope for D.C. fans. Orioles management patronized D.C. fans, setting up an office in downtown D.C. and holding appreciation events that won the hearts of young fans. Yet the sight of those old Senators hats and jerseys mixed in among the orange and black at Camden Yards gave voice to the unspoken truth that D.C. residents knew in their hearts. The Orioles were a substitute team. When the time of Ripken passed, when there was less and less waiting at the other end of the long drive from Washington, the longing of Washington fans for their own team germinated in the fertile soil around the nation's capital and would not go away.

In the spring of 1999, after Sosa and McGwire's famous home run duel, Mayor Tony Williams was the first to promise with some credibility that baseball would be back at Robert F. Kennedy Stadium, the setting a final exhibition game between the Cardinals and the Expos. Before the ceremonies began, Mark McGwire delighted the fans by depositing batting practice pitches high up into the yellow seats where Frank Howard's moon shots are recorded by open white seats. One McGwire shot hit the light standards high above the roof. It was baseball legend on display, there where it had once belonged.

The promise from Mayor Tony Williams was not an idle one. He had erased the economic and political cloud under which the city of Washington had lived for so long. Could he bring baseball back as well? If Tony Williams could exorcise the ghost of Marion Barry, was he up to the task of handling Bud Selig and Jerry Reinsdorf? That spring day the mayor introduced the Montreal Expos with knowing asides about their potential as the next Washington baseball team. They were prophetic words, and with McGwire's autograph in hand, my young daughter and I savored them and waited.

It has been a frustrating and seemingly endless interlude. Thirty-plus years for some, less for others, but by any standard a long wait, and wrestling it to the ground has been fraught with emotional costs. Mayor Williams and others have had to confront more than just Bud Selig. The last indignity came from the Orioles' owner, Peter Angelos.

Angelos, who purchased the Orioles franchise during the final years of Ripken's career, put a different mark on Baltimore baseball. The "Orioles Way" was never about big money, but about developing great pitchers, playing good defense, and getting the three-run home run. Yet Angelos made big money as a lawyer and it seemed more natural for him to create a winner by buying talent rather than by building it.

The Orioles' owner made his view clear from the beginning, that the only way to compete with wealthy teams like the New York Yankees and the Boston Red Sox was by creating a regional franchise, uniting Washington and Baltimore into a single megamarket whose media wealth could match even New York's. He ignored the ethic of small market teams who compete successfully with the Yankees, and in doing so positioned himself squarely in the path of all attempts by Washington, D.C., to obtain a franchise. Finally pulled kicking and screaming out of the way, he made a last attempt to sabotage the team by freezing local television distribution and carving out a very limited piece for the new Nationals team. For many who had once been Orioles fans it was the last straw.

Parting ways with Baltimore was like a divorce, an ugly one where the property is split contentiously and the friends all take sides. As with any divorce, the toughest part is the children. How do you tell the children who grew up reading the Ripken Life Story, who have the autographed picture of his three thousandth hit hanging in their rooms and still occasionally wear the faded T-shirts that commemorate those days?

The best way Washington fans have found to get their children beyond despair is to immerse them in the joys of life with their new family. Children are everywhere at RFK. Kids with tongues blue from cotton candy, kids standing along the rail yelling, "Mr. Wilkerson, Mr. Wilkerson, sign my glove!" There is no Cal Ripken, but that transition had already been made; learning a whole new set of heroes has become part of being a mature fan.

This new family is uniquely Washington, from the commuters taking the subway to the games, to the federal workers taking the afternoon off to catch a game. We are all Washington Nationals fans now, the kids, the parents, the feds, the lobbyists, the pundits and the lawmakers. It all dawned very quickly. First there was no team, then there was, then maybe not, then there was and it was March and only a month to learn the new players, to get tickets, to finish the improvements to the stadium, to find out where and how to get the games on TV or radio.

Finally, in April when the Mets and the Nationals played an exhibition game, there was no denying it was going to happen. What had taken forever, or, more precisely, 33 years, emerged, and when Washington, D.C., fans walked through the turnstiles at RFK stadium for the first time the thrill was compounded by all those years of waiting and wondering. Washington fans had lived with a nice adopted family up in Baltimore, and that family deserve thanks for the good times they shared with us; but getting your own baseball family was like coming home; and there is nothing that can compare with it.

Opening night at RKF affected me deeply for some reason, and as I took it all in through the haze of fireworks and shimmering lights I resolved to record my impressions about a unique moment in Washington's sports history. This is a collection of notes I took as a fan watching dozens of games at RFK stadium where the Washington Nationals played their first year. Unlike many people in the area, I was lucky enough to have cable access to the Nationals' games and to take in games narrated by the Yale-educated Ron Darling— sounding for all the world like James Woods—and Mel Proctor, Darling's well-traveled broadcast partner.

Darling is a constant source of intelligent insight into the game for a town that has an average educational attainment level some years into graduate school. His career with the Mets is well remembered by baseball fans my age, and his storied duel with Frank Viola when Darling pitched for Yale and Viola pitched for St. Johns is a great and memorable bit of baseball lore from 1981, especially as recounted in *The Web of the Game* by Roger Angell (*Late Innings*, New York: Simon and Schuster, 1982).

When the games are *not* televised they are available on the radio. As a federal worker, I am proud that the radio broadcasts emanate from WFED—fed radio—for all us bureaucrats our very own radio station. On some evenings, and in certain locations around town, WFED is barely detectable, its tiny signal reduced to a whisper. It is a detriment to the team that it cannot be heard more easily. But there is an eerie familiarity to the situation when I glue my ears to a radio, tuning desperately to hear what has happened as the signal fades in and out. It's almost like it was when I was a kid in high school, those summers with nothing special to do, trying to tune my car radio or a hand-held transistor to KMOX radio in St. Louis that beamed games to all of us Southerners too small-town for major league baseball. What a team that was: Lou Brock, Bob Gibson, Kenny Boyer, and Curt Flood. They beat the Yankees and the Red Sox, and they should have beaten the Tigers, too. But 1968 was not a good year for much of anyone, except Richard Nixon. It was worth straining to hear Jack Buck even when the signal faded. It was all we had. Now we have much, much more.

At my age there is no further need for exploration. I have arrived at my baseball destination and I will be a Nationals fan regardless of what else comes down the pike. This is a story of settling in by the Washington fans, of their coming to know and understand the various players and other complex personalities that make up the Washington Nationals.

One's experience of a team and a season stretch across the broad field. There is so much more than the games, though they are the highlight. Apart from the games, fans embrace topics such as the steroids controversy, while deeper discussion is saved for questions such as where statistical analysis makes sense and old school doesn't. Discussing the Nationals and how the team fits into its era is as much a pastime as the game itself. For me, a big part of the Nationals' story has been watching and listening as new families of fans discover all they have missed these long years. Covering that part of this drama has been an especially compelling joy for me.

The people who share space at RFK for baseball D.C.-style are distinct and absolutely without rival. The stands are awash with political pundits, with conservatives to be found in left field and liberals in right, and the melting pot of ethnicity offers up a richer roux than elsewhere. In noting the games I have tried to share the random interplay of fans in this first year at RFK, their mundane and perceptive insights into the game and into life itself, some of which rise to the level of wisdom and others to a higher threshold, that of wry humor.

It has been fun to watch my wife, who had never been a fan, pay attention to the game for the first time. She has even on rare occasions settled in before the TV screen and enjoyed the athleticism she sees on display. New to ESPN's play of the week countdown and Jeter's long throw from the hole, she has adapted remarkably well to my fixation with the Nationals and faithfully watched me through this venture of recording the season.

In recent years there have been too few occasions to go to games with my now almost-grown daughters. My baseball history with each of them is as different as my daughters are unique in their humanity. My daughter Julia, a junior at Beloit College, encouraged me in this project from the start and has gotten me over a few rough spots with kind words and a trip or two to RFK. Claire, my younger daughter and quite ready to graduate from high school, is my oldest baseball buddy. Exploring the game with her when she was growing up made it all the more important to me.

Sometimes baseball is not a smooth ride on a Sunday afternoon, even for the fan. The game is also about the political and economic culture in which it plays itself out. The story of the Washington Nationals' first season is about how things can be put back together after a fall and about how possibility and potential can be reborn. The Nationals are a story of resilience, of swimming upstream against baseball's inability to resolve the conflict between owners and players. That conflict carries forward today largely underground, yet its tensions define much that happens in the still unfolding story of the Nationals.

Who will own the team? Who will wear the crown—local or outsider? The answer to these questions appears caught in the maelstrom of current discord; but by looking back over the history of the team we can see these same issues have been there from the start. Whether Ban Johnson, Judge Landis, or Bud Selig, every era has a defining personality at the top, and in Washington that fact has taken on more importance than it should. Yet a resolution to these issues has not yet occurred and even the longer term perspective illustrates just how important a successful settlement can be. Clark Griffeth brought baseball success to a town that had never known it, the same way Bobby Cox brought it to Atlanta and Theo Epstein to Boston. Washington fans more than any others deserve better than they have gotten from league management.

The 2005 season has shown that Washington will have its day again. Seeing the way through the clouds may be difficult, but this magical season has ultimately been about blue skies. The wife of a friend told me at RFK that she had not seen me this happy in many years. I thought about it and realized she was right. I have had many proud and glorious moments as a parent; but there has not been enough of what my friend Reverend Ed Winkler calls "happy feet." Baseball and this singular season have brought me a happiness I have not known in a while, serving as an enduring distraction that defies whether the threat level is elevated, whether social security is in crisis, or whether my triglycerides are peaking.

I would like to thank my many friends, who helped bring me out of the doldrums and created the true spirit of this endeavor. My wife has looked on with bemusement as I labored to bring this idea forth. But when Tom Goldstein was kind enough to publish a piece of it in *Elysian Fields Quarterly* and my wife said how proud she was, I cannot think of a moment since our wedding and the birth of our children that brought more joy. Our friend Maida Tryon deserves special thanks for her kind words, but more importantly for helping to edit the manuscript. Bernie McShane and Bill Seedyke, fresh from their writing classes, were there to help get the idea off the ground. Our oldest friend, Melissa Greene, shared many years ago what fun writing can be and offered helpful insights at several junctures this season, despite being busy at what I know will be a very special task.

George Clark and his wife Mary, who got the season tickets and took the many wonderful pictures, deserve grateful recognition, as does Brent Bolin, who scored the opening day tickets and prowled RFK with me. Then there is my friend, Reverend Ed Winkler, who can counsel from so many perspectives, even from his membership in the Society of American Baseball Research. The sharing that goes on at the ballpark crosses many disciplines, yet the magic of baseball is for fans a simple but essential beauty: there is no more precious alchemy than the company of family and friends, and the unique opportunity baseball allows us to spend a little time together under the stars.

# Part One

In its beauty and design that vision of the soaring stands, the pattern of forty thousand empetalled faces, the velvet and unalterable geometry of the playing field, and the small lean figures of the players, set there, lonely, tense and waiting in their places, bright desperately solitary atoms encircled by that huge wall of nameless faces, is incredible.

—Thomas Wolfe, *Of Time and the River*

# 1

# Do You Believe in Magic?

Your eyes are drawn immediately to the field, the green, green field. The construction workers who queued around portable canteens in front of Robert F. Kennedy Memorial Stadium during the cold days of February and March 2005 made RFK ready for opening day in April. Yet there must have been unseen hands helping them, leprechauns, no doubt, who made the field so green. It is the first thing the fans see on Opening Night as they pour through the main gate for the inaugural game at RFK, in this the inaugural season for the Washington Nationals. The aura of wide-eyed disbelief is in every face as their eyes take in the red, orange and yellow bands of seating across the field. They can see the stands filling, the multicolored array of Nationals T-shirts and caps, but the thing of greatest beauty is that field and its magic emerald color.

The sky is clear, the temperature perfect, and those secret service agents with the cool shades—who could ask for more than this. A dozen or so snipers patrol the roof, hundreds of gun toting, Kevlar vested gym rats search bags, wanding the butts of fans as they stream into the stadium. None of the secret and not-so-secret service can suppress the joy of a beautiful spring evening and a historic event so alien to the veneer of false drama that it is gone in the snap of a finger, replaced by the slooshing sound of a keg full of dark Irish beer jetting into a plastic cup, rinsing away any thought other than the joys of the ballpark on a great day, the stadium filling with a great sea of fans.

This Washington baseball team has stirred interest at every social level with its mere presence as fans adapt to the idea of the retread Montreal Expos, now the Washington Nationals. Their record heading into opening night stands at five wins and four losses against the best of the National League East. The winning record, even so early, is a surprise and generates a rush of enthusiasm across D.C. It's not just any team, it's a winning team; it's ours, and people are starting to take notice. Players like Brad Wilkerson, the center

**The soaring stands, the 40,000 empetalled faces.**

fielder, have hit for the cycle—a home run, triple, double, and single in one game. Kids are reading of Wilkerson's feat in the box scores around the same breakfast tables where their older brothers and sisters followed Cal Ripken for years. They spend the afternoon looking through their baseball cards to find out about this new hero. Now they want to see him manning center field in the opener.

"He hit 32 home runs last year," says one kid holding up a shiny paper card.

"Says he holds a record for home runs in college," says his friend.

"No kidding. Where'd he go?" asks kid one.

"Florida. Think we can get his autograph?" asks kid two, tucking the card into his shirt pocket beside a Sharpie pen.

The Nationals, like any major league team, have an impressive array of talent to delight any young fan. Wilkerson set collegiate home run records that have yet to be broken at the University of Florida, was a "Mr. Baseball" in the basketball crazed state of Kentucky, and looks as boyish as any of the youngsters straining chest forward across the outfield rail and calling to him to sign

The crowd.

their hats and gloves before the game. He is just the first of many heroes wearing a Nationals uniform with which kids will identify, the first of many who will bring to mind the games at RFK as naturally as the kids cram a hot dog down a hungry throat.

Long lines of dour fans stand grumbling during the seventh inning stretch, waiting as plates of empty buns languish while frozen hot dogs thaw slowly on the grill; but by then Livan Hernandez has struck out Troy Glaus and Shawn Green with nasty slow stuff that has the Diamondbacks off stride all evening. Hernandez allows only one hit over the first eight innings. After a three-run homer in the ninth pulls Arizona to within two at 5–3, Frank Robinson takes the ball from him on the mound. For his masterful performance, Hernandez receives a long, noisy standing ovation. He does not doff his cap, as is the tradition, as if he has grown used to adulation. Yet his strides to the dugout are measured and slow. They allow him to bask in the appreciation, and he looks toward the stands as he nears the dugout. The sight of the standing multitude brings a smile to the face of the wily veteran as he goes down the dugout stairs and departs.

Dick Bosman hands the game ball to Livan Hernandez to start the opening night game against Arizona.

The fans get a great look at the ace of their pitching staff on opening night, but the cool evening also features the hitters whom the fans will come to love over the course of the season. Vinny Castilla, the veteran third baseman added to the roster in the off-season, has a triple, homer and double in that order to account for four of the Nat's five runs. Castilla has a chance to repeat Wilkerson's cycle that thrilled fans in the second game of the new season up the road in Philadelphia, and now Castilla faces Arizona reliever Lance Cormier in the eighth with a chance for another of these rare baseball events, needing only a single.

When Cormier gracelessly plunks Castilla in the back with his first pitch, the fans rise in anger, showering the field with words of derision, showing an appreciation for the moment and the game. Cormier finishes the inning quickly but is greeted by Nat's fans hanging over the Snake's dugout, pouring forth their righteous indignation in words that can easily be guessed at.

With the game suddenly close in the ninth and the Nats up only by two, Robinson turns the ball over to the 23-year-old closer, Chad Cordero, with his goofy unsculpted hat. Cordero exemplifies the fine young players with whom the Nationals are blessed. Nick Johnson, whose neat fielding and sweet swing were in evidence that night, and the two starting outfielders, Ryan

Church and Jose Guillen, all are in their mid twenties, as are several of the starting pitchers. It is this blend of youth and experience that gets the Nationals off to a surprisingly good start as they win six of their first ten.

Cordero puts away the bottom of the Snakes' order. The Nationals cap off their opening night win, the sixth of the young season, while the fans cheer themselves hoarse. Then, after staying until the final out is recorded, the fans stream happily past the event staff manning each gate, who give each fan a souvenir medallion with which to mark the occasion. For the fans, the game itself will serve as a mental image that needs little burnishing. The joyous and smiling crowds on the Metro, children sleeping on their parents' shoulders or eagerly clutching a cherished piece of baseball history, are tired but warm testimony to a great evening and a successful change in history's flow, a change that brings baseball back to Washington, where it was at the beginning of the last century, and where it will—it's to be hoped—ring out this one.

The games continue on Saturday. The crowds come back in near sell-out numbers for game two with Arizona and nearly 35,000 are in attendance on Saturday. John Patterson, a 27-year-old Texan who sports a red glove with the words "Texas" stitched along a seam, will pitch against the Diamondbacks, for whom he pitched during his two first seasons in the National League in 2002 and 2003. Patterson gives credit to the great pitchers on that staff, Curt Schilling and Randy Johnson, for helping him achieve his modest level of success. The Diamondbacks' pitcher will be the veteran Russ Ortiz, who pitched for Eastern Division champs Atlanta for the past two seasons and for the National League champion San Francisco Giants in 2002.

It is Patterson who pitches the masterpiece on this day. He limits Arizona to four hits and a walk, Royce Clayton's double in the third the only extra base hit. Ayala follows him in the eighth and begins what will be a run of shaky outings, but the bullpen finishes the game without further damage, the final score 9–3. Vinny Castilla is once again outstanding with the bat, a perfect three hits in three official plate appearances with a walk. His third home run in the third inning breaks the game open for the Nationals, and his single to lead off the seventh ignites a seven-run inning.

The Sunday game is the end of the series and there are 35,000 fans again. Could it be the same eager fans? They scream and yell; they drink and eat. Who's to know? For this game the Diamondbacks send the young pitcher to the mound against the veteran. Esteban Loaiza led the American League in strikeouts in 2003 and has pitched well enough during the first two weeks of this season that some are hoping he has returned to the form that won him twenty games in 2003. His downturn in 2004 after being traded to the New York Yankees remains one of those mysteries that seem to happen only with the Yankees. On this Sunday, Brad Halsey, who also pitched for the Yankees in 2004, opposes Loaiza. Halsey is a rookie, however, whose time with the

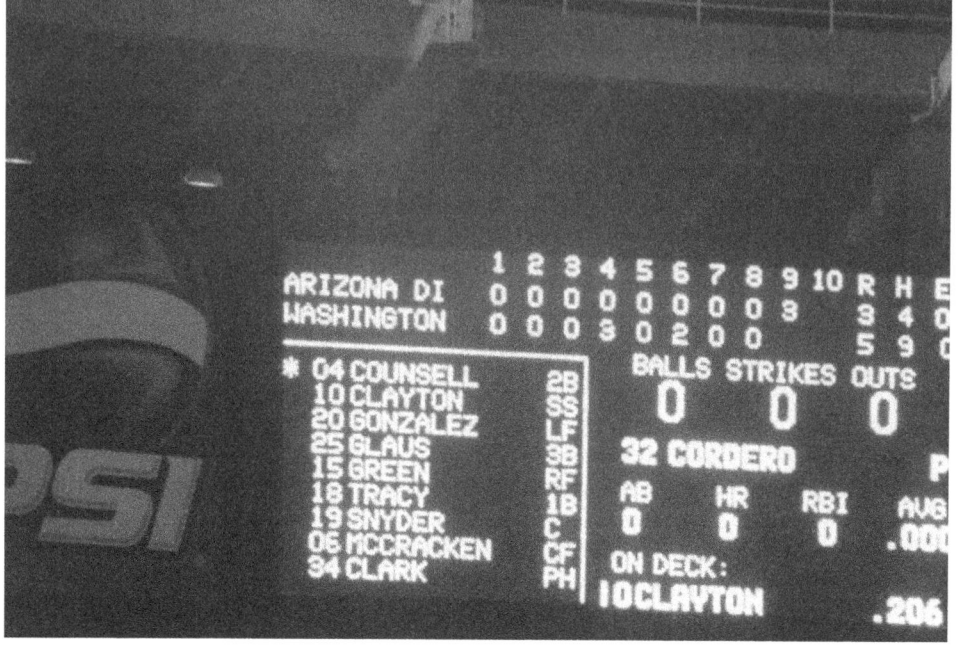

The opening night win puts the Nationals' record at six wins, four defeats going into the third week.

Yanks amounted to only a "cup of coffee," baseball parlance for a brief late season call-up when the games do not matter.

Halsey and Loaiza both start well, but Loaiza seems to lose concentration in the second, and sandwiched between three strikeouts are two singles, a walk and a double which lead to three runs. The Nationals get back one run in the fourth on a Wilkerson double and a sacrifice fly by Vidro, but Halsey seems very much in command until the seventh. After Vidro leads off the inning with a single and Guillen doubles him to third, Halsey gives way to the Arizona bullpen that has been less than overwhelming so far in the season. Mike Koplove enters the game and gets Castilla to grand out, but Nick Johnson rips a triple deep into the gap in left center and two runs score. A walk and a single force in two more runs and then Vidro bats for the second time and his second single plates two more runners.

This seventh inning uprising is an emerging trend by the Nationals to strike late in the game, primarily against the bullpen pitchers of the opponent. The Nat's bullpen in contrast has been a strength for the team and four young relievers come on and pitch three perfect innings against the Diamondbacks to end the game with the final score of 7–3.

The win is the fifth in a row for the Nationals and the fans are unbelieving. Can this be the same team they have read about for the past three years, the lowly Montreal Expos, the orphans of baseball?

# The Wedding Party

They gather in twos and threes as cheerful and animated as guests at a wedding party. They can be seen in the workplace or at lunch stands, recounting their afternoon or evening at the ballpark.

"RFK is not so bad. It has the feel of an old park, you know, the peeling paint, the water pooling in the bathrooms. I kind of like that already worn feeling to the place," says one fan.

"Camden Yards is beautiful, but it's kind of artificial, ya know what I mean? RFK is the real thing," says another.

"I love the stadium. I can't believe how good it looks. I haven't been this excited about baseball since I was a kid," says the first fan, speaking for many.

They in fact *are* smiling, like children on Christmas morning with new toys. This first season reminds every fan in town of nothing so much as those great seasons of youth when baseball was sheer joy, when we woke to the adventures of the likes of Sandy Koufax and Bob Gibson, when fireballing pitchers were unbeatable, unhittable, and only until they ran into their match in the World Series could we sort out for certain who was best.

The Nationals start the season at home in such a way that kids brag for hours. There is an aura of faith in the fantastic about it. A day of reckoning will come, but, oh, for the present, ain't it grand. In the early games of the season the team has rallied, coming from behind to beat great teams like the Braves, the Diamondbacks, and the Marlins, winning several series before the sweep of their games against the Diamondbacks. These are teams that have won it all, like the Marlins, who were world champions just two short seasons ago. The old Expos grew accustomed to watching them from too far a distance.

In the young season Washington's record stands at eight wins and four losses. It is good enough to keep them near the top of the very competitive NL East. The Major League schedules concentrate the competition within each division so that the Nationals will play the preponderance of their games against the Atlanta Braves, New York Mets, Philadelphia Phillies and Florida Marlins, who share the NL East with Washington. The long season will wind its way toward conclusion in September, when head-to-head play against these teams will settle it all.

The third week of the young season brings the Florida Marlins to town for a two game series. In the second series of the season, the Marlins' young pitching staff show why it is so highly regarded and take the measure of Washington by winning two of three. For the first game in the series they send out

Dontrelle Willis, whose nine-inning shutout in the fourth game of the season is still fresh in the minds of Washington's team and the fans most familiar with the sports pages.

The game seems a repeat of the first game almost exactly. Willis is dominating. With a 9–0 lead, Willis takes the mound in the seventh inning. Tomo Ohka struggles and allows four runs in five innings. Joe Horgan, an effective relief pitcher for the Expos in 2004, is pounded for five runs in the seventh inning. It looks like Willis has another easy win in the offing. But the quiet of the seventh is broken by a solo home run from Jose Vidro that rises quickly into the darkness over the open dome of the stadium. Vidro's shot lands well up into the stands in left field, sends the souvenir hounds chasing, and suddenly the impossible is possible again, even the steep grade of a nine-run lead seems doable suddenly.

Willis may be tiring, although he has thrown less than ninety pitches. The next batter, Jose Guillen, laces a ground ball through the right side that just eludes the shortstop's outstretched glove and the fans can see a hint of worry on D-train's face. Castilla hits a liner into right that arrives on the outfield grass in front of Cabrera almost as quickly as Vidro's homer mounted the outfield seats. A double by Nick Johnson bounces over the short wall in right center in a single bounce and D-train's run is over, that much is obvious.

Willis is lifted for a new pitcher and the fans look at the scoreboard, anxiously seeing what is still a large gap between the runs in their column—three—and those on the Marlins' side—nine. After a sacrifice fly and a double play ball by Schneider pinch-hitting at the end of the order, the Nats score another run, but fall short. The Marlins bullpen rises to the test and closes out the eight and ninth innings quietly. The Nats lose to D-train one more time, 9–4. It is the first loss by the Nats in the new stadium and the first home loss for the fans ever. They leave the park more quietly, still smiling but quieter than they have been for the magic run during which, for four games at least, RFK was an impenetrable fortress and the Nats unbeatable.

"We will get them tomorrow night," they say, but they are less sure now, now that the spell has been broken.

The scouts, the old hands of baseball, watch and wait. An old scout in his ragged cap looks to the young scout, whose sleek shades perch on his buzz cut like a second pair of eyes on the top of his head.

"What do you make of the Nats now?" asks the young scout, noting the speed on Majewski's fastball.

"Wait til they hit a rough spot," says the old scout. "Wait til they lose five in a row and Loaiza starts to get hit hard in June."

"Yeah, they could lose 10 in a row, 15 of 20 and we'll see who comes to see them then," says the young guy, looking disdainfully at the cheering crowd around him.

The fans return 26,000 strong for the second game of the midweek Marlins series hoping that the Fish's fifth starter, Brian Moehler, will be an easier mark than D-train, and that the Nationals ace, Livan Hernandez, will silence the bats of Florida's formidable young hitters.

The early innings offer promise as Hernandez not only keeps the Marlins off the board but, in the bottom of the second inning, executes a perfect squeeze play, laying the ball softly out into the green no-man's-land between the pitcher and first baseman where Moehler is fortunate to field the ball cleanly and get the slow footed Hernandez. As he does, Schneider comes in to score from third and the crowd erupts appreciatively, knowing how difficult the squeeze play is to execute, and what a statement it makes about Hernandez as a well rounded player, able both to perform with the bat and to pitch remarkably well.

The fans also hope that this early run signals a rebound from Monday's game against Dontrelle Willis. Early promise leads to frustration, however, as Hernandez begins the third inning by walking the Fish pitcher Moehler. The crowd groans as Moehler stands on first with no one out. Then the lead-off hitter, Juan Pierre, adds to the growing depression as he singles. Delgado pushes the first run across with a sacrifice fly and then Cabrera continues to bedevil the Nats as he singles cleanly and the Nationals lose their brief 1–0 advantage. An Encarnacion double, another single and the Fish end the inning 5–1. It is clear that Livan Hernandez does not have his good stuff today.

In the fifth inning, Carlos Delgado deposits a Hernandez pitch well up into the right field bleachers and the Fish take a 6–1 lead in the fifth. The Nationals bats are silent until Schneider homers in the eighth. Nick Johnson pushes Wilkerson across in the ninth to make it 6–3, but the rally fizzles and another frustrating game ends poorly against Florida. There are signs of life, though. The bullpen pitches well and Cristian Guzman's three hits in four at bats seem to signal that he is coming around; the fans hope for better things against the Braves, who were beaten two out of three in Atlanta. They come to town for a two game series to end the week.

## April Showers

On Wednesday night, the Nats had rallied from their back-to-back losses to the Fish. Dontrelle Willis is a memory, but the Atlanta Braves, back for a two-game set, bring to any baseball series one of the finest pitching staffs assembled in the past decade, whose names are long tenured in the annals of post-season play. Fortunately for Washington, the opening game features their fifth starter, Horacio Ramirez, pitching in only his third season, although his rookie campaign placed him at the upper reaches of young star hurlers. Under Leo Mazzone, the Braves' storied pitching coach, the California-born Ramirez has thrived and given the Braves more than they could reasonably expect from the minimum salary of $300,000, providing 12 wins in his rookie season alone.

Against him, Washington sends out an equally young pitcher, whose first two years in the National League have shown similar potential to Ramirez, although pitching for the lowly Montreal Expos has yielded fewer wins for him than Ramirez saw at the top of the league. Zach Day, the Washington pitcher, is the rare, "crafty" right-hander. Soft-tossing lefties achieve an enigmatic success that is best described by sports writers as crafty. Right-handed pitchers are more commonly successful with speed or sharp breaking curves, and only occasionally do pitchers such as Day last with sinkers and sliders that never come close to the 90 mile per hour benchmark.

Under a clear sky that night, both pitchers have their best stuff for the crowd of 30,000 patrons, remarkable attendance for a midweek game. It has been the hottest day of the year in Washington at 85 degrees, and the warm slightly muggy evening provides a test of the theory forming among the writers that RFK will play shorter once the summer heat arrives. Currently, the lack of home runs and the plethora of very long flies that have died in front of the fence have raised concerns that RFK may play long all year.

However this debate may resolve itself in the future, only Jose Vidro is able to breach the barrier that warm April evening. His two run home run in the third inning provides the only scoring. After seven masterful and scoreless innings, Day gives way to Luis Ayala who combines with Chad Cordero in the ninth to shut out the Braves for the game. The 2–0 final score provides a win that brings the Nats back from the two losses to Florida and renews optimism among the fans.

The weather gods predicted a gorgeous afternoon for baseball, with the temperatures in the mid–60s and bright sunshine. They are horribly, horribly wrong. The fans fill the midday, off-peak Metro trains, streaming toward RFK through the Metro caverns underneath the city like some subterranean river of red hats and red shirts. They pour out of the Stadium Armory subway exit with its new Euro-dome glass canopy, past the hawkers with the ten-dollar T-shirts and five-dollar hats.

"Anybody need a ticket?" cries the scalper, and in the background the lonely sound of the old saxophone player wails from the top of the escalators and follows the crowd around the bend toward the stadium.

"Hot dog two dollar, peanut three dollar!!" cries the Middle Eastern concessionaire, his clipped accent out of place.

"Get the little lady a tee shirt, mister," cries an African American hawker. "Everybody wants a Nationals jersey."

There are Asian vendors as well, the long line of them winding their way to the stadium, a vast potpourri of peoples on the outside, modern-day

Frank Robinson, bench coach Eddie Rodriguez and umps on opening night.

ragmen plying their humble trade along the edge of the crowd, crying out to the folks with tickets to the game on the inside.

No sooner do the fans take their seats at RFK, looking out over the players stretching in the outfield, than the first drops of rain fall. The first hint of worry settles in as the scant sunshine of the morning disappears completely. The cold front that had hovered north along the Mason-Dixon Line but was forecast to remain there has slipped southward and brought a gray sky as impenetrable as a Pynchon novel.

The players are still stretching and running in the outfield before the game. Nick Johnson signs autographs along the left field stands and Jamey Carroll, the utility infielder, is doing the same near home plate as he recounts for an acquaintance his difficulties finding an apartment in his new home and furniture with which to furnish it. The Nationals are sending out another young pitcher. This one, John Patterson, is another lanky right-hander, who has pitched less than 200 innings in three partial seasons in the big leagues. Patterson's father was drafted by the Baltimore Orioles as a young man and spent four seasons in their minor leagues, never making the majors. He taught his son John the mechanics of the big breaking curveball that harks back to Bert Blyleven and the great curveball artists of the 1970s when Patterson senior played the game.

*Above and opposite:* Nationals fans are introduced to the home team on opening night.

In stark contrast, the opposing hurler is the consummate veteran John Smoltz, who has been at the top of baseball's list of star hurlers, part of the Braves' celebrated threesome along with Maddux and Glavine during their long run at the top of the National League East. He has taken on a new role for the team the past two years, closing out games in the ninth inning with remarkable proficiency. Now, he is back to his more familiar starting role and fills out a pitching rotation that features native Georgian Tim Hudson, who is joining the team after five very successful years in the American League, where he has been a 20-game winner and near the top of the Cy Young Award voting several times. Along with 10-year veteran Mike Hampton, the Braves have one of the deepest and most experienced pitching staffs in baseball.

With the beer venders pounding down the aisles as the last chords of the national anthem fade, a few scant raindrops return. Both Smoltz and Patterson are masterful as they take their turns in the first inning, each recording two strikeouts as batters seem unable to get good wood on anything either is throwing. As the second inning begins, a slight but steady drizzle begins but few pay it any heed, although some in the stands break out umbrellas or colorful plastic ponchos. Patterson begins the second inning kicking at the mound and summoning the umpire, and in short order the grounds crew arrives for

what will prove to be the first of many appearances in this game, although the last will be the most fateful.

The rain increases in the second inning and the faithful begin to scatter to other parts of the stadium. During the next two innings the rain becomes a steady downpour and the fans become a crowded mass under the overhangs in both the first and second levels. Patterson ends the third inning having faced the minimum number of batters, perfect to this point, and Smoltz has surrendered only a first inning single to Termel Sledge.

Then in the bottom of the fourth, Wilkerson breaks the monotony with a line drive into the gap. The ball is chased down but not until Wilkerson is standing on second base. With the leadoff man aboard, Robinson orders Guzman, batting second, to lay down a bunt. Guzman executes the play perfectly, Smoltz's fastball deadened in the grass halfway between the pitcher and the catcher, where the only play is to first base. Guzman is out by a half step, but Wilkerson moves on to third, where he can score easily on a fly ball to the outfield. Bobby Cox, the wily skipper of the Braves, pulls in his infielders almost to the fringes of the infield grass so that any ground ball fielded cleanly

**The opening night flag ceremony.**

will deny the runner on third time to break for the plate. Nationals fans sense a golden opportunity at hand with Vidro at the plate, but he hits a hard one-hopper to Marcus Giles, who fields it, looks Wilkerson back, and flips to LaRoche at first.

The fans still huddled in the covered seats rise to their feet as Jose Guillen strides to the plate. The noise echoes beneath the upper deck girders and Guillen delivers a solid line drive single in front of the left fielder hustling in to make the play, but Wilkerson scores and the Nationals take the lead 1–0. The lead holds, Patterson breezing effortlessly through the rather formidable Braves lineup until the seventh inning. Then he walks his first two batters, temporarily losing the command that has to this point been almost perfect. He pitches around the mistakes and gets Mondesi and Langerhans at the bottom of the order to end the inning.

The rain slacks off during the middle innings, but as the Nats come to bat in the seventh it begins again in earnest and increases during the inning until it is again a steady downpour. When the teams take the field in the eighth, the grounds crew spends considerable time lining the infield positions with dirt.

"Do you think they really use kitty litter like some say?" asks a fan.

"I hope so, 'cause they sure got a hell of a mess to clean up," says his friend under the canopy, watching as the grounds crew rakes in the fill, leaving what looks like a dry infield. Yet within minutes there is water puddling in numerous locations in the infield. Carrasco pitches a perfect eighth inning in relief of Patterson and keeps the score at 1–0, but the fans are nervous, booing lustily as the umpire squeezes the strike zone like a wet rag, denying a quick exit from the worsening weather conditions.

Again the grounds crew is summoned as the ninth inning begins. The infield is a heavy, muddy mess and the crew can do little to keep it dry. The Nationals begin the ninth with their reliable closer, Chad "the Chief" Cordero, on the mound again. He seems to have his good stuff despite the difficult conditions and gets two quick strikes on the first batter, but Giles singles through the wet infield to start the inning. Chipper Jones runs the count full and draws a walk, with the fans grumbling on each call and wondering how anyone can pitch in such conditions. But when Estrada lines a Cordero offering into right field, the fans fall silent. Giles holds at third, respecting Guillen's arm and uncertain whether the ball would be caught. The bases are loaded and there are no outs.

There can be no resolution to the situation that will leave the 1–0 lead intact, yet Cordero rises to the occasion. He strikes out Jordan and Laroche and the Braves are down to their final out. The fans rise in anticipation, the risers pound, the stadium shakes with the noise of the faithful. The Braves fans, who have ventured north from Virginia to cheer for what has become "their" team, are silent again. But when Cordero goes to two balls and no strikes on Mondesi, the Braves fans begin to shout again. Their fondest wishes seem dashed, however, when Mondesi strokes an easy grounder toward the sure handed Guzman at shortstop. Guzman is lost amid the puddles and makes his way to the ball like a truck driver battling to see through a foggy windshield. The ball skids through the water toward him and he gloves it, but as he picks it out of his sodden mitt it slips from his grasp. Water and kitty litter fly from his hand as he flings the ball across the diamond. It arcs crazily to the right and the normally sure handed Johnson moves with the throw, hopeless to scoop it from the wet grass. It careens under his glove and over the wet grass into the Braves dugout. Two runs score; the Braves have taken the lead. The Richmond fans begin the one-armed chopping motion that looks like rehab exercises for tennis elbow. The Nats fans are quietly disgusted.

"That's the last time we see Guzman at short for a few games," ventures one fan, echoing local writers who have begun to question his play.

"Who they gonna play, Cabrera?" asks a fan in a red hat with the big *M* in the middle—a Montreal Expos hat—his voice dripping with irony.

Cabrera was the very athletic and gifted regular shortstop for the Montreal team, a gem from the minor league organization. Before the team was sold to MLB, Inc., for plunder, he was considered one of the better young talents in baseball. Now he is playing in Boston—or is it Los Angeles? It is difficult to remember which Expo is where, like sweaters left around the house by teens.

The rainfall is relentless. The Nationals can find no way to push across a single run in the bottom of the ninth. Danny Kolb, the Braves' new closer—coming over in a trade from Selig's old team, the Brewers—finishes the game. His outing is in stark contrast to one a week earlier when he gave up three runs in the bottom of the ninth to allow Washington a thrilling come-from-behind victory in Atlanta. The Nationals fans stay until the bitter end, the rainfall gushing in torrents out from the stadium as they exit after the final bitter out is recorded. As they walk back toward Metro, they mull Guzman's error.

"Hell, the frigging umps shoulda called the game in the seventh when it started pouring again, when we still had the lead" says one.

"Yeah, no way you can expect people to play ball in that mess," says another, forgiving sort.

The newspapers the next day join the debate, but the reporters are more severe with Guzman. Robinson echoes the general disappointment. But news of the game is lost among headlines of another fiasco in the making. The television deal struck by MLB, Inc., fails to hold any better than Guzman. The local cable network is suing to get back their rights to broadcast games from Orioles owner Angelos. The wet fans, willing to endure damp, soggy conditions to watch their team take on the best in the National League, are once again at the mercy of corporate millionaires far away from rainy afternoon games. The article proclaims no hopes for TV broadcast of Nationals games. Everyone has problems and what does Robinson do with Guzman?

# 2

# In for the Long Haul

Frank Robinson, the manager of the Nationals in their first season, was a great player who was inducted into the Baseball Hall of Fame on the first ballot. He is a veteran manager as well, and his rich history in the game offers a look at how it has developed and changed during the last half of the 20th century. Both the styles of play and the approach of managers have changed markedly in recent decades, when Robinson was a player and manager. During his heyday in the sixties and seventies, great players like Maury Wills and Lou Brock brought to the fore a brand of baseball that had been popular in the Negro Leagues, where brash base stealers danced around the base paths to the delight of fans. Ricky Henderson was both the best at that craft and its last modern practitioner, as the Oakland Athletics team that he played for also featured Jose Canseco and Mark McGwire, who would usher in the long-ball era-the one with the asterisk for steroid use.

The 21st century brand of baseball has yet to be defined, but so far Billy Beane, the general manager for those same Oakland Athletics, has dominated the discussion. His strategic philosophy is described in a recent best-selling book by Michael Lewis, *Moneyball* (New York, W.W Norton, 2003). Whether 21st century baseball looks like the ideas of Billy Beane or something else entirely, it is unlikely that it will look anything like the game Frank Robinson mastered over the past half century. But Frank Robinson is a fiercely proud traditionalist.

Robinson is the first African American ever to manage a team in Major League Baseball. There were, of course, great managers in the Negro Leagues, but Robinson successfully crossed an important color barrier in 1975 when he took over as skipper for the Cleveland Indians. He was successful then and has known both success and failure as a manager. In 1988 he took over the

Baltimore Orioles from Cal Ripken, Sr., after that team had lost six in a row, only to see the streak of losses run to 21. He brought the team back to finish second the next year and won the Manager of the Year Award for the feat. Yet of all managers within comparable longevity, he has the fewest post-season appearances and the lowest winning percentage, well below .500.

Robinson's tenure with the Nationals began when Major League Baseball, Inc., took over the team. His appointment by Bud Selig gave legitimacy to baseball's bizarre arrangement whereby the owners of the other 29 teams owned the Expos; Robinson had to compete against teams owned by his employers—a conflict of interest that could exist only in baseball. Robinson was a great choice for the job because of the respect he commanded in the game. His age when he was hired may have exceeded that of many of his peers, but he is not old by historic standards, where great managers have continued to manage well into their 70s. For three full years he has guided the team quietly and with dignity.

Most fans know the basic history of the Expos and baseball in the modern era, but from their perspective the game is not about owners, luxury taxes, corporate boxes, or other economic variables. For fans the game is played on the field and on the field, Frank Robinson is boss. Fans love managers who win and they give them as much, if not more, deference than they do players.

Washington sports writers and broadcasters are talking in April about Robinson's "instincts," a term he uses to describe his approach to management and decision-making. He is instinctive in choosing his lineups, evaluating players, making decisions about who is hot, or who is best in a given situation. It is a dated approach in a baseball world that is developing increased dependence on the electronic assist that comes from computer generated statistics and video analysis of player performance.

As the game has changed over the past two decades, three great managers have dominated: Bobby Cox of the Atlanta Braves, Joe Torre of the Yankees, and Tony LaRussa of the Cardinals. Only Bobby Cox, who is 64, approaches Robinson in age. Other than Cox and a few other elder statesmen like Jack McKeon and Felipe Alou, the active managers at the helm of major league teams are considerably younger than Robinson, and many got their playing experience in the decades after Robinson retired, when baseball was beginning to change direction toward its current, more analytically driven model.

General Manager Billy Beane's analysis of the game was not new, as *Moneyball* establishes. Rather it began with the striking impact of Bill James and other statistical consultants and analysts. Their obsession with statistical modeling of player performance can be seen in certain managers, as well as in GMs like Beane. Some managers dwell for hours each day on statistical performance data about the players on their team. Tony LaRussa, currently the manager of the St. Louis Cardinals and accumulating wins faster than any other manager in baseball history, is widely known to rely on an approach aided by statistics and other objective analysis.

According to *Three Nights in August*, by Buzz Bissinger (New York, Houghton Mifflin, 2005), LaRussa takes into each game a set of statistical data on game situations. He keeps this information on index cards in his pockets and leafs through them as the game situation dictates. His book also touts the facility of videotape, the large libraries of tape his team and other teams maintain, and its ability to allow players who use it extensively to project themselves into the very game situations they will face on a day-to-day basis. Several general managers who were hired from Billy Beane's staff in Oakland cultivate all of these new analytic tools and use them prior to each game to inform their on-the-field managers about how they want game situations addressed. Some of these GMs, like Theo Epstein, the 32-year-old in Boston who hired Bill James, have Ivy League pedigrees and are quite young in comparison to Robinson.

There is sharp disagreement within baseball about the value of these young analysts. Robinson and many of the old veterans perceive this new approach as a radical polarity existing on the fringes. ESPN's Joe Morgan, whose career overlapped Robinson's, has been critical of it in game broadcasts, although in temperate terms. Morgan's era and his own Hall of Fame career valued the sacrifice, the hit-and-run, and many other managerial moves that *Moneyball* declares are wasted outs that undermine offensive productivity and are needlessly risky ventures.

Some of the philosophical differences can be explained by differences between the American League, where Beane is located, and the National League, where Robinson and his Washington Nationals play. The need to have the pitcher bat makes the sacrifice bunt a required part of the NL game. Yet it is not just Robinson's skillful deployment of his pitchers as batters. What sets him apart from Beane is his glorying in the unconventional, playing hunches rather than the odds. His approach can be both exciting and very frustrating. When he is right and his long shot pony ends up in the circle of roses, everyone cheers, but the accumulating losers become more worrisome.

Several facets of the approach in Michael Lewis's book seem to be gaining popularity with other GMs, players, and managers, especially in the American League. One example is Beane's contention in the book that starting pitchers are the best pitchers each team has. Relief pitchers are in effect the second string. Therefore, Beane's strategy is to use patient approaches at the plate from the very beginning of the game, in every batter, to force the starting pitcher to throw as many pitches as possible. This tendency to extend the pitcher throughout the course of the game reaches a successful conclusion when the opposition is forced to bring in the relief pitchers in the sixth or seventh inning. The poorer quality bull pen pitchers afford the opposition better chances to score and to prevail in the end.

The wisdom of this approach is apparent in the Nationals' early season statistics. Constantly facing many of the best pitchers in baseball, the Nationals are batting less than .250 in the first six innings of their games. In the seventh, when relievers have faced them, they are hitting over .300, a remarkable contrast.

Frank Robinson may not *believe* in the hegemony of statistics, but he does not ignore facts. His lineups may not be perfect from the perspective of Moneyball analysts, but they show the evidence of similar knowledge to arrive at its construction, much as a building designed by computer aided designers may not look remarkably different from one whose designers used only pencil and pen.

A statistical analysis of, Frank Robinson as a manager shows that over his career he has a winning percentage of .476. In managing four major league teams, he has had slightly more losing seasons than winning seasons and has never finished higher than second, which he did with a pathetic Baltimore team in 1989 that lost over 100 games in his first year. It is considered the highlight of his managing career, although his 1982 Giants team finished 12 games over .500 and was in contention most of the year. From his record as a manager, one can only conclude that he was a vastly better player than manager.

His current tenure, that began with the Expos in 2002, is an animal of a very different stripe, however, and the data could arguably be excluded. In 2002, when MLB hired Robinson, the Montreal team finished in 2nd place in the NL East, four games above .500, with Vladimir Guerrero, Bartolo Colon and Javier Vasquez, who were recognized as marquee players in the National League and all of baseball. But MLB soon stripped these valuable assets from the team with the aplomb and lack of apology one would expect of corporate raiders. Robinson's tenure can be viewed only as part of MLB attempt to dismantle the team under the guise of respectability he lends.

The 2005 Nationals represent what appears for now to be a complete change of direction. Robinson now lends the operation more than just respectability. He and GM Jim Bowden have kept afloat what was fast sinking from the stern. They have pumped out the bilge water and found the superstructure generally sound, the crew remarkably fit. They have set sail and the ship seems trim and remarkably responsive to the tiller when the wind is up at old RFK.

In the first three weeks of the season Robinson's largest problem with the Nats has been the lineup. He has not used the same one very often, if at all. Robinson has had only two consistent lineup slots all year. Brad Wilkerson has consistently batted leadoff, and Jose Guillen has hit fourth, the traditional cleanup spot reserved for the strongest and best hitter on the team. Jose Vidro has batted third quite often, but other than these few positions, and the pitcher's position as the ninth batter, each lineup card has presented new surprises, for both the fans and the players.

The first experiment was with Guzman in the two-hole. Guzman embodies some traditional traits thought essential for number two hitters. He can bunt and earlier in his career he showed speed. This emphasis on the "little ball" player in the second slot in the lineup is traditional and well known to the era in which Frank Robinson played. The great base-stealing threats usually had a patient hitter behind them in the order, one who could take a pitch or two and still feel comfortable batting with two strikes if necessary to get a Brock or a Wills to second or even to third with stolen bases.

Guzman is not a patient or a selective hitter historically. His highest walk total is 30 and in one season where he had 620 at bats, he drew only 17, a remarkable display of impulse hitting. If left alone in a supermarket line, Guzman might come home with a cart full of tabloids and candy bars. In a *Moneyball* approach, Guzman is poorly qualified to bat second. Additionally, batting in the Minneapolis Metrodome, with its artificial turf, he has become accustomed to an approach that maximizes ground balls that get through the very fast infield there. At RFK the infield is intentionally slow and Guzman hitting behind anyone hits into more than his share of double plays, killing fledgling rallies repeatedly.

Beane and his followers have settled upon players for the top of the order whose on-base percentage is high and who can hit comfortably even if the pitcher gets the first two quick strikes and the situation shifts clearly in the pitcher's direction. In this scenario the player must be both patient and skillful with the bat. He must be comfortable making the pitcher throw as many pitches as possible, happy to get a free four pitch walk to first base, or as many as he can generate. The logic compounds itself if the batting order as a whole can make use of numerous patient hitters. Frank Robinson is blessed with several of these types of hitters, but Cristian Guzman is not one of them.

What Robinson calls an instinctive approach is clearly what Beane is critiquing. Lewis's book ungraciously characterizes managers in general as old-school hacks. Yet Robinson comes to conclusions remarkably similar to Beane's, though it seems to require more experimentation to get to that conclusion. For example, the logic of Beane's approach can be seen in Robinson's Nationals roster. Robinson does not have on his roster a player who fits the traditional leadoff hitting model he might wish for. He wants a speedy, base-stealing threat who will rattle the pitcher by dancing off the first base bag every third inning and disrupting his focus on the batter. He tried Endy Chavez, a speedy light-hitting outfielder, as his leadoff hitter for much of 2004, but Chavez's failure to get on base became a clear drag on the team and Robinson discarded him in favor of Wilkerson.

Robinson does have a bumper crop of players who get on base with remarkable proficiency. Vidro, the second baseman, has a career .360 on-base percentage, in sharp contrast to Guzman's .303. More impressive still is Nick Johnson's .381 career on-base percentage. Both of these players would make excellent hitters at the top of the order. Neither has displayed exceptional power, although both can hit the long ball. For this reason, Robinson has chosen to move them around in the order, generally batting them third through sixth, but never both of them at the top of the order. Instead, he has used Wilkerson and Guzman most frequently by late April.

Wilkerson also has a high on-base percentage, averaging .360 for his career. But he has the most impressive power credentials on the team. His slugging percentage of .498 in 2004, as he approaches the prime of his career, reflects the fact that he hit 32 home runs, as well as 41 other extra base hits, a remarkable year for any player, much less one only 27 years of age. Only Jose Guillen's power numbers approach Wilkerson's. Guillen in 2004 had 27 home runs, 57 total extra base hits with a slugging percentage of .498. These statistics would support a lineup structure that took advantage of the power of Wilkerson and Guillen, and the on-base capabilities of Vidro and Johnson.

In addition, the Nationals are blessed with Vinny Castilla and Termel Sledge. Although in the latter stages of his career at 37, Castilla showed last season in Colorado, where the thin air produces exaggerated power numbers, that he *can* still hit. However, his career slugging percentage is only .411 and he is notoriously slow and does not walk exceedingly often. Termel Sledge was the Nationals' Minor League Player of the year in 2003, and in 2004, in 400 at bats, had a slugging percentage of .460 with 15 home runs. These two hitters, at opposite ends of their careers, provide excellent hitters to follow the Nationals' power and on-base strengths that should be slotted at the top of the order.

Robinson has played Sledge hardly at all during the first weeks of the season, preferring two rookies, Ryan Church and J. J. Davis. Neither is a proven major leaguer, and, although Sledge has not exactly established himself as a reliable star, he has clearly demonstrated he can hold his own, and is in his baseball prime at 28. Church and Davis have each batted in the five-hole numerous times. This spot in the lineup has great importance, as it provides cover to Gullen, the cleanup hitter. Without sufficient power or presence in the five-hole, the pitcher will walk or pitch around the best hitter in the lineup when necessary because he knows a lighter hitter waits on deck. For example, Billy Beane is babysitting his young prodigy, Nick Swisher, hitting him every game seventh or lower in the lineup.

Although Robinson has batted Castilla and Nick Johnson fifth sensibly enough on occasion, finding hitters like Church, Davis and other rookies without proven major league batting must put a smile on the face of the opposing pitcher. They know they do not have to give Jose Guillen much to hit when he has runners on base. This is a reasonable explanation for Guillen's league-leading number of home runs in mid April without driving in many runs. Pitchers pitch to him only when there is no one on base. Additionally, Guzman is not getting on ahead of him and is eliminating runners as well.

Finally, on April 22, with the Nationals beginning to lose traction after their five-game winning streak, Robinson bats Guzman second for the last time, moving him to the seventh and eighth spot in the lineup for every game that follows. Down in the lineup, Guzman begins to hit, slowly but surely he comes out of the funk he has been in, as though he had been uncomfortable in the role Robinson had cast for him. During the week immediately following Guzman's descent to the lower reaches of the lineup, Robinson begins to appear consistently along the dugout rail during games. Initially, he was more often sitting in the shadows back in the dugout, as if stewing over the unresolvable dilemmas presented by MLB's failure to provide him a full set of parts. He has looked unengaged, but actually he was just sorting things out, his worry beads there all along just out of sight, hidden from the intruding cameras.

"See Robinson standing out along the top rail of the dugout?" says one fan, taking note of the change.

"Yeah, what of it?" says the fan at his elbow.

"Well he hasn't been up there much this year."

"Yeah, they showed him sitting against the wall on TV a couple times at the start of the season," says fan two.

"I think he's starting to get into the games more, now. You can see it."

Frank is indeed up out of the shadows now. He stands, keeping the same tense watch on the game that so many other managers do. He watches the game in deep concentration, staring out at the mound wondering whether Zach Day will last the third inning of the Mets game in New York, his trusted lieutenant, Eddy Rodriquez, is at his side and they share their thoughts on the progress of the game.

Last year, the ESPN cameras caught Robinson napping during a game, sleeping so soundly, in the shadows of the dugout that his mouth was slightly open and he was totally unaware of his surroundings. Last year, the team jetted from Montreal to Puerto Rico and any number of other locations and Frank could be forgiven for catching up on a few sleepless nights in Seattle, or wherever that camera found him.

Now he is awake. The team's energy, the fans' energy, has become contagious and Frank is finally fully engaged. Maybe it is the jumping fans back at RFK rattling the risers, making the whole left side rumble and pound like deep base drums from an approaching parade. More likely it is the enthusiasm of his players; they are playing hard, legging out every ground ball in the infield, even Castilla, who is slow enough that it is sometimes hard to tell. This is a team worth watching, even for someone who has seen a lot, seen almost fifty years of major league baseball. Frank Robinson is *watching* the Nationals now. They have earned his respect and that is no mean accomplishment.

"Frank Robinson has been with these kids through the hard times," Joe

Morgan remarks on *Sunday Night Baseball* on ESPN. It is certainly true. This team has been sold down the river and left for dead: it is unfair to look the survivors in the eye and say that, although they were good enough while the show was on the road, now that they are going to Broadway a new leading man is necessary. This show is attracting huge crowds. It is Zero Mostel's worst nightmare, a show designed to be so bad it had to flop, but the crowds love it. They are buying up every ticket in sight and demanding more. Robinson is in it for the long haul now, and the team needs him, deserves him, because that is what a manager is-part of the team.

He has been thrown out of his first game. The fans are hoping he has taken his blood pressure medicine. They are getting used to seeing him along that rail.

# 3

# After the Thrill Is Gone

The first ever Nationals home stand is over. The team wins four and loses three and, even with the tough loss to the Braves the previous day, the team still has two more wins than losses and its 9 wins and 7 losses puts it in the upper reaches of the National League East. It is a good beginning.

"You think this is for real?" wonders a fan.

"Should I wake you for the play-offs, or after?" he asks, smiling slyly. "I'll wake you when it's over," offers his friend, who thinks for a minute

Is this team really better than last year's team? Fans are mulling the possibilities. What is so different from last year's team that lost 95 games, almost reaching the landmark of haplessness-100 losses? Has this team so taken to their new surroundings, so responded to the cheers and enthusiasm of the fans that they are playing up to their real potential? Are they like a stray dog brought home by a child, from which a purebred emerges after a good shampoo and cleaning? The fans at RFK want to think that they have brought forth the real Washington Nationals. A quick comparison between the new 2005 Nationals team and the old 2004 Expos team bears out such an assertion to a degree.

In 2004 the Montreal Expos were led by a different group of players. For example, third baseman Tony Batista's 32 home runs provided important punch for the 2004 version of the Nationals and Orlando Cabrera was the anchor of the infield at shortstop. Both of these players are now gone and their offensive punch has not been replaced by the addition of Cristian Guzman and Vinny Castilla. Juan Rivera and Carl Everett were outfielders that Jose Guillen replaced, an upgrade but a risky one. Overall the offense in 2005 is no better, unless Castilla can provide as much power as Batista, an unlikely bet for an aging player no longer in the rarified air of Colorado.

The improvement is seen in overall pitching and team defense. Guillen and Castilla are much better defensive players than their predecessors. The major personnel upgrade is in the addition of Esteban Loaiza. A proven pitcher who had difficulty pitching in the high stress New York Yankees uniform, Loaiza adds much needed veteran presence to a rotation that features far too many young pitchers. Young pitchers will struggle and if they are forced to carry a ball club largely by themselves, the outcome can be dreadful, as the Tampa Bay Devil Rays continue to learn year after year. Loaiza takes pressure off these young pitchers and gives them room to develop.

Loaiza is tall and as good-looking as a Mexican don, but not young anymore in baseball terms. He is thirty-three and his hair is disappearing like snow melting in the mountains. One of four Mexican ballplayers on the team, Loaiza contrasts with the other great Mexican player on the team, Vinny Castilla, like some before and after ad for hair growth stimulants. Loaiza is thinner than Castilla and taller, and Castilla is too busy with his three children to spend time with Mexican president Vicente Fox at Los Pinos, the presidential compound in Mexico City, where Loaiza was in January before the season started.

There is another factor. The additional year of maturity for young players can be very important. Many of the Nationals were rookies in 2004 or still new to the major leagues, still developing as players and people. Now, after another year, they are growing into more mature versions of their former selves and the Nationals fans at RFK will act like adoring grandparents to help facilitate the growth process.

There is a minor league team long tenured in the Sally League as the Asheville Tourists. The Tourists are today what the Montreal Expos were in 2004. The Expos had no real home and were like foster children trying out new places to stay. For example, they played 22 games as the home team in Puerto Rico. Rumors were floated from MLB. that Puerto Rico was a potential new home for the team, and then it was Mexico City. In contrast to the Expos' scheduling problems, this year's Nationals adventures in scheduling seem pedestrian indeed, but they do not go away. Amtrak's Acela trains are halted suddenly before the Mets series in late April, and the Nationals lose their means of travel to New York. But ad hoc arrangements are commonplace.

The New York Mets, also-rans in the National League East and playing second fiddle to the Braves and Marlins since their glory days with Daryl Strawberry and Doc Gooden, are coming off a week when they have scored 26 runs in two games. But in typical fashion, after their drubbing of the Phillies they lose the next game and in the same fashion split two with the Marlins. For the Friday night game against the Nationals, the Mets send to the mound former Brave starter Tom Glavine, who may one day join his friends Greg Maddux and John Smoltz in the Hall of Fame

Glavine faces Loaiza, who has pitched in play-off and all-star games and has been in the Cy Young voting as well. It is a match-up of equals. That would not be the case if the Nats were again sending Zach Day or Claudio Vargas against pitching legends like Glavine. The game also features two of the best fielding first basemen in the game in Doug Mientkiewicz and Nick Johnson.

The game starts with Glavine struggling to find his spots, unable to convince the home plate umpire that the edge of the plate extends several inches out from both sides. He gives up a double and two walks and the Nats push him to the precipice, but he has been there before and coolly pitches out of trouble without giving up a run. Then slowly he extends the umpire's sight lines, using Leo Mazzone's skillful tutoring, and after the first inning he settles into his groove and the Nationals flail helplessly for his seven innings of work on this May evening.

Loaiza by contrast is sharp at first, but has the same problem coaxing anything from the same home plate umpire. Frustrated, he loses his concentration and walks five over the course of the game. In the third inning he gives up three hits and two runs, and, after struggling through five innings, with base runners in scoring position constantly, Frank Robinson lifts him.

Three of the Nationals' bullpen corps, Joe Horgan, brand new call-up Hector Carrasco, and Luis Ayala, combine to keep the game within reach. But the offense manages nothing more than a homer from Cristian Guzman in the 6th and the Mets bullpen closes out a 3-1 score, the Nationals' 8th loss. Uncharacteristically, Nick Johnson and Castilla boot easy chances and the errors do not help offset the appearance that Glavine and the Mets are in control and the Nationals still a work in progress.

The worry going into the Nationals' first season is that they do not have enough power to compete. The Mets have added great players like Carlos Beltran to hit in front of perennial superstar Mike Piazza. They add one of the great pitchers in the game, Pedro Martinez, to a staff that already included Glavine. Jose Guillen is an excellent, multitalented player and Loaiza an excellent pitcher, but they are not of the caliber of Martinez and Beltran. So a Nationals team that finished several games behind the Mets in 2004 seems likely to lose further ground in 2005.

On Saturday it is the Mets' turn to send out an unproven pitcher in Jae Seo, a Korean once regarded as having promise, but who, at 28, has outlived most of those predictions without achieving notable success. He pitched poorly in 2004, walking almost as many as he strikes out, and seeing as much of the Mets' Norfolk franchise as the majors. His opposing number for Washington is Tomo Ohka. Just when Ohka seemed to have reached his potential, pitching nearly 200 innings in 2002 and 2003, and winning a total of 23 games over those two years, he was struck with a batted ball in June of 2004, suffering a badly broken arm and not returning during the season.

Ohka seems the better bet, yet Robinson appears vexed by having the upper hand. He fields a ragtag lineup that has Carlos Baerga batting fifth at third base. No mention is made of an injury to Castilla, but Baerga has not played every day in the field since playing for these same Mets in 1998. Since then he has been consistently overweight, and has been waived or released by numerous teams. To add to the amateur status of the team, Robinson puts Tony Blanco, a 23-year-old rule five draftee with no major league experience in left field. Getting playing time for either one of these walk-ons might be understandable. It is a day game after a night game and reasonable to rest a 37-year-old like Castilla, but playing both together is asking for trouble, which is what Washington gets.

Ohka continues Loaiza's lack of strike zone command, walking three batters in three innings. Leaving balls over the plate constantly, he gives up six hits and four runs in three awful innings. Majewski puts the fire out in a scoreless fourth inning. But Robinson is leaning on the back wall of the dugout again, clearly frustrated. He sends Horgan out again in the fifth. He is not hit hard, but his teammates desert him, Vidro misplaying a pop-up into a double, Baerga letting a ball go between his legs, and Blanco falling down while chasing a fly ball that also goes for a double. Only as a comedy would the game be a hit, but Frank Robinson is not known for his humor.

Robinson does not budge from his place against the back wall. He leaves Horgan to absorb the embarrassment and Horgan, realizing that no help is on the way, strikes out the side to end the brutality on his own. True to form, the Nationals' bats come alive in the late innings. Against the Mets' relievers they bang out six hits in three innings and score four runs. It invites second-guessing by the fans watching back home. If Robinson had remained on top of the game and limited the beating that Horgan took, could the team have come back?

The Washington record after the shellacking by the Mets is nine wins and nine losses. Still, playing even in the National League East is above expectations for this team and when the curtain rises again on Robinson and his players on Sunday there is hope. The Mets series concludes with another situation in the Nationals' favor. Livan Hernandez, the Nationals' best pitcher, goes against Victor Zambrano, who before Seo's performance the previous day had been the club's fifth starter, barely. Zambrano's lack of command is legendary. He has walked almost a batter an inning since he was converted to pitching in 2000. There are few pitchers in the history of the game to match that statistic, and, taken with his record number of hit batsmen, he seems one of those millennium oddities.

After a ringing Wilkerson double off the wall begins the game, Zambrano walks Nick Johnson as if on cue. Vidro singles to right, but Wilkerson waits a millisecond too long to see if the ball will drop. There are no outs and Zambrano is as likely to airmail a pitch to the backstop, but third base coach Dave Huppert sends Wilkerson home. He slides wide reaching out for the plate, but Piazza manages to tag him out, giving the Mets a break they do not need. Johnson scores on a Jose Guillen sacrifice fly and hit after hit by Termel Sledge and Castilla the bases are loaded with one out.

Gary Bennett, the veteran backup catcher subbing for Brian Schneider, walks to the plate. He is a lifetime .247 hitter and largely unknown to Nationals fans. He is a bit short and squat. Backup catchers always seem like runts of the litter, slow-footed and awkward, so the faithful can smell a double play ball to end the inning. But Bennett is a solid backup, and his line drive single to center scores Vidro and Sledge. Guzman makes the final out dependably, but the Nationals have salvaged three runs and a 3-0 lead with their ace taking the mound in the bottom half of the inning.

The Mets come out in their half of the inning bunting, trying to take advantage of scouting reports about Livan Hernandez's injured knee. First Jose Reyes, the young shortstop, reaches on a bunt back to Hernandez; then with runners on first and second, Beltran, the young phenom, lays a bunt into the no-man's-land between the pitcher and third base for a hit. The bases are loaded and no outs. It is slugger Mike Piazza's turn at bat, but Piazza is no longer young. Squatting every day behind the plate has taken a toll and he enters the game batting .200 with only two home runs.

Hernandez, however, seems undone by his inability to field his position. Piazza laces a long drive to the wall in left and all three runners score. The Nationals' lead evaporates with only four batters faced by Hernandez. It is hard to imagine a much worse scenario after the previous two days. Cliff Floyd walks and now there are two men on base and still no one out. Mientkiewicz, the next batter, pops weakly to third. Then, Hernandez loses it again and walks the Mets' young third baseman, David Wright. The bases are loaded for Victor Diaz, who bedeviled the Nats on Saturday with four hits that scored three runs. As though the governor has issued a last-second pardon, Diaz grounds to Guzman, who turns a nifty double play, ending the Mets' threat, with the score tied 3-3.

Hernandez rights himself in the second, while Zambrano continues his struggles. The Nats squeeze in a run on a walk and an error to lead 4-3. Then in the fourth Zambrano plunks Livan Hernandez with one out and Brad Wilkerson pulls another inside fast ball from Zambrano over the right field fence for a two run homer. Livan Hernandez has another three run lead at 6-3.

Whether it is the indignity of Zambrano's beaning him, or just warming to the task, Hernandez puts down the Mets in the third and pitches four more scoreless innings, leaving the game at the end of seven with a 8-3 lead. Wilkerson and Castilla continue their torrid pace at the plate, each getting four hits for the game. Eischen comes on in relief in the eighth and sets down the Mets with only a single run. The game ends a laugher at 11-4. The Nationals maintain a winning record at 10 wins and nine losses.

On Monday the forecast for the 4:30 start time against Philadelphia is rain, but the skies are clear and blue in the morning and only a few frumpy clouds scoot across the sky in the afternoon. Temperatures reach into the high sixties as the sparse crowd of fans settle slowly into their seats. The Nationals players come onto the field for warm-ups and stretching, and behind them the U.S. Navy Band enters through the center field bullpen gate. The band takes up a smart-looking position in straight away center field. They play Sousa marches and an occasional armed service theme. In the stands the wives of sailors sing along to "Anchors Away." It could be a hundred years earlier—the beginning of a different century, a band in a park gazebo entertaining the crowds with the same martial music. An admiral throws out the first pitch, the band plays the national anthem, and baseball as it is played only in the nation's capital begins.

Along the rail, a young fan looking only slightly older than his hero begs a departing Wilkerson to sign his ball.

"Brad, that was some poke last night," the boy opines, holding his ball as far out as his skinny arm will stretch.

"Thanks," Wilkerson responds politely, as though he were talking to his mother, signing one last ball before going back to the dugout and the beginning of play.

"It was upper deck, man, right out there in section 468," the young fan says to his friend, showing him his new trophy.

Wilkerson and Nick Johnson are common sights as they sign autographs along the left field foul line, standing along the rail with laundry pens inking whatever kids hand them. They are building fans, making friends. These same kids will watch the two players who have signed balls for them and cheer for them long and loud. Nick Johnson has long been considered one of the most gifted young hitters in the game. His future was forecast as extremely bright, but he has spent major portions of his first four years in the major leagues on the disabled list with a panoply of ailments dating back to 2002 when he came up to stay with the Yankees.

Johnson hit 15 home runs in '02 in slightly more than 300 at bats. He spent much of the second half of the season with a bruised wrist. The following season, he again was sidelined with hand and wrist problems and the Yankees gave up on their prodigy, trading him to the Expos. He is having what may be his break out season, but it is early. If these young fans' luck holds, Nick Johnson's autograph could be something special.

Loaiza will take the mound for the Nationals against the Phillies. The Phillies are in last place in the National League East with a record of nine wins and 12 losses. They are several games behind the Nationals, who won the first series, their first meeting two hours away to the north.

The Phils send a young pitcher to the mound who has been very good in the early going. Brett Myers is only 24 years old, an age when most pitchers are just moving up the ladder, leaving Triple-A if they are lucky, but Myers has already had two full seasons with the Phillies, winning his first major league game at the age of 21. He is a ground ball pitcher, but one who gave up more home runs than he should have last year but, last year no Phillies pitcher had much success.

"They say you have to get to Myers early," offers a fan.

"Yeah?" says the other fan, watching Myers fall behind on Wilkerson to start the game. "Glavine's like that, too, you know?"

"Yeah, we let Glavine slip off the hook last week. Had the bases loaded, should've finished him then and there. But we lose to him three to one, go figure."

"Yeah, well, Myers ain't Glavine."

"Got a point there."

The afternoon sun washes across the diamond, bathing the outfield in bright colors while the grandstand is in gray shadows. The ball in the pitcher's hand is a golden orb, but as he finishes his delivery his arm moves toward the shadows very quickly, so that the ball goes in a flash from the bright sun to dull gray. The batter's eye has difficulty adjusting to the change and less time to calculate the angle of the pitch, less time to pick up the rotation on a curve. The effect makes the fastball much quicker and the curve more deceptive.

The light-to-dark effect does not help if the pitcher does not throw the ball over the plate, however. Wilkerson draws a five-pitch walk and trots down to first base. Ryan Church steps to the plate, filling in effectively for Nick Johnson, who has banged a foul off his knee at the plate the day before. Wilkerson is caught leaning, looking for the stolen base against Myers who whips the ball over to the first baseman who tags Wilkerson out. Church works another walk from Myers, but Vidro strikes out and Guillen bounces out to the shortstop, and what could have been a promising first inning is quickly over.

Loaiza faces Jimmy Rollins, the Phil's leadoff hitter. Rollins is emerging as an all-star shortstop in a league where there are no stars at the position. The American League has veteran stars like Derek Jeter and Miguel Tejada who put up monstrous offensive numbers from shortstop, and also perform with ballet precision in the field. Loaiza works quickly to Rollins and throws the ball past him, notching a quick strikeout to start the game. Kenny Lofton, the veteran of many campaigns, bats second. He has no better luck against the 91-mile per hour fastball of Loaiza than Rollins. He swings through two pitches and is the second strikeout in an afternoon when Loaiza will record many. Bobby Abreu, the Phillies' fine right fielder, lines out to first baseman Johnson and the inning ends quickly and quietly.

The pitchers settle into a classic pitchers' duel. The sun is now well behind the pitchers' mound, but there are only zeroes on the scoreboard. In the middle innings manager Frank Robinson is visible from the left field stands, holding forth along the railing at the top of the dugout.

Loaiza strikes out his seventh batter in the sixth inning. In 2003, when he was an all-star game pitcher, he struck out over 200 batters, a benchmark for pitching mastery. He also allowed fewer than three runs per nine innings, a feat seldom achieved in the era of buff batsmen whose performance is assisted by several forms of chemical enhancements. Loaiza looks more and more like the pitcher he was in 2003. It is a long year and he has a long way to get back to that level, but he is getting close on a sunny April afternoon.

In the eighth, Loaiza strikes out second baseman Utley to begin the inning. Then Jason Michaels his second hit of the afternoon. It is late and the fans wonder if Loaiza is tiring. He answers the question quickly, fanning Polanco with a fastball that is still topping out at 90 miles an hour.

Lieberthal draws a walk and the worry beads are out again. Charlie Manuel, the Phillies' new manager, pinch-hits Jose Offerman, a DH in the American League for several years and now closing out his career as a pinch hitter. He has no luck and fans to become eleventh K in the scorebook against only two hits. There will be few games by the Nationals over the course of the season that are pitched as well, but Myers is matching Loaiza, at least on the scoreboard.

"Somebody's going to hit a home run and win this game one to nothing," says a fan.

"Yeah, and we got Myers out of the game last inning," says the other fan hopefully.

Now the pitcher for the Phillies is Rheal Cormier, a French Canadian from the sea-weathered town of Moncton, New Brunswick, fifty miles inland from the frigid North Atlantic. Cormier has seen 14 seasons and is 38 years of age. He overwhelms the young Nationals Wilkerson and Sledge with left-handed mush. Vidro gets a good swing but bounces out to second and the game goes to the ninth as quietly as it began.

Loaiza comes out for the ninth, still pitching though Myers and the shadows are gone now. He faces Jimmy Rollins, who started the game a short two hours ago. Rollins has the advantage now. He has seen everything Loaiza is throwing, and none of it is as sharp as it was when he saw it the first time around. Rollins demonstrates why he is a rising star by depositing the second pitch over the right field wall into the Phillies bullpen. It is not hit far, but far enough to send a chill through the air; a sag in the risers can be felt thoughout the stadium.

Robinson lets Loaiza have one more chance. One more chance to finish out the inning in hopes that the Nationals will come from behind again in the bottom of the ninth and Loaiza can get a win. But the second batter up, Kenny Lofton, singles on a line to center and Robinson mounts the steps and walks slowly across the infield to take the ball from Loaiza. As the Nationals' newest star pitcher departs, the fans rise to their feet, all 27,000 applauding loudly in appreciation of a great effort. Loaiza tips his hat as he nears the dugout and departs with no chance to win.

Joey Eischen, one of the many veteran relievers on the team, takes the ball from Robinson. He faces Abreu, who singles Lofton to third. Jim Thome is the Phillies slugger who swings hard on every pitch, harder than any other batter in the game. He comes to bat and rockets a one-hop grounder to Wilkerson, who is playing first base for Nick Johnson. Wilkerson skillfully plucks the ball from the infield and stabs back toward the bag with his right foot, then, seeing Lofton dancing down the third base line, he screams the ball across the infield to Castilla, who gloves it just as Lofton slides back toward the third base bag. The tag beats him and Lofton is out, but Wilkerson misses the first base bag, and with another chance, the Phillies score twice more to take a 3-0 lead.

Billy Wagner, the left handed closer for the Phillies, comes on to close out the game. The Nationals send up the heart of the order in Jose Guillen, Sledge, and Castilla. But none can do anything with Wagner. The 3-0 shutout moves the Phillies one win closer to pulling themselves from the National League East cellar while welcoming the Nationals to it. The Nationals' record stands again at 11 wins and 11 losses. They have not been below .500 since April 11. The fans remain content, but as they leave the stadium and head toward Metro they wonder which way this season will break.

The home stand continues with three games against the much-improved New York Mets. Not only are the Mets another key NL East rival, playing at or near .500 ball like the Nationals, but after the series the Nationals also make their first trip to the West Coast, where they will play eight games. These trips are always difficult, but three games against the league-leading, red-hot Los Angeles Dodgers will be tougher still. Any advantage Washington can build before beginning the arduous trip will help.

In the first game of the home stand, New York sends to the mound young Jae Seo, a Korean born pitcher who, like Tomo Ohka, is part of an increasing Asian presence in the major leagues. Seo beat Ohka and the Nationals in a 10-5 second game of the last New York series. Livan Hernandez will pitch for Washington, and, though he is the ace of the staff, he has been inconsistent so far. But he beat the Mets 11-4 on Sunday, just five days ago, and Washington is hoping he will build on this developing pattern of excellent starts. Like Washington, the Mets have 11 wins and 11 losses, and the winner of the game will take sole possession of third place, bragging rights for a day.

Hernandez has established a pattern of pitching poorly in the first inning, looking for a comfort level with his pitches, with the ball itself. He gets Reyes on a can of corn to center, but then Matsui and Beltran single and he loses Piazza after running the count full. The fans hold their breath. Is this another game where Hernandez gets shelled early, or can he right himself?

Cliff Floyd steps to the plate as one of the hottest hitters in the league. He had a good series against the Nats a week ago and hit the home run that undid another of Loaiza's wasted efforts. Floyd hits a high arching fly ball that gets in only a single run and everyone breathes a sigh of relief; but there are still only two outs. Doug Mientkeiwicz, who looks more like a hockey player, comes to bat and ends the inning with a grounder to Nick Johnson, who is back at first, his deep thigh bruise healed enough that he can play.

Seo struggles slightly in the first inning but the Nationals do little. Hernandez has an easier second and seems to be getting into the same kind of rhythm he did on Sunday, but the Nats take a 1-0 lead into the bottom of the fourth when Jose Guillen gets a pitch to hit and does not miss it, depositing it over the left field wall convincingly. The Mets go quietly in the top of the fifth and the Nats send the bottom half of the order to bat.

Castilla flies out, but Brian Schneider catches a pitch on the sweet part of the wood and the ball clearly seems headed for the stands. There have been many balls that have been hard hit and stayed inside the fence, sparking discussion about the physics and wind patterns inside RFK, but Schneider's ball carries over the fence and gives his battery mate, Hernandez, and the Nats the lead at 2-0. After Guzman makes the second out, Livan Hernandez shows his remarkable athleticism once again. He catches a get-me-over pitch from Seo and lifts a solid home run over the left field fence to add comfort to the margin at 4-0.

Castilla doubles in two runs in the sixth inning and Hernandez cruises through eight full innings, throwing 130 pitches, perhaps a few too many but it gives the bullpen a needed night of rest. Cordero and Ayala close out the ninth and it is the Nationals who stand in third place when the papers are delivered Saturday morning.

# 4

# Playing in the Shadows

On May 1 the *New York Times* sports page announces it, "The Birds Are Back in Town." Even the New York papers are convinced of the bona fides of the resurgent Orioles. The Orioles are in first place with a solid four game lead over the Red Sox in the AL East. The attention paid to the Nationals at the beginning of the season has faded. They were a novelty for a while, but they have slid from view as fans pay attention to the emerging pennant races that will capture imaginations over the summer. Now the newsprint focus is on the Orioles' seven game winning streak that has them ahead of the perennial favorites, the Yankees, who languish in the nether reaches with Tampa Bay.

The article on the Orioles features their recent head-to-head wins over the Red Sox, offering the Yankee faithful at least the good news that the hated Red Sox have hit a snag as well. More deserving of attention is the wonderful start that Oriole shortstop Miguel Tejada is having. He is leading the league in runs batted in and is tied for the lead in home runs. He had a landmark season in 2004, when he led the American League with 150 runs batted in. He established himself in 2004 as the best shortstop in the game, playing in a town that is synonymous with great shortstops. Tejada would relish any comparison with Ripken, not because he seeks to better his predecessor, but because he appreciates the legends of the game and wishes only to join them. Since 2001, no other player has played in more games than Tejada, the 21st century's iron man.

The New York paper makes no mention of the Mets game with the Nationals because it was finished late in the evening. Even so, both teams are playing in the shadows now. High hopes for the Orioles make stories about the Nationals less compelling copy, but flying beneath the radar is nothing new to D.C. baseball. There was a lot of baseball played in D.C. during the twentieth century and some of the best went largely unmentioned by the national press.

The Nationals game that ends their very successful April run is about the rain and the nearly 41,000 fans who attend the game despite the dreary forecast. The game is played concurrent to a Washington Wizards play-off game at the MCI Center. The Wizards' poignant season offers a return to prominence by a once proud franchise. The attendance at the MCI Center is a record 20,000 fans-half what attend the Nationals game. The Wizards beat the Chicago Bulls in game three of their play-off series. Attendance at these two events draws attention to the fact that D.C. is becoming a big-time sports town. It's not the same town that hosted the Washington Senators. The Washington that gives rise to the Nationals has seen a lot of things change.

The Wizards offer what is at first glance a sharp contrast to the Nationals. They are an inner city team, playing an inner city sport. Basketball belongs in Washington, D.C., because African Americans claim it with pride as "their game." The Nationals are built on a suburban fan base, typical of all of baseball. Which is not to say that Washington African American community and the affluent middle class blacks in Prince George's County are not baseball fans. Truly, if one thing distinguishes D.C. baseball it is the substantial minority fan base.

It is not a new thing, African American support for baseball in Washington. The Washington Senators drew more minority fans than any other franchise, even though Old Griffith Stadium decreed segregated seating for much of its history. Baseball in D.C. stands in marked contrast to Baltimore, where minority attendance is—to put it kindly—less commonplace. Baltimore is an industrial town where the African American community never formed a bond to what was perceived as a largely white game when Baltimore joined the American League in 1954.

The huge federal workforce and federal career opportunities in Washington have provided an affluence and stability for African Americans in D.C. than cannot be found in most other cities in the country. Federal jobs supported an affluent African American community in Washington for many years and Old Griffith Stadium was located in the middle of it. The now departed ballpark was also adjacent to Howard University, one of the most prominent of Historic Black Universities and Colleges. The unique economy of Washington's African American community explains why minority attendance always has been, and remains, commonplace for D.C. baseball teams.

Overall, however, the modern game of baseball does not draw well in the black community. Baseball is just not as popular among African Americans as football or basketball, for whatever reason.

It has not always been this way. When baseball was the "national pastime," black Americans played the game with the same dedication and enthusiasm as whites, and certainly brought as much athletic talent to it. In the stands at RFK one can find evidence of a golden era when black ballplayers were among the best there were and their accomplishments mythic. It can be see in the many African American fans wearing old Negro League jerseys and hats. Some of them herald a team known as the Grays, whose ties to the Nationals are not well understood going into this new season and new century of baseball.

The team was the Homestead Grays, an African American barnstorming team from western Pennsylvania that first appeared in 1912. It settled into Pittsburgh as Negro League ball established itself. During the depression era, the Grays joined the prosperous and growing National Negro Leagues and outgrew their humble origins and even the small park in Pittsburgh. During the depression era and the Great War, baseball attendance outstripped prior decades by far and the Grays moved some of their games to Washington at Old Griffith Stadium. The arrangement both helped the Grays to dip into the affluence of Washington's black community, and kept the stadium in use when the Senators were away.

The Grays brought to Washington some of the greatest men ever to play the game, and black fans attended the games in numbers that often topped their white counterparts at Senators games. Many of the Grays stars from that golden era have been recognized now as baseball greats, some of them having been inducted into the Baseball Hall of Fame. Their feats have taken on mythic proportions because they were accomplished outside the spotlight of the American mainstream. There is no denying the vast talents of these players and the vast importance of the Negro Leagues to the culture of the times. Donn Rogosin, in *Invisible Men* (New York: Atheneum, 1983), says the totally African American operated league, was one of the great economic achievements by blacks during the Jim Crow era. The very best of the Negro League teams in attendance, fame and accomplishment was the Homestead Grays, playing before a packed house at Griffith Stadium.

The most famous Washington Grays included Josh Gibson, the star catcher, Buck Leonard, the heavy-hitting first baseman, and James "Cool Papa" Bell, of whom Satchel Paige made the famous claim, "He could turn off the light and be in bed before the room was dark." During the nine-year period between 1938 and 1947, the Grays won eight Negro League Championships, is quite a record considering the level of talent playing in the league at the time. The rosters of teams like the Kansas City Monarchs and others were studded with now famous names. Much of the excitement under the lights at Old Griffith Stadium took place with little notice by Washington's mainstream press. The city elite, the lobbyists and congressmen who make this town what it is, were largely ignorant of the boiling baseball caldron just a few blocks from the Capitol. It is a neglected but amazing piece of American history and folklore. A wonderful book details the history of the Grays, *Beyond the Shadow of the Senators* (New York, McGraw Hill 2003), written appropriately enough by a Baltimore sports writer, Brad Snyder.

Some of the RFK fans, aging black men with salt and pepper hair, proudly wear the shirts and hats of the Grays. As young boys, a few may actually have seen them play and can tell the stories. Many black fans went to see both the Grays and the Senators. For Senators games they sat just beyond first base out along the right field line in the bleachers, the area restricted to black patrons. Before the Grays came along, the Senators provided great baseball for both blacks and whites, winning the World Series against the old New York Giants in 1925, and appearing in their last World Series in 1933, again against the Giants. But as the Senators faded the Grays became more prominent, especially during the Second World War when many prominent black players were too old to go to war but were still famous athletes in the neighborhoods around Old Griffith Stadium.

People may not know enough about the history of the Grays, but that team is an important part of what is going on down below on the field at RFK. Jackie Robinson, the great player who broke the color barrier in Major League Baseball, played for the other great Negro League franchise, the Kansas City Monarchs, whose long-standing competition with the Washington Grays was legendary. Robinson's historic transfer to the Brooklyn Dodgers in 1946 is reflected in the players on the field for Washington whether they are black Dominicans like Cristian Guzman and Jose Guillen, or black Cubans like Livan Hernandez. The break in the color barrier opened the game to many, regardless of what language they spoke, regardless of where their ancestors came from.

It is unfair to compare the obscurity of low expectation that plagues the Nationals with the forced obscurity of the Grays. Yet the Nationals are still playing outside the glow of the bright lights because the baseball establishment is unsure whether to take the Washington team seriously. The final April game on Saturday night concludes too late to make some of the early editions. But the Nationals win another impressive game. Tomo Ohka bounces back from several rough outings and shuts down the Mets. These are the same vaunted Mets who paid top dollar for the best in free agent talent.

When the Nationals were shopping in the bins for old vinyl, long-playing records like Vinny Castilla, the Mets were getting the latest CDs. When Washington took a flier on bad boy Jose Guillen, New York got proven, tools-laden Carlos Beltran. When the Nationals plucked stressed-out Esteban Loaiza from the busy streets of the Big Apple, the Mets got perennial all-star Pedro Martinez. Somehow, though, the Nationals seem to have done the better shopping. Sometimes there is nothing like those old 33s for quality.

The last game in April features showers once again, but this time the Nationals survive. The overcast skies do not open until the fifth inning. Before the umpires call a delay, Washington scores three runs for a commanding 3-0 lead. Jose Guillen and Vidro score the first two runs driven in on a double to left by Vinny Castilla. Victor Zambrano continues to provide assists to the Nationals, forcing in a third run on a walk to Nick Johnson. Johnson has a .380 lifetime on-base percentage, and the fans at RFK are relieved to see him returning healthy after the foul ball crashed into his thigh on Tuesday. Careers have been lost on similar bad luck.

After returning from the rain delay in the fifth inning, Zambrano gives up solo home runs to Church and Nick Johnson, and Washington extends its lead to 5-0. Ohka departs with his best performance of the season and hope that what could be an excellent pitching rotation may yet round into form. As Robinson stands on the mound to give the ball to the new pitcher, Gary Majewski, the rains pick up and the field is again getting treacherous. Robinson and Mets manager Willie Randolph complain about the condition of the infield, where puddles form the same as they did in the afternoon game when Guzman's weather-forced error cost the Nats a hard fought win. In the inclement weather, Majewski allows a bases loaded double to Cliff Floyd, always a source of trouble for the Nats, and three runs cross the plate.

Robinson turns to journeyman reliever Hector Carrasco, who has been perfect in five appearances. As Robinson departs the field he collars the umpire crew chief, Joe Crews, and gets into a shouting match over the condition of the field. The Mets blame the mess on the Nationals grounds crew, but it is the umpires who have let games carry on with heavy rain falling, now for a second time in April. Robinson is not just engaged, now he is enraged. In his animated protest he draws verbal pictures for the umpire of Guzman's play days before. He demands that the MLB umpiring crew respect the health of the players. He is heaved from the game with a long arm by Crews. The fans applaud Robinson's show of faith.

Carrasco shuts down a Mets rally in the eighth and the umpires have no choice, as the rains are too heavy for the game to continue and show no sign of abating. The game is declared over. The Nats win 5-3 and their record for the month of April stands at 13 wins and 11 losses. They are in third place. They are ahead of the Mets and their hundred million dollar payroll. They are only a game behind the Braves and two behind the Marlins, who are in first. April showers have not dampened the spirits of the fans, and the team is rounding into fine shape as the month closes. The papers may be covering the Orioles, but the Nats' pitching is strong.

"Hey, they still got that head case Ponson pitching don't they?" asks one fan.

"Yeah, they won't be in first place come August, hell, they won't be there come June," says the other fan.

These are smart fans. There will be 2.7 million of them who will see baseball in D.C. this season if the April pace holds. There have been no promotional advertisements for this team. Their games are televised less frequently than any other major league franchise, impossible viewing for most in the area. Their presence is definitely shaded by events elsewhere, in the commissioner's office in New York and in Baltimore, where the TV franchise deal is stuck in Peter Angelos' flypaper. Yet the fans come and they will keep coming as the summer sun heats up. Baseball in D.C. is real and it will be coming to a town near you, soon.

## California Dreaming

The first game in May features John Patterson, who leads the team in allowing the fewest runs scored against, the earned run average or ERA. His ERA stands at the lowest reaches of the scale, not even one run per nine innings. Young pitchers like Patterson are notoriously inconsistent. For that matter, almost any pitcher can be inconsistent, and only the great ones hit a groove that lasts for years. Patterson has not reached that level yet, though he does show signs of promise. His opposing number on the Mets is Aaron Heilman. Heilman is a few months younger than Patterson and has a year less major league experience. Those first two hundred innings of experience are important to young pitchers. Patterson is just reaching this milestone. Heilman is several months away.

Patterson has his first rough stretch right off the bat in the first inning. Two singles by Miguel Cairo and Carlos Beltran put runners on first and third base with one out. Patterson catches Beltran leaning toward second base in an apparent steal attempt. Patterson runs toward the runner, which is textbook for rundowns, but Cairo is not at third in the case study Patterson is following. Cairo breaks for the plate and Beltran points to him. Patterson peeks and loses his focus completely, but refuses to take the bait and runs Beltran down. But he loses Cairo, whom he could have kept at third with smarter play. The Nationals are immediately behind 1-0, and Patterson is rattled.

Heilman pitches well in the first two innings, allowing only a scratch infield single to Guillen. Patterson has a perfect second and third inning with two strikeouts, one on a beautiful 94 mile per hour fastball to Mientkiewicz. Guzman, who has hit in eight straight games now, gets a single to center field after a hit by Bennett to start the bottom of the third inning. There are runners on first and second base and Patterson lays down an effective bunt, moving the runners to second and third with only one out. Wilkerson walks and there are runners on every base when Nick Johnson has a great at bat, fouling off pitch after pitch until he rips a clean liner to right that scores Bennett and Guzman. Guillen's sacrifice fly gets Johnson in from third later in the inning and the score is Nationals 3, Mets 1.

Patterson starts the fourth easily enough, getting Cairo on a bouncer to second, but the heart of the order explodes on him. Beltran gets a ball past

Nick Johnson at first and it skips into the left field corner for a stand-up double. Cliff Floyd doubles him home and Piazza walks, the Mets trailing only 3-2 and only one out. Mientkiewicz flies out, but Wright, the Mets' third base prodigy, gets a solid hit through the infield into left and the score is tied. Valent is walked intentionally to bring the pitcher, Heilman, to the plate. He gets solid wood on the ball and the fans sink for a moment, but Guillen tracks it down and the inning ends with the score tied.

Both Patterson and Heilman leave after six innings with the score still tied 3-3, giving way to the respective bull pens.

"We're gonna win this. Our bull pen has been lights out," asserts the proud Nationals' fan.

"Yeah, we've won our share in the late innings," affirms his mate.

This time, something unforeseeable happens. Eischen, the experienced left-handed setup pitcher, comes in and leaps athletically to grab a high hopper that would have been better let go through to Guzman. Eischen gloves the ball and falls to the ground hard on his wrist. His face is twisted in pain and he lies on the ground for several minutes as his teammates and manager look on with concern. Two trainers are necessary to get Eischen off the field with a broken arm. Suddenly the bull pen is less deep, less sound. Carrasco comes on for Eischen and pitches a perfect inning, followed by Ayala, who has an easy eighth inning. The Nationals have no greater luck with the Mets bull pen and the game goes to the ninth tied.

Ayala is a young pitcher, still. He is the same age as Patterson, although he has distinguished himself for two consecutive seasons as a relief pitcher with the game on the line. It is the ninth and the game is tied, but Ayala is facing the bottom of the order and the fans are expectant. Ayala starts with consecutive singles to the first three batters and there is no one out. Suddenly it is not the weak sisters but the top of the order facing him. Cairo sacrifices a run home and then Beltran, the multi-year signee making $12 million this year alone, gets his second double of the game that drives in two runs. The Mets bull pen seals off the Nationals in the bottom of the ninth. The Nationals lose 5-3 in a game they might have won. The Nationals get ready for the flight to L.A., only one game over .500, with a long West Coast road trip before they are back before the friendly fans at RFK.

## The Other Side of the Moon

May's schedule will be very different from April's. The road trip to the West Coast is a test of any team. Like American astronauts that disappeared on the other side of the moon, baseball played in California is lost to fans on the East Coast. Games that start after 10:00 p.m. in California do not conclude until midnight and fans in the east do not wait up.

The games are not on TV and are played so late that no one back in

Washington knows anything about the outcomes until the late news editions are printed or they appear online. (Ah, but the wonders of the modern age. The insomniac fan can grab a few winks late at night, then get up in the wee hours restless and worried, turn the computer on, check the scores and, if things go right, go back to sleep and make it to work on time.)

The team has a late game on Sunday and the paper reports that their plane did not land until six in the morning. One wonders whether there were white clad nurses leading the wounded from the plane as the Nationals continue to lose players to injury. Eischen's surgery is performed in Baltimore in the morning as his teammates try to sleep before practice in the afternoon. He will be out for half of the season.

Esteban Loaiza took an early flight to the coast on Sunday. The team sends him ahead because he is starting the Monday game in Los Angeles and will give the team at least one key member who is rested. As the game starts and the players meander about the field wanly, this measure of precaution takes on added importance.

The book on Loaiza is that he is an April pitcher who founders as the season wears on. It is May and he still looks sharp, the two-seam fastball running and sinking at 91 miles per hour, and his cutter good enough to strike out seven in six innings. He gives up three hits and three walks but leaves for a pinch hitter in the seventh, trailing 1-0 against an even better Scott Erickson, a veteran of numerous arm and shoulder surgeries. Baerga pinch-hits for Loaiza in the top of the seventh with the bases loaded and no one out. He repays Robinson for his enduring vote of confidence with a line drive single to right to score the first run, chasing Scott Erickson and getting to the Dodger bull pen. Here, as in so many games in the early part of the season, the Nationals score their runs, first two in the seventh, then two in the eighth and ninth as they go on to win 6-2.

With Eischen out, the Nationals' patched together bull pen gets the Dodgers, nonetheless. Gary Majewski pitches the seventh, Carrasco the eighth, and then the six-foot-ten, left-handed Jon Rauch closes the ninth allowing only a solo home run to Milton Bradley, the Los Angeles center fielder.

Although the game puts the Nationals back over .500 by two games, the injuries continue to mount. Termel Sledge is helped from the game after coming up lame chasing a fly ball in the green outfield grass. He is diagnosed the next day with a serious hamstring injury. He is placed on the disabled list after the game, and the following morning the Nationals call up Endy Chavez and Jeffrey Hammonds from New Orleans. Both players are outfielders with major league experience, although at different ends of their careers. Hammonds is 34 years of age, hanging on to legitimacy by a whisker. Chavez is a good utility outfielder who is only 27 years old.

For the second game on the coast, the Dodgers starting pitcher is Jeff Weaver, who, like Loaiza, fled the Big Apple in ignominious defeat, only to resurrect his career after a suitable time of decompression. Weaver is having a fine season after reestablishing his career with the Dodgers in 2004. He is still only 28 years old and suffers the same inconsistency many of his peers experience. His counterpart for the Nationals is Zach Day, on this Tuesday evening when 41,000 southern Californians pay to see the newest National League franchise. Day has said that he knows Robinson has him on a short leash, meaning that he believes his manager lacks confidence in him and takes him from ballgames earlier than Day believes is warranted. All pitchers believe this to be the case, but Day proves prescient, as Robinson lifts him in the fourth after a long inning that sees the Dodgers score twice and runners to inhabit every base for most of the time Day stands on the mound. Robinson watches Day depart and rubs the baseball as he waits for Rauch to arrive from the bull pen.

It is not Rauch's day, either. Although he retires J. D. Drew in the fourth to end Day's rough inning, the Dodgers are back again in the fifth and collect two seemingly innocuous runs. The Nationals score single runs in the second and third on doubles by Guillen and Wilkerson, but Weaver makes the 4-2 scored stand up until he is relieved in the sixth inning. Then four Dodger relievers close out the game, allowing the Nationals numerous scoring opportunities but keeping them off the scoreboard until the game is over and the series is knotted at one game apiece.

The next day is a double whammy. The long plane flight and cumulative effects of sleep deprivation are taking a toll on Frank Robinson. He delivers a lineup card to the aggregation of blue-suited umpires at home plate, a lineup card with the names Endy Chavez and Cristian Guzman hitting in the first two spots. To replace the seriously injured Sledge, Chavez has been called up from New Orleans where he has not learned to appreciate either the joys of Dixieland jazz or patience at the plate. Wilkerson is slumping and Chavez is a suitable enough replacement, but the combined on-base percentage at these two happy hackers at the top of the order is .303.

The long-term impact of this evening's lineup is disturbing, given that Sledge is out for months. Frank Robinson has another variable to enter into the already capricious Lineup Bingo that he plays, sending chills into the sabermetric community of Nationals fans. Robinson drops Nick Johnson, with his career on-base percentage approaching .400, to sixth place.

The key for the Nationals continues to be their pitching. Livan Hernandez, who starts the game, is a veteran of the West Coast wars. He pitched for the San Francisco Giants from 1999 until the 2002 season, and started games three and seven of the World Series in October of 2002 for the Giants. He lost both games of that series against the Anaheim Angels in what is probably the low point of his career. He was forced from game seven in the third inning, eventually taking the loss in the final and deciding game of the series for the Giants.

He showed early and exciting promise pitching for the Florida Marlins and was showcased in the 1997 World Series with them. Livan Hernandez was a rookie pitcher that year for Florida, having signed with the Miami based team after fleeing his native Cuba the year before. Called up from the minors that summer, he started seventeen games for the Marlins, generating some of the same excitement that Dontrelle Willis now sparks for that team. Hernandez that year won nine games and lost only three, with an earned run average of only 3.18. He started game one of the 1997 World Series against Cleveland, imperturbable in the face of great hitters like Manny Ramirez, David Justice, Jim Thome and Matt Williams. Aging Dodger legend Orel Hershiser pitched for Cleveland in game one, but Hernandez scattered three runs over six innings and got the win, and then went on to win game five of that series as the Marlins won in their first ever World Series appearance.

The Marlins were a baseball phenomenon, an expansion franchise that managed to put together a World Champion team after joining the league in 1993. Hernandez never realized the star potential Miami fans saw in him that first season of 1997. He remains one of the game's most durable starting pitchers, however, pitching over 200 innings in each of his full seasons since 1997 with the exception of 1999, when he joined the Giants in mid season and only made 30 starts for 199 innings.

On this Wednesday, slightly less than a decade removed from Cuba, Hernandez has his good stuff against the Dodgers. He has struggled in the early innings in his starts so far this year, but on Wednesday night he is that same pitcher who had "Star" written all over him back in Miami. He limits the Dodgers to seven hits over nine innings and allows only two runs, winning the game for the Nationals 5-2. (As he throws in the second inning, back in downtown D.C. the Gilbert Arenas shot floats through the net, the final horn sounding to give the Wizards their third win in their series against the Bulls and sending them home for the sixth game to D.C., where they can win their first play-off series in almost twenty years.)

Nick Johnson, hitting near the bottom of the order is unfazed by his yo-yo status in Frank Robinson's order and knows nothing of the drama unfolding at the MCI Center in D.C. He hits a solo home run in the fifth to start off Washington's scoring, tying the game at 1-1. He then singles in the middle of a rally in the 7th to drive in Castilla with the third and winning run after Vinny Castilla's RBI double. Endy Chavez ends the scoring with a double that drives in Jeffrey Hammond's, the other New Orleans call-up. Cristian Guzman, batting second, goes 0-for-four after raising his average to .247 over the two weeks he has batted at the end of the order.

The Nationals leave Los Angeles with a win in the series. They leave without Jose Vidro, the veteran second baseman has who turned an ankle and is lost for at least two weeks, adding to the growing number of players hurt. However, there is reason for optimism. It is another victory against a team that won the NL West Division in 2004 and has one of the best records in baseball in the early going of 2005. The win lends additional credibility to the Nationals' growing reputation as a team to regard with respect—no longer globetrotting pushovers without a home. If they can only get healthy they may surprise many in June. First they have an appearance at the Fillmore, in old San Francisco, that is going through a tough fit of withdrawal.

# 5

# Cream at the Fillmore West

It has been a dozen years since a lithe young ballplayer named Barry Bonds came west from Pittsburgh. He hit 46 home runs in his first San Francisco season and became a fan favorite whose legend and notoriety grew with each year until he broke the single season home run record with 73 only three years after McGwire had set the bar at 70; both records seemingly perched on some superhuman plateau. Like Cal Ripken before him, Barry Bonds made a new stadium—now called SBC Park—a regular on the highlight reels, with his home runs being fished from the bay by waiting kayakers. During his tenure, the Giants as a franchise have taken a back seatonly to the Braves in overall winning percentage. It is no overstatement to say that Bonds is the "franchise."

Yet Bonds has not played a single game in 2005. The allegations of his steroid use, including his admission under oath to the use of a "cream and a clear substance," have made many sportswriters and fans secretly hope his days and his now questionable hitting feats will fade quietly into San Francisco Bay's darker waters.

"The San Francisco team has remarkable depth that will make them contenders with or without Bonds," says ESPN commentator Peter Gammons, his Boston twang twanging on *Baseball Tonight*.

"You cannot replace a player like Barry Bonds," counters Harold Reynolds, his slight southern drawl complementing Gammons perfectly.

They are both correct. San Francisco has tremendous talent even without Bonds. But the average age of the talent is 33. Like the Yankees on the other coast, they are a team of aging wonders. San Francisco is managed by the oldest of the grizzled veterans, Felipe Alou, whose weather-beaten countenance is matched only by Frank Robinson's. The Giants in 2004 failed to make the play-offs and finished behind Los Angeles in the West. In 2005 they are struggling to stay even after the first month.

Bonds begs the larger question as to what baseball will look like without the puffy-faced pitchers still throwing plus fastballs well into their 40s, and aging sluggers with their cartoon physiques still capable of sending homers arcing into the night sky game after game. Do the fans need the legendary exploits of the steroid era to capture their interest? Will interest sag and fans look for other sports where there is more blood in the water? There are those who believe baseball's owners have been betting on the seat-filling capabilities of increased home run drama and hockey style fights spurred by headhunting pitchers unchecked by the "Commissioner."

Buzz Bissinger, in a *New York Times* op-ed article in early May, blames the owners, his article appearing with an apt cartoon depicting the players with their uniforms spattered by tomatoes hurled by fans while the owners beam sunnily and prosperously in the foreground. The article cites the steroid testing adopted by other sports at earlier points in their history as evidence of the purposeful negligence by MLB, Inc., on performance enhancing drugs. Testing in basketball was initiated with far less overt evidence than to surfaced in the late eighties in baseball, and football, that had obvious problems predating in baseball, has had a testing regime since 1987, just prior to the first allegations about steroids and Oakland's Jose Canseco. Recently published books have created this turn in the controversy. *Juicing the Game* (NY, Viking, 2005), by the Boston sports writer Howard Bryant, correctly characterizes the owners' implicit endorsement of performance boosters as their grasping not only for control of the game, also, for the very soul of the game itself.

The soul of the game lies in the magic between fans and players, both of whom love the game and appreciate the art of it. Owners may love the game, but it is also a business and their concern is the bottom line—putting more fans in seats, getting more television sets tuned to baseball. Steroids have increased the brute element of the game and supposedly enhanced its animal appeal. The chemical array of performance enhancements is larger than just steroids and includes amphetamines, human growth hormones, and anything else that increases the intrinsic muscle of the player and his ability to focus on the game at hand over a very long season.

Making the batter larger is the most obvious enhancement, however, and it tilts the fundamental equation of baseball that occurs between batter and pitcher in favor of the batter. Pitchers have responded by enhancing their own performance and the 100-mile per hour fastball has become more common; and with relief pitchers it is a staple of their game, their coda to strike fear at the plate. Relief pitchers have always relied on the simple elegance of the exploding fastball, and they have always pitched inside. But in recent years, baseball has condoned a more bloodthirsty approach by pitchers, and the essential equation of the game has been altered even further. Teams spilling onto the field to defend the honor of their brothers drilled by these pitchers have also added an element of appeal to games, like NASCAR where tragedy sells tickets. The owner think that anyone who believes otherwise is naïve, that they are just selling the game. Critics believe that rather than selling the game, have the owners already sold it out.

Barry Bonds' absence in 2005 presents a great test of the owners' hypothesis. A quick look at the attendance figures in 2005 offers surprising insights. In Los Angeles, for example, the Tuesday, Wednesday, and Thursday games with the fledgling Nationals draw an average of 36,000 fans for three mid week games. Neither the Dodgers' nor the Nationals' lineup offers muscle bound brutes poling long shots into the night. Shawn Green, Jeff Kent, and Jose Guillen are at the heart of the two lineups and both Green and Guillen are relatively lean ballplayers who harken back to Yaztremski and DiMaggio, the great athletes whose power was generated in the precision of their swing, not its brute force.

In San Francisco the three weekend games are almost completely sold out and paid attendance averages almost 40,000. If the lack of home run production that is being documented in the early games of the 2005 season is an issue of great importance the numbers do not show it. Fans are coming to see "their" team play. They come to see Vinny Castilla rope one into the corner and the home team go on top. They come to see Livan Hernandez struggle through eight innings but emerge victorious.

It is the tension of the games, subtle in comparison to football, no doubt, but there for those who appreciate the game. Fans who display that appreciation are not hard to find. They are there in San Francisco, even while Bonds is undergoing another knee surgery, his doctor now linked to a new controversy. Are the fans at the SBC Park learning to love the game without him? Time will tell, but one can hope that phenomena like the Nationals will convince players and owners that it is the thrill of the game and who wins it that matters most, whether it is won on a squeeze play laid down by a pitcher who can handle the bat, or by a home run looking for a record book to fit into.

## Playing for Heart in San Francisco

The series by the bay is sold out and the Nationals continue to play to full houses, like a Broadway play that is being fine-tuned on the road rather successfully. The Giants send Noah Lowry, a 24-year-old left-hander out to face Tomo Ohka for the Nationals in game one of the series. Lowry, called up in the second half of 2004, had remarkable success at his home park, winning five games without a defeat. This season he has been less successful, but he is making his first home start and is no doubt hopeful his luck is about to change.

Ohka is still trying to find his rhythm for the 2005 season. He has been up and down and Robinson still is concerned that there is something unsound that Ohka is hiding. Starting the game, Ohka again looks uncertain on the mound. He walks two in the second inning and gives up a double to Pedro Feliz, a single to Edgardo Alfonso, and the Giants score twice to take a 2-0 lead. In their half of the second inning the Nationals counter with four runs off Lowry. The bottom of the batting order gets the rally started with Gary Bennett, the reserve catcher, and Guzman getting singles to start. Wilkerson bunts for a single to load the bases. Carroll playing for the injured Vidro singles in a run, Castilla singles two more, and Nick Johnson ends the scoring with an RBI-single to center. The Nationals take the lead 4-2.

Ohka continues to search for the plate in the third inning, and gives up a homer to light-hitting Devi Cruz. Robinson loses patience and lifts Ohka for Rauch, who has looked good but has gotten dinged a few times. Rauch responds with three scoreless innings and the game remains 4-3 until the top of the eighth when the Nationals put another crooked number on the score board, this one more crooked than the last.

Alou begins the eighth by going to the bullpen and bringing in journeyman reliever Jason Christianson, who gets Jeffrey Hammonds; but Nick Johnson singles and Guzman walks, and a run-scoring double sends Alou to his bullpen again. He brings in Scott Eyre, another journeyman, who walks the pinch-hitting Baerga to load the bases, and then forces in a run with a walk to Brad Wilkerson. Losing patience, Alou goes to the equally well-traveled Al Levine, who surrenders a bases clearing, three-run double to Ryan Church, and the Nationals take a 9-3 lead into the bottom of the eighth inning. Ayala pitches a scoreless eighth and Cordero pitches a shaky but scoreless ninth, preserving the first Nationals win for Rauch.

The Nationals go into the second game in San Francisco with three wins on the road trip and are now 16-13. The Mets have starting winning games as well and are pushing them for third place in the East. Needing to keep the pressure on the Mets, the Nationals send their best young pitcher, Texan John Patterson, out to get the victory. San Francisco counters with their number one starter and their most durable pitchers over the previous four years, Jason Schmidt. Schmidt won 18 games in 2004, striking out 250 batters. He is big and throws hard.

The scouts say his fastball has lost something this year. He joins other hard-throwing pitchers who have lost velocity, about whom rumors swirl that fears of testing positive for steroids have taken away their chemical edge. Whatever the source of Schmidt's edge, his performance was off in Arizona in the previous series, and he walked five while only striking out four in less than seven innings. Yet it is Patterson who clearly does not have his good stuff on this Saturday night in May. Moises Alou hits a three run homer in the third to give the Giants an early 3-0 lead.

In the fourth inning, with the bases loaded, Robinson pinch-hits for Patterson, bringing in Jose Guillen to hit. Robinson's strategy takes on the aura of brilliance when Guillen singles in two runs. Wilkerson brings in a run with a sacrifice fly and Nick Johnson doubles in two runs, which forces Alou to lift Schmidt. The Nationals now lead 5-3. The age of Alou's bullpen becomes more obvious when Jeff Fassero takes the mound. The left-hander is 42 years old and has seen a lot of baseball over the past two decades. He cannot staunch the bleeding however, as Church and Schneider single in additional runs and the Nationals lead 7-3 in the fourth.

Unable to stand the success, Zach Day returns the favor as he replaces Patterson. At the bottom of the fifth inning he gives up a single and a walk, and then hits Moises Alou with a pitch that prompts a warning from the umpire, who thinks Day may be responding to Alou's homer in the third. The convoluted ethic of retaliation in baseball is explored through the eyes of Tony LaRussa in Buzz Bissinger's book. Whether Robinson controls his pitchers as tightly as LaRussa claims is unknown, but it proves a poor time for retribution, as Day faces Pedro Feliz, who has had a very good series, with only one out. Predictably enough, Feliz singles in a run and Robinson counters with Hector Carrasco to face Edgardo Alfonso, the bases still loaded. Alfonso doubles in two runs, and the Giants retake the lead 8-7.

Alou goes to his bullpen again, and again, and again. He brings in Jason Christianson and Scott Eyre for their second appearance in the series and Matt Herges bridges another inning, getting the Giants to the ninth still holding a one-run lead. Alou brings on a 23-year-old rookie, Jeremy Accardo, who has been in the show, as they call it, less than a week. He says after the game that he was less nervous than for his first appearance, but he gives up two walks and a wild pitch that belies calm. Wilkerson's sacrifice fly drives in a run and Alou brings in Jim Brower to relieve Accardo, making seven pitchers total for the game. Brower fares little better, walking Castilla to load the bases and bring up Ryan Church. It is déjà vu all over again, as Church laces a bases clearing double to left, giving the Nationals an 11-8 lead heading into the bottom of the inning. Cordero, Frank Robinson's sixth pitcher of the day, pitches a perfect ninth inning for the save. The Nationals are four games over .500 for the first time since their five-game winning streak that included the home opener in mid April. They play on Sunday afternoon for the sweep against the Giants.

The final game of the series with the Giants is telecast and the team can be seen for the first time since leaving on the West Coast road trip. Loaiza pitches another fine game going into the eighth inning with a 3-2 lead. But he gives up a run-scoring double to Edgardo Alfonzo with two out and the games goes into extra innings when the Nationals cannot take advantage of run-scoring opportunities in both the ninth and tenth. Jamey Carroll has four hits and Jose Guillen hits his eighth home run, but the Giants push across a run in the tenth and the Nationals look tired, happy to leave San Francisco with two wins.

The trip ends in Arizona with the Snakes. Since the Nationals swept them in three games in April at RFK, the Snakes have seen happier days. Troy Glaus, their third baseman, leads Jose Guillen and all others in the National League in home runs. Their young pitchers are doing well; Brandon Webb and Brad Halsey have six wins and are averaging fewer than three and a half runs per game. Webb will pitch the first game in Phoenix on Monday night.

It appears as though some of that opening night magic still lingers for the Nationals with Arizona, or maybe it is just Livan Hernandez's Cuban voodoo. He pitches another masterful game against the Snakes, keeping them scoreless until they tie the score at 3-3 in the seventh. Nick Johnson and Ryan Church home runs lead the scoring, but it is Johnson's double in the eighth that scores the winning run and gives Hernandez an impressive five wins for the season.

The last two games of the series look dreadfully like the Sunday game against the Giants and beg the question of the team's fatigue. Guzman goes down hurt and the team is limping all over the field. In the Tuesday and Wednesday games they lose by identical scores, 3-2. Tony Armas comes off the injured list to pitch in the first game and goes five innings without giving up a run. Wilkerson knocks in two runs with a double, but the Nationals cannot make them stand up. Baerga's miscue allows Arizona to score three in the sixth and to take the contest 3-2.

In the last game of the road trip, Javier Vasquez, formerly the ace of the Expos staff before trying Manhattan and the Yankees, pitches extremely well. He allows only six hits, two doubles by Brian Schneider being the main damage, and takes his fourth win of the season away for his trouble. Claudio Vargas, a hard thrower who came up in 2004 for the Expos, is back from injury like Armas, and he also pitches well. He gets out of trouble several times and does not walk a batter, which had been his weakness as a rookie. The addition of two healthy pitchers gives Bowden something of value to dangle in front of the many GMs in need of pitching. The trade publications are abuzz with rumors.

# 6

# Seven Days in May

The road trip is over, and everyone sighs in relief as the team returns. The Cubs are in town for their first look at RFK and the first three games of a seven game home stand for the Nationals that will include four games with the Milwaukee Brewers. Neither of these two Central Division teams has won anything in a long time. The Cubs' record of futility is as legendary as that of the old Senators and the Brewers have been cellar dwellers in the National League Central since they fled the American League in 1998. The Cubbies have a retinue of loyal fans second only to Fans of the Yankees and the Red Sox. All three teams have fans in every city, especially places, like Washington, with numerous transients. For these fans it is an opportunity to see their team; for the Nationals the seven-game home stand offers a chance to get ahead of the curve, to build a cushion.

On this Friday night the ceremonies that occur in the home plate area prior to many games are a tribute to fourteen surviving players from the Negro Leagues. The aging greats from another era gather slowly behind home plate while their modern era counterparts run sprints in the outfield grass to warmup. Around the old timers a gaggle of fans look on from behind the railing, hoping to see the source of the commotion. There are Kansas City Monarchs uniforms as well as Homestead Grays suits. Celebrities and journalists are popping pictures.

"Who are the ones with the Homestead Grays uniforms?" asks a white fan, nodding toward three aged men wearing their old uniforms. An African American holding a pad and pen and looking knowledgeable offers guidance.

"Well, the one in the wheelchair is 104-year-old "Double Duty" Radcliffe. He used to catch a game in the afternoon and then come back and pitch the night game of the doubleheader," explains the journalist.

"No kidding," says the initiate.

"The Negro League teams couldn't afford 25-man rosters like these teams," says the journalist. "They didn't have minor leagues, so players filled in however they were needed. Satchel Paige hit, Radcliffe pitched, they were great players who could do it all," he says with pride.

From his wheelchair Radcliffe plops the ceremonial first pitch into the mitt of the catcher; the Jumbotron pays tribute to one of the greats of the Negro Leagues, Buck Leonard, as the crowd begin to take their seats; the anthem is sung; and the game begins.

Two years ago the Cubs' pitching looked like it would take them in to the play-offs, if not the World Series, which, like the Braves before them, would create a dynasty for years to come. Mark Prior and Kerry Woods were the showcase talents, but, behind them, pitchers like Carlos Zambrano and Matt Clement were equally talented. Since that time of promise, Wood and Prior have succumbed to a growing list of injuries and Clement has left town for Boston. The residue is one of the great pitching talents of the late 20th century, Greg Maddux, who heads a staff that goes in and out of the surgical wards.

During the three-game home stand, the Cubs will send out perennial underachiever Glendon Rusch on Friday, followed by Zambrano and Maddux. Frank Robinson will counter by skipping Patterson, the young developing pitcher, in the rotation, pitching Hernandez and Loaiza, the veterans, first, with Patterson against Maddux on Sunday. It is a good idea unless you are Patterson. The cold front goes through town on Friday and game time temperatures are in the low 60s, but this does not dampen the spirits of a near sellout crowd. The subway ride to the stadium is the first indication that the crowd will be a "bipartisan" one in a town where the term was minted.

The Cubbies, like the Red Sox, have blood loyal fans, love of their team heated in the red-hot frustrations of losing seasons that stretch back to 1908, and forged in some of the most historic swan dives in the history of the game. The Cubs have had some of the game's great talents, but all of them were somehow undone in the heat of the September pennant drives when they failed. Their fans have endured all of that but still believe that someday, like the Red Sox of 2004, they will have their due. It is a great object lesson for the Nationals fans, the Cub fans here to share with them this lovely night of baseball.

This will not be the year of redemption for the Cubbies. Though the Metro is littered with the names of Cubs players lined across the shoulders of faithful fans—Maddux, Prior, Patterson, and other current heroes—the lineup that last year boasted Sosa and Derrick Lee, two great sluggers, now has only Lee. The pitching staff has lost Mark Prior again, after regaining Wood. Maddux is 39 years of age and is just pitching out the string of years, a great run but a show that will soon close.

Frank Robinson has no such ghosts to patronize. His lineup card each night is like the creation of some artist trying to get in touch with his inner self, trying to draw forth the masterpiece within, all the while not knowing whether it is really there. In LaRussa's book on managerial strategy, he talks about how the little decisions a manager makes add up. They are inconsequential for the most part, but they have a cumulative impact that can spell defeat or provide a prevailing wind that helps the home team come down the stretch a winner. Robinson's team has not been scoring runs. Of late, Castilla, Wilkerson and Guillen have tailed off. Robinson counters with Jeffrey Hammonds, hitting a lusty .125, including an 0-for-4 a week ago, an 0-for-4 on Sunday, and an 0-for-2 on Tuesday. Robinson sits Ryan Church, who has nine hits in his last sixteen at bats over five games. Robinson will find an imperfect way to get him into the game later.

Glendon Rusch has pitched well in the early going. His ERA is under three runs per game and he starts the game throwing strikes. Both he and Loaiza have a one-two-three inning and there is no score at the end of the first inning. But in the second, Vinny Castilla sends a grounder that hugs the dirt down the third base line and skips over the bag just in fair territory heading into the outfield corner. Before it is chased down, Castilla stands on second with no one out. Hammonds fouls out weakly, but Nick Johnson ropes a liner into left after getting two strikes. Castilla is too slow to score on the single and stops at third.

It is up to Gary Bennett subbing for Schneider. He delivers a dying quail single that falls softly into the center field grass. Castilla scores and Johnson gets all the way to third, still only one out. Henry Mateo, a 28-year-old journeyman, steps to the plate. On the first pitch Johnson takes off from third as Mateo squares around to bunt. The squeeze play is on. The Cubs are not taken unawares, though, and Rusch pitches out to the catcher as Mateo bunts through the wide pitch. Johnson is dead to rights, caught in a rundown, and tagged out. Mateo walks but the pitcher is up and the inning ends with the Nationals scoring only a run.

Loaiza settles in and retires the Mets in order until the Cubs pitcher gets the first hit in the third. Rusch quiets the crowd and small children turn their attention to watching the puffs of pink and blue carried above the crowd by cotton candy vendors making their way up this aisle and down that one—a drama lost on adults but a fascination for the five-year-old girl wiggling in her seat as her mother watches and casts her eyes after her child's and softly whispers, "Not tonight, sweetie."

Two businessmen talk shop and hardly see a pitch. A stunning auburn lass flounces her hair from side to side like a thoroughbred's mane, inviting stares as her beau eyes the action. Two boys still enthralled by the action in the second inning debate what could have been and yell "Go, Nats," to spark excitement where there is none.

In the fourth inning, Loaiza continues his gem by striking out Derek Lee

## 6. Seven Days in May

**Keeping Derek Lee quiet keeps the Cubs quiet.**

for the second out. But for the first time during the evening the Cubs fans make their presence known as Aramis Ramirez walks and Jeremy Burnitz hits a nubber down the third base foul line that leaves Castilla helpless except to watch it hit the third base bag and softly bounce into his glove, a fair ball and an infield single. With men on first and second and two out, the Cubs fans stir

"Go, Cubs," yells a fan, taking off his Nats hat and replacing it with a Cubs hat. "Go, Nats," he yells, completing the flip-flop and laughing to the consternation of his friend in a red cap with the trademark *W* for Washington.

The Cubs fans try their hand at bouncing the metal risers as Jason Dubois, the young Cubs outfielder, gets the first solid hit off Loaiza, scoring Ramirez. Then Michael Barrett, the catcher, lines another one to center and the Cubs take the lead for the first time, 2-1. Jerry Hairston, the former Oriole now playing second base for Chicago, pops out, but the damage is done. There is no action for the Nats in the fourth and after a quiet fifth inning both pitchers head for the finish.

With the Cubs still leading the game, Rusch blinks rather than Loaiza.

In the sixth inning he gives up a single to Jose Guillen and a walk to Vinny Castilla. With two on and none out, the Cubs bring in Latroy Hawkins, a right-hander, to replace Rusch the lefty. Robinson counters by replacing Hammonds with the left-handed Church, a platoon that has worked well for the Nationals. Church again delivers with a single to right that scores Guillen with the tying run. There are runners now on first and third with no one out. It looks like a big inning, but Nick Johnson pops out weakly and Robinson brings in his professional pinch hitter, Carlos Baerga, who bounces into an inning ending double play, the score still tied 2-2.

At the beginning of the seventh inning Cristian Guzman appears in the field at shortstop. Mateo sits. After Loaiza sets the Cubs down at the top of the inning, Robinson sends Loaiza out to hit for himself to lead off the inning. It is a tie game and there are but few chances for the Nationals to score the winning run. Leading off the inning with a pinch-hitter is the call. Had Robinson thought ahead, knowing that Loaiza is due up, he could have pinch hit Guzman now and done a double switch. Fans are left to assume that Loaiza is pitching too well to lift. He makes a puny out and Wilkerson and Carroll do likewise.

Then as the eighth inning begins, Luis Ayala comes running in from the bull pen to start the inning. If Loaiza was to be lifted, why did he bat? Blanco, who is a right-handed hitting outfielder, could have pinch-hit against the left-handed throwing Will Ohman, who pitched the seventh against Loaiza. So Baerga in the sixth and Loaiza in the seventh do nothing to jump-start the offense. Then the Nationals begin to seriously self-destruct in the eighth inning.

Ayala gives up a home run to the first batter, Alexis Ramirez, to start off the inning. Nationals trail 3-2. Then Burnitz doubles and Barrett sacrifices him to third with one out. The Cubs have a perfect chance to add an insurance which they will need with the Nationals having two at bats against the weak Cubs bullpen, a source of huge problems for them this season and last. Ayala plunks the weak-hitting Jason Dubois after getting two strikes on him. Robinson lifts Ayala and brings in Cordero, "the chief," to give the Nats any chance to salvage the game. The Nationals have an immediate opportunity to scramble back into the game.

Turning the tables on the Cubs, the Nats anticipate the squeeze and Hairston cannot get the bunt down on the pitch away. Burnitz is caught halfway down the third base line exactly the way Nick Johnson had been. Now, though, Bennett cannot execute. He fires to third baseman Castilla, who runs Burnitz toward the plate, but on the throw back toward Bennett he misses the ball and Burnitz scores, 4-2 Cubs.

The Cubs fans have become a raucous and obnoxious presence in the stands and the sour expression on the faces of Nats fans could curdle milk. Hairston walks, but Cordero strikes out pinch hitter Todd Hollingsworth for

## 6. Seven Days in May

the second out. There are still runners on first and second when Corey Patterson hits a slow roller to Cordero's left. Patterson's speed rushes Cordero as he fields the ball and he tries a scoop toss that goes over Johnson's head. The two runners who were moving on contact race around to score, making it 6-2. The Cubs fans react as if Patterson had put one over the fence. Nationals fans head for the Metro in disgust. The Nats rally in the ninth. Blanco gets his pinch-hitting opportunity and singles in a run. The final score is 6-3.

The Cubs fans are quieter on Saturday. Robinson sends out the "A" team, Guzman is back at shortstop and Church is in left field. There are 42,000 fans for the Saturday night game, trying out the new weekend entertainment in D.C.—a night out with the Nats at RFK. The most reliable Cubs starting pitcher in recent years, Carlos Zambrano takes the mound against the Nationals ace, Livan Hernandez. It is a great match-up of two established pitchers, although Livan has the long resume, replete with postseason theatrics. The Cubs cannot, of course, claim postseason experience.

Zambrano displays his usual dominant stuff, a 95-mph sinking fastball and hard slider, for the first three innings and the Nats are helpless. In the fourth inning, however, things unravel for him. Wilkerson doubles and Carroll sacrifices him to third, but Zambrano's errant throw gives Carroll first base. Guillen strikes out and Zambrano seems to have recovered his focus, but then, inexplicably, he hits Nick Johnson to load the bases. Castilla comes through once again, and singles in both Carroll and Wilkerson. The Nationals get back the run that Livan Hernandez had allowed in the third and take a 2-1 lead.

With only one out, Church singles in Johnson and then Zambrano hits Schneider, his second batter of the inning to put. After a Cristian Guzman singles Castilla, Dusty Baker goes to the mound to get Zambrano, who complains about his forearm and leaves to be examined by the trainer. Cliff Bartosh, of the much-maligned Cubs bullpen, gets an inning-ending double play. Three other relievers follow Bartosh and completely shut down the Nationals for the rest of the game. The damage has been done.

Livan Hernandez turns in another steady performance, pitching well enough to win, leaving the game with one out in the seventh ahead of the Cubs 4-2. He, like Zambrano, complains of minor ailments—his knee—but says that he is on the mend and pitched through the pain. Chad Cordero pitches a rocky ninth, allowing a run, but closes out the game for a 4-3 Nationals win. The Nationals' bats do not boom, but they group their hits judiciously, their best lineup proving that it can score enough runs to win.

General Manager Bowden is busy during the day and completes a deal with Philadelphia that relieves each team of problem outfielders who have under achieved for their respective teams. The Phillies send Marlon Byrd, who had significant success in 2003, to the Nationals for Endy Chavez, who has played almost the entire year at New Orleans after a disappointing spring training that continued his 2004 problem getting on base. Byrd declined markedly in 2004 and the complaint has been that he is overweight. Frank Robinson thinks Byrd's problems are not physical but with his approach at the plate—something Frank tells the media he can fix, and it stands to reason he may.

    On Sunday an even larger crowd is on hand, 44,000 paid to see the rubber match of the three game series, an afternoon game on a cloudy afternoon that provides a sprinkle in the third inning. Greg Maddux, the eighteen-year veteran whom his pitching coach, Leo Mazzone, called the smartest pitcher he has ever seen, goes for the Cubs. His last outing was a combined shutout, Maddux leaving after six innings, and the bullpen keeping the New York Mets off the board. The Mets passed the Nationals on Friday night for third in the NL East.

    John Patterson, the lanky Texan, pitches for the Nationals. He was skipped for his last start and has had seven days' rest. In the first inning the layoff is evident, as he walks Corey Patterson, the Cubbies' leadoff batter, who promptly steals second. Patterson gets Nefi Perez on a foul bunt and strikes out the dangerous Derek Lee, who has been neutralized completely by the Nationals pitchers so far in the series. Then, with the inning almost done, he walks Burnitz and uncorks a wild pitch that moves the runners up to second and third. Michael Barrett, who has had the big bat Lee should be swinging, drives them both in with a single.

    Patterson finds his focus and Maddux quietly but quickly dispenses the Nationals until the third. Patterson is "on," his switch suddenly flipped to hard focus, his big bender toppling across the strike zone—"falling off the table—suddenly, with the hitter rushing his swing to catch up with it but missing. His fastball sweeps through the strike zone without touching a bat. Ron Darling, who broadcasts the game, discusses the contrast between the two pitchers, something he is eminently qualified to do. He states that Maddux pitches looking for the hitters' bat, looking for ways to get the batter to put the ball in play but off balance and compromised. He says that Patterson, who strikes out six through the first three innings, should think about this more, because he could economize with his pitches—throw fewer of them—and pitch further into games.

    Prophetically, Maddux's pitches begin to find the Nationals bats in the bottom of the third and they group three two-out singles together, Wilkerson and Carroll, then Guillen driving in Wilkerson with the first run, and the score is 2-1. But Patterson seems undone by the success, and as if to outdo Maddux, he gives up four straight singles, and only Maddux hitting at the end of the inning and a beautiful double play, Guzman-to-Schneider-to-Johnson, ends the inning without further damage. The Cubs now lead 4-1. The Nationals peck away, getting a single run on a single by Castilla, who steals second and is singled in by Guzman.

Then, in the fifth inning, Nick Johnson, sporting a new clean-shaven look, pulls a Maddux pitch into the right center upper deck. The home run is one of the longest of the year and with Guillen aboard gives Patterson the lead for the first time at 4-3. The sixth inning starts on a downbeat with another walk, this time to Burnitz. Barrett grounds to the left side, advancing the runner to second, and Jason Dubois, the young left fielder with 34 home runs in Triple-A Omaha in 2004, shows his potential, doubling into the gap to tie the score. Patterson struggles through three more batters, but on the fourth walk of the afternoon to load the bases, Frank Robinson comes to the mound to give the ball to Hector Carrasco. In one pitch, at the top of the strike zone where Hairston cannot get good wood on it, Carrasco gets a pop-up to third and it is the Nationals' turn in the sixth.

Dusty Baker lifts Maddux and brings in Cliff Bartosh for the bottom of the inning. Ryan Church leads off and cues a fastball off the end of the bat. The ball spins oddly through the infield until it arrives at Nefi Perez's glove,

Nick Johnson pulls Greg Maddux's pitch into the right center field upper deck.

where the spin seemingly takes hold, sending the ball careening away for an error. Church is on first. Robinson asks Schneider to bunt him over and he executes the play perfectly, Church moving to second, but with one out. Guzman hits what should be the second out of the inning, a grounder to Perez. Perhaps thinking still of the last grounder, perhaps watching Church heading to third base in the corner of his vision, Perez lets the ball go through his legs, kicking off his calf into center field just far enough out of reach of anyone to allow Church to come all the way from second to score what will be the winning run at 5-4.

The Cubs bullpen pitches well again, but the Nationals are better. Ayala pitches two scoreless innings in the seventh and eighth and Chad Cordero comes in for the ninth. Throwing harder than he has thrown all year, the warm afternoon sun limbering his arm, he strikes out Nefi Perez for the final out, ending what is a frustrating day for the Cubs' second baseman. Cordero pumps his fist across his body and does a little Jackie Gleason kick after the final out. It is a sweet victory after listening to the Cubs fans who invaded the home turf. The Cubs fans leave much quieter on Sunday than on Friday night, settling into the lower reaches of the NL Central Division, while the Nationals are climbing, 20 wins and 17 losses, nearing the quarter pole in the season. They are closing on the Marlins, who are beginning to fade a little, D-Train at 7-0, but the rest of the team lagging.

## Milwaukee Brewskies

The trend toward microbreweries has not been kind to traditional beer brands, many of which were once headquartered in Milwaukee, Wisconsin, their vast grain elevators still a visible part of the city's Midwestern skyline. Baseball trends that have diverged to feature small boutique teams like Oakland and megamarket teams like the Yankees have been no kinder to Milwaukee Brewers baseball, whose competitive teams made the World Series as an American League team in 1982 with Hall of Fame players like Robin Yount and Paul Molitor, but they are a distant memory. The team's shift to the National League during the last expansion of teams in 1998 has put it at a competitive disadvantage with great franchises, like the St. Louis Cardinals and the Cincinnati Reds, who play in their division now.

Before the series starts, the Nationals announce the trade that brings Marlon Byrd, a 27-year-old center fielder from Philadelphia, to Washington in exchange for Endy Chavez, who had been demoted to New Orleans twice during the 2005 season. Byrd was excellent in his first full season with Philly in 2003. Batting .303 and showing speed and defensive prowess, he looked like a player who had arrived, but in 2004, his sophomore season seemed to belie the early promise. Frank Robinson announces after the trade that he believes he can reshape Byrd's swing effectively. More importantly, however, is the ability to platoon the righty Byrd with the lefty Church. Church's numbers in his career favor a platoon.

The Monday night game starts with a slight chill in the air, but the sky is clear and crisp. An attractive girl leans over the outfield rail watching Gary Bennett warm up the Nationals pitcher, Tony Armas. She begs Bennett for a ball, pointing to her outstretched hand and asking him to hit it with the ball. He pegs one her way and she does not move an inch, catching the ball with aplomb and showing it to her mother, smiling. These small encounters are how fans are made. The girl once watched Cal Ripken and does not know these new players well. But now she knows Gary Bennett has a great arm and she will look to see his name in the box scores and will start to notice other players. One at a time, the fans are watching, learning, and forming bonds to their team.

Armas, starting only his second game after coming off the disabled list, is hoping to recapture the form he had in 2002 when he was a budding star. His father, Tony Armas, Sr., was an outfielder who played thirteen years in the seventies and eighties with the Athletics and Red Sox. He had 35 home runs for the Athletics in 1980 and four years later had 43 for the Sox. His son is a pitcher, though, who has been plagued by ill health since winning 12 games as a 24-year-old. Tony, Jr., is still a young player and developing, though, like his teammate, Nick Johnson, he has not reached his potential because he has not been able to stay healthy.

The Brewers pitcher is Ryan Glynn, who came up with the Texas Rangers and has had little success. The game runs true to form, with Armas continuing to round into form, pitching seven strong innings and allowing only two runs. Glynn is in trouble much of the evening, allowing five runs in six innings. The Nationals' bats continue to show life, but it is the addition of Marlon Byrd that is most remarkable. He gets three hits off Glynn in his first three at bats as a National and is in the middle of each Washington rally, knocking in three runs. The Nationals fans are jumping and the stands are shaking in the first six innings as 26,000 show up for the game and go away happy with the 5-2 win, the third win in a row on the home stand. It is also a great way to start the series with the Brewers.

The second game will provide a higher hill to climb for the Nationals. The Brewers are throwing Wes Obermuller, who, like Glynn in game one, has never had a successful season in the majors. It will be hard to understand Obermuller's mediocre numbers later in the evening. Prior to 2005, Obermuller has experienced greater relative success as a hitting pitcher than as a thrower. Claudio Vargas, like Armas in game one, is coming off an injury; he pitched well in his prior game, but this Tuesday will not be his night, it will be Obermuller's.

The first batter up is Brady Clark, a journeyman 32-year-old whose career has been spent in the minor leagues until getting a chance with the lowly Brewers in 2003. Clark blasts Vargas's first pitch over the wall in left.

"Not a good sign," says a fan sitting in the left field stands behind David Brooks, the syndicated columnist.

"That was the first pitch, wasn't it?" asks the fan next to him.

"Yeah, I did not even know the game had started," says a third. "Damn!"

Geoff Jenkins, the Brewers' third batter, singles, and Carlos Lee, the cleanup hitter, walks as Vargas continues to struggle. Then Lyle Overby laces a long line drive into center that Wilkerson almost runs down, and holds the damage to one run, with Overby stopping on second base and Lee on third. Vargas wiggles off the hook facing the bottom of the Brewers order, but in the second inning he is chased from the game when he loads the bases and Carlos Lee comes up for his second at bat in two innings and hits a convincing home run that carries well beyond the same left field wall that Clark found with the first pitch. Manager Robinson comes to the mound and hands the ball over to Tomo Ohka, who has been banished to the bullpen after several poor outings. Ohka ends the inning without further runs scoring and the fans let out a collective sigh.

As the innings pile up, fans keeping score and watching the board begin to notice that the Nationals are going down in order in every inning. Obermuller has a perfect game and the fans take note at the end of the fifth inning.

"In a couple innings, he'll be a little more nervous making that play," a fan says, watching the shortstop end the sixth inning with an athletic pickup of a hard hit grounder.

"They'll be saying, 'don't hit it to me' if he stays perfect," says the other fan, sitting behind David Brooks.

"Some banjo hitter'll break it up."

"Yeah, and it's always someone like Guzman."

True to form, the perfect game is broken up in the seventh inning. With one out, Jamey Carroll, the prototypical banjo hitter, gets a sharp single to right. Nick Johnson gets a weak hit on a fly ball that the fielder loses in the lights. Then Frank Robinson does the inexplicable again. With runners on first and second, one out, he lifts the cleanup hitter, Vinny Castilla, for a pinch hitter, Tony Blanco, the rule five minor leaguer who will stay with the team all year as a bench jockey. It is only the seventh inning. Obermuller is not Nolan Ryan, he may be flustered by the error and the Nationals have a history of scoring late. Robinson should come out on the field with a white flag and lead his troops off to early showers.

"Maybe Castilla is hurt?" says the fan behind David Brooks.

"He did not look hurt in the field last inning," says the fan beside him.

"Robinson is getting senile," says fan three.

The game plays out and ends with the Brewers winning 8 runs to 2, after

Nick Johnson salvages a smattering of home team pride with a two-run homer in the ninth off the Brewers bullpen. The Brewers have tied the series at one win for each team and the chances for success on this important home stand seem to narrow.

Wednesday night's game brings long-suffering Esteban Loaiza to the mound, thirsting for a win. In his last six starts he has averaged almost seven innings per game and has allowed less than three runs per outing. Yet he has not a win to show for his efforts and has only one win this season despite being much more than the Nationals bargained for at the beginning of the season. The Brewers pitcher is Chris Capuano, a smart lefty from Duke University, who in two brief tryouts with the Brewers in 2003 and 2004 has shown promise. In the early going in 2005 he has pitched well and been remarkably consistent for a lefty.

Someone in Milwaukee seems to have the book on the Nationals. Capuano picks up where Wes Obermuller left off on Tuesday. Brad Wilkerson starts the game with a double, but Robinson commits the egregious *Moneyball* sin: he gives up the out to get Wilkerson to third, except this time Wilkerson is thrown out at third when Jamey Carroll's bunt is fielded quickly. Carroll is then thrown out trying to steal second after the Brewers throw over five times, daring Robinson to run. Then Castilla flies out and the Nationals settle in to eight innings of futility. Loaiza is even more effective. He gives up nothing, nothing beyond first base, six singles and no walks over eight masterful innings with no runs for the Brewers; but following the season-long record of futility the Nationals cannot even score a run to support him.

Then in the ninth, against the Brewers bullpen, the Nationals rally. Wilkerson is hit by a pitch, Castilla scratches out an infield single, and Johnson is intentionally walked to get to Hammonds. The lack of respect motivates Jeffrey Hammonds, who jumps on the second pitch and pulls it past Russ Branyan at third base and knocks in a single game-winning run to end the game in the bottom of the ninth. The team congregates in the infield, happy to win the tension-filled affair, clapping the broadly smiling Hammonds on the back repeatedly. Washington is now back at four games over .500 and is once again pushing Florida for second in the NL East. Livan Hernandez will go in the series finale on Thursday afternoon.

Hernandez has a chance to tie Dontrelle Willis for the National League lead in wins by a pitcher with seven, and the Nationals have a chance to go over .500 by five games, their best mark of the season. The Brewers pitcher is Victor Santos, another marginally successful journeyman who is having success in the early going in this year where reduced power and offense is being experienced baseball wide. The Nationals get on the board first—a good sign for them this year—on a fourth inning double by Vinny Castilla. They extend this lead to 2-0 on a single by Jamey Carroll, whose second hit of the day pushes his batting average to .330 to lead the team.

Hernandez has what is becoming his trademark game, despite having fluid drained from his knee early in the week. He gets runners on base with a walk and a hit, but he is able to pitch to get the tougher hitters in the lineup and keep the easy outs off base. This economy fails finally in the top of the sixth inning and the Brewers push across a lone run, but the Nationals come back in the bottom of the inning with a run on a walk, a hit, and an errant pitch that the Brewers catcher cannot corral until Vinny Castilla crosses the plate with the Nationals' third run for a 3-1 lead.

Hernandez is lifted in the sixth to give his ailing knee a rest and Hector Carrasco begins the seventh inning by hitting the first two Brewer batsmen. Gary Majewski comes in and gets the side out in order, but the Brewers get their second run on a sacrifice bunt and a deep fly ball by Geoff Jenkins. Luis Ayala is effective in the eighth and keeps the score at 3-2, and Chad "The Chief," Cordero, gets the Brewers out in the ninth, although he allows two walks and keeps the game interesting until the final out. The Nationals take three out of four from the Brewers with the win, and at 23 wins and 18 losses they have their best winning percentage of the season. They win both series of the home stand with five wins and only two losses.

# 7

# Oh, Canada

When Major League Baseball conceived the original schedule for its 2005 season, Montreal was still the home of the Expos. For that reason interleague play was masterfully planned so that when the Toronto Blue Jays hosted the Expos the series began on Victoria Day, an important holiday for English-speaking residents of Canada's Ontario Province where Toronto is located. Conversely, the return engagement, whereby the Expos hosted the Blue Jays in Montreal, was planned for June 24, known in Quebec Province as "Vingt-Quatre," an emotional holiday that has been a celebration for the Quebecois Separatist movement and its hopes for independence. This testament to intelligent human design was spoiled when Major League Baseball moved the Expos to Washington for the 2005 season.

Interleague play is meant to increase attendance, drawing on sectional rivalries. The rivalry between the French-speaking Quebecois and the English-speaking citizens of Ontario is as old as Canada itself. It has at its core a more intense emotional cause than say, the one between the Mets and the Yankees. The Separatist violence in Montreal caused many citizens and businesses to leave Montreal during the late sixties, and even more in the late '70s and early '80s when the vote to separate Quebec from the rest of Canada seemed poised for victory. Those who left Montreal return periodically to visit old friends and families and you can overhear them in restaurants along fashionable rue St. Laurent if you are careful.

"Can you believe the service in this place?" asks a returning diner from Toronto.

"It's why we left," says the companion, "*that* attitude."

The emotions are still raw and not far from the surface although they have receded. Yet the angst of regional rivalries is more easy to fathom than the apparent contradiction between a Major League Baseball that tries to increase attendance in Canada through a carefully planned schedule—using province holidays no less—and one that did so little to protect the Montreal franchise in the first place. While the schedulers were artfully plying their trade, the corporate CEOs who own baseball were plying theirs, refusing Omar Minaya, the fill-in GM for the Expos, the ability to offer Vladimir Guerrero a long-term contract and then refusing salary arbitration so that the Expos would get no compensatory free agent picks in the next amateur draft.

Washingtonians are largely ignorant about how the Montreal franchise came to wither and die on the vine after bearing such great fruit in the 1970s. The Expos gave baseball "Le Grand Orange," as Rusty Staub, Montreal's most popular player, was known, and Tim Raines, Andre Dawson, and Gary Carter. Gary Carter recently was inducted into the Baseball Hall of Fame in a Montreal Expos cap, forever bronzing the memory of the team. If asked, Washingtonians say that the lack of success of the franchise in Montreal doomed it.

"They never had a winner."

"Besides, hockey is their favorite sport anyway."

Washington fans believe their own team will do better; that they are a larger more vibrant city. Yet there is an exhibit in Montreal that every Washington Nationals fan should see. It is at the Museum of Architecture in Montreal, in Centre Ville, and it is called "Montreal in the '60s." The exhibit features a slide show up on a screen suspended artfully from the middle of a white-walled museum room. Pictures from old newspaper archives roll on a five-second interval on the screen, headlines and photos from the '60s popping up one after the other. There are photos of the Quebecois insurrection, stories about the kidnappings and the killing of a British diplomat. Immediately following those stark scenes are the happier shots of the new Expos team that started in that city in 1969. There are the city fathers standing along the first base line with the team lined up along the foul line itself. They are all beaming proudly, shaking hands with the players.

Then there is a page from the *Montreal Gazette* in April of that year with the headlines, "Guess Who's In First Place?" The team's first game of that spring was a winner and the team started well that year. It all seems so familiar, despite the thirty-six intervening years: first place, proud political leaders. The Senators were still playing in 1969, although they would leave in three short years.

The Montreal Expos were seldom in first place, although the team knew great success over the years, certainly more than did the Senators. Maybe their inability to win a championship hurt, but articles written in Montreal since the move of the team cite economic realities commonly overlooked in this country as having more to do with the death of baseball in Montreal than winning or losing. Two trends converged in the 1990s that pulled the rug out from under the Expos.

The first trend emerged in the run-up to the baseball strike in 1994. That labor conflict came to symbolize the new economic structure of the game. The rich teams were getting ever richer and paying ever larger salaries from the pots of gold that flowed from TV revenues. The bargaining agreement coming out of that strike allowed the steady escalation of salaries with only a revenue sharing requirement among the teams to counter it. The Expos were in first place at the end of the strike-shortened 1994 season, but from there it was a gradual slide to oblivion.

There was no *Moneyball* strategy for small market teams then, just teams like Montreal trying to develop great talent from their minor league system faster than the players could go elsewhere for the American dollar. Montreal stayed ahead of the game by scouting, signing, and developing Latin players better than anyone else. They brought up Vladimir Guerrero, Pedro Martinez, and a host of the best Latin players in the game today. But they could not fight the second damaging economic reality: the plunging value of the Canadian dollar against the American dollar.

When the Montreal franchise began, the relationship of the Canadian dollar to the American dollar was relatively even and fairly static. Then, in the boom years of the mid eighties and beyond, the dollar became much stronger and the differential between the Canadian dollar and the American dollar was heavily weighted toward the American currency. At its worst, the Canadian dollar slid to almost 60 cents on the dollar and baseball players, regardless of their point of origin, wanted to be paid in American dollars or the equivalent. The Montreal franchise took in revenues in cheap Canadian dollars and was forced to pay salaries in the more expensive American dollars.

The team could not keep up and in the second half of the 1990s, as attendance began to lag, it became more and more difficult to make the equation work. Attendance slipped lower and lower because the Montreal ballpark was not an attractive venue for baseball. Olympic Stadium was built for the 1974 Olympics, its mammoth structure intended for track and field events at those games. It did not configure well for baseball and was aging and uncomfortable.

A new stadium was sought by team owners, and Major League Baseball tried to pressure the city to move forward and commit their money. It was the same bait-and-switch tactic Bud Selig used to build new stadiums in a dozen American cities, threatening to pull the team unless the city agreed to use public dollars to build the park. Yet the Quebecois spirit has endured for almost 250 years and did not bend to dictates from Americans who seemed more and more British with each passing year, and less and less like their revolutionary allies from the 18th century. The Quebecois got on their painted ponies and the new stadium was General Custer and the Little Big Horn, a short-term victory that led to ultimate defeat.

A very similar dynamic has occurred in hockey. Hockey is the quintessential Canadian sport. The National Hockey League was once the domain of great Canadian franchises—the original six—including the Montreal Canadiens and the Toronto Maple Leafs. The expansion of teams brought successful franchises like the Edmonton Oilers and players like the Great One, Wayne Gretsky.

Gretsky is perhaps the best example of how the Canadian dollar hurt sports north of the border. The most beloved player of the upstart prairie franchise in Alberta, Gretsky left all the love behind, left streets named after him, statues outside the arena, all of the Michael Jordan trappings before there was a Michael Jordan. He left it as if Jordan had left Chicago because the money was better in New York. Edmonton could not match the wealthy offers from Los Angeles.

Money not only spelled the exit of great players, it meant the demise of whole teams. Before the Expos left for Washington, the Quebec hockey team, the Nordiques, moved to Colorado in 1995. Then came the Winnipeg team that moved to Phoenix. Hockey in Phoenix and Tampa, Florida, while the ice is empty in major Canadian cities? The economic realities of sport seem an isolated reality, but in truth are no different than textile manufacturing and other industries that moved first to the south and now to Asia. Hockey in Singapore is perhaps not as incredulous as it might seem.

Only a few of the baseball players currently on the Washington Nationals roster played any significant amount of time in Canada. At the beginning of the Toronto series in May, the Canadian anthem, "O Canada," was sung, but few if any of the Nationals felt any emotional tug. For the Nationals it is just another day in the long season, just the beginning of a series they needed to win to stay in the thick of the fight in the National League East.

Their interleague opponents, the Toronto Blue Jays, are the success story of Canadian sports. The city is the financial center of the country and has the wealthy patrons who can pay to keep baseball and hockey there. Much of that wealth came from Montreal during the separatist era in Quebec, and there are no doubt "Anglais" in that province who believe the Quebecois have no one to blame but themselves for the demise of baseball.

Toronto grew to dominance at the expense of Montreal, getting a franchise only in 1977, but building one of the great baseball venues quickly. SkyDome, the huge entertainment complex that hosts the Blue Jays, held over 4 million fans in 1991 when the Blue Jays won the American League Pennant and went on to win the World Series for the first of two back-to-back wins. The Toronto franchise is backed by the wealth of the LaBatts Beer label, much the same way St. Louis has been backed by the Busch family brewers. They have been able to pay out American dollars to their players when Montreal could not. There is little concern for the health of that franchise, and no one calling for a new stadium or the team to be relocated.

In 2006, Major League Baseball has adjusted the schedules, and interleague play for the Washington Nationals will feature as its sectional rivalry the Baltimore Orioles. A very real bitterness has sprung up between Washington and Baltimore over the two baseball teams. The moves by D.C. Mayor Anthony Williams and wealthy backers for the team were blocked by Baltimore owner Peter Angelos and the feud continues as TV revenues are disputed in court and back room rumors continue to swirl about the intrigues between Angelos and Major League Baseball, which still owns the Nationals. Many fans in D.C. speak with some anger about the conflict and refuse to go to Orioles games, refuse to take their children, who once cut their baseball teeth on Cal Ripken, the "Iron Man."

The history of the Toronto and Montreal franchises in the last two decades of the 20th century should serve as a cautionary tale for the two mid–Atlantic rivals, Baltimore and Washington. At what point do regional rivalries begin to hurt teams and diminish the whole as something less than the sum of its parts? Most importantly, at what point is cooperation a better tool for survival than isolation? Home run bashers pumped up on steroids and sectional rivalries may increase ticket sales, but the history of the Toronto and Montreal franchises is a cautionary tale for the two Mid-Atlantic rivals.

The ever cocksure Mr. Angelos might have the greater cause for concern. The long-term demographic trends favor Washington more than Baltimore. Washington's population growth and its depression-proof economy fueled by government spending pose problems for the Baltimore team and ownership if fans and viewers to the south become alienated. Washington has more ability to endure economic vagaries than does Baltimore. So who more resembles the French-speaking Quebecois in the Baltimore-Washington scenario? Who is most at risk if baseball in the mid–Atlantic area suffers a downturn of circumstances? It is not a question either Baltimore *or* Washington should risk answering.

In the first game against the Expos reborn in 2005 as the Nationals, Toronto will send out left-hander Ted Lilly, who has been as steady a pitcher as they have had recently, but he has been awful so far in 2005. The Nationals are forced to pitch Claudio Vargas for the Friday night game at SkyDome. Vargas was hammered in his start on Tuesday, lasting not even two innings before giving up a grand slam home run to Carlos Lee prior to exiting.

Vargas starts the game in Toronto on a more even keel, but Lilly seems a better pitcher than his record would indicate. Lilly has established himself with three consecutive seasons of double digit wins, first in Oakland and then with Toronto in 2004. He gets touched for a run by the Nationals in the fourth, but Vargas runs into trouble in the bottom of the inning and gives up a two run homer to Vernon Wells that seems to rob him of the focus he had maintained in the first three innings. He gives up three more runs before leaving, with Toronto ahead 5-1 and on their way to an easy win. Lilly holds on for six innings, striking out eight. Journeyman reliever Pete Walker finishes the job as Vernon Wells hits a second home run and the game ends 8-1 for Toronto.

The Saturday game pits Halladay's well-placed 95-mph fastballs, his excellent curve and cutter, against the Nationals hitters, who are struggling to score runs against anyone. Tony Armas starts his second game since coming back from injury. It is never a contest. The Blue Jays score two runs in each of the first two innings off Armas, and Halladay dominates, never allowing a threat to materialize for seven innings. The Toronto bullpen completes a shutout of the Nationals, who lose for the second time on the road trip series by a final score of 7-0.

The team's offensive production is declining and Robinson announces on Sunday that Wilkerson is going to be given an extended rest to determine the seriousness of a sore elbow and forearm. The toll of injuries is staggering the team. The Blue Jays lose Cory Koskie on Thursday and call up promising minor leaguer Aaron Hill, who has hits in each of the first two games against the Nationals. Washington can only hope that Jeffrey Hammonds can find some magic to return him to a form he has known only rarely in the major leagues. The pitching match-up for the Sunday afternoon game with the sun shining and the stadium roof open will favor the Nationals for the first time during the series. Tomo Ohka will face Josh Towers, who has struggled for several years to achieve consistency; he can be very good, but rarely puts together quality starts. Ohka pitched well in relief of Vargas on Tuesday and has the longer record of success.

True to form, Ohka pitches the better game. In the fourth Ohka gives up a two run home run to Shea Hillenbrand. There is further bad news as Vinny Castilla leaves the game in the third with a sore knee that the SkyDome's hard turf has aggravated. Given that the Nationals have scored only seven runs in the past week's five games and one of their best hitters is out, two runs looks like quite a lot. In the fifth inning, however, the Nationals get three straight singles from Ryan Church, Hammonds, and Gary Bennett to score their first run. Guzman singles to load the bases and Marlon Byrd hits a sacrifice fly to tie the score. Carroll walks to load the bases again. Frank Robinson realizes that the game is at a crossroads. Jose Guillen is up and he has been cold since getting three days off to rest his sore rib cage. Robinson comes up off the bench and walks to the end of the dugout, where he stops to watch Guillen.

The Nationals hitters have started jumping on Tower's first pitch when they are strikes, which seems to be a strategy they adopted before the game but had forgotten until now. Guillen seems to remember as well and makes solid contact with a fastball low in the zone that he pulls just to the left of the center fielder, over his head and bouncing off the wall just two feet from going out of the ballpark. Bennett, Guzman, and Carroll all come in to score and there is fisting and back slapping in front of the dugout for the first time in many days. The Nationals lead 5-2.

Robinson replaces Hammonds with Carlos Baerga, who goes in to play third. Tony Blanco, who replaced Castilla at third base, now moves to left field. Ohka has the lead and is pitching the fifth inning when the normally sure handed Jamey Carroll pulls Nick Johnson off of the first base bag with a poor throw. With a runner on first, a sharp fly goes toward Blanco in left. Misjudging the ball, he moves back several steps only to realize that the ball is not hit nearly as hard as his first read indicated. He lunges forward and stabs the ball just off the turf for the out and disaster is averted. Ohka puts away the next two batters easily and goes on to pitch eight innings, with only the two run homer against him. Tony Blanco comes up at the top of the seventh inning with two runners on base and sends the ball well into the center field stands for a three run homer that makes the score 8-2. The Nationals go on to win with nine runs, more runs than they had scored during the preceding five games combined.

The Nationals are slightly past the quarter pole in the season. Their record stands at 24 wins and 20 losses, far ahead of the pace from the previous year in Montreal. There is a lot of baseball and a lot of teams for which swoon rhymes with June. But first there are three games with Cincinnati, which has one of the worst records in the National League. It is Jim Bowden's old team, although he will not be greeted by cheering crowds.

# 8

# Where's That Famous Golden Touch?

Washington Nationals General Manager Jim Bowden has gathered about him his trusted staff from his days in Cincinnati like a deposed monarch exiled to a lonely Mediterranean isle. He and his generals plot their return to glory from his office at RFK and the early campaigns are going well. Many give Bowden credit for the success of the Nationals in their first season. The additions of Jose Guillen, Esteban Loaiza, and Vinny Castilla have added talent that has elevated the team from the misery it knew in Montreal in 2004 to the magic of Washington in 2005, and their play as a team is a feather in his cap.

As Washington fans await the outcome of the bidding to determine who will own and manage this exciting new toy, D.C. Baseball, it is worth a test drive around the block to get a better feel for the late model Bowden. The golden locks and beaming smile look good on TV, but a kick of the tires, a peek beneath the hood seem in order to see if it is worth keeping for 2006. Whether it is George Soros and the Democrats, or Fred Malek and the Republicans, new ownership will need to take a long, hard, evaluative look at the wonders Jim Bowden has wrought, because Bowden has been auditioning for a job, the Nationals job or any job, since MLB, Inc., gave him the Nationals to play with late last year.

There are writers who believe Bowden was hired to tend the Nationals until the new owners arrived. That theory has it that new ownership will feel no compunction about hiring their own GM and letting Bowden go after grateful thanks in the off-season. These early season prognosticators did not foresee the huge success that Washington has enjoyed in the first half of the 2005 season, nor do they seem to notice the large hand of Bud Selig behind Bowden, pushing steadily.

It was written of Bowden, fresh from his dismissal in Cincinnati, that he had rubbed many people the wrong way during his years there, that his phone calls are not returned, and that he is not allowed access to Cincinnati Reds personnel on any level. He was given his current job with the Nationals ostensibly because of favors he has done for MLB and friends he has made there. They are the ones who selected him for the Washington job. Bud Selig, or Bob Dupuy, or some other official at MLB remembered the good deeds Bowden did for MLB back in 2002, and offered him this rung on the ladder as a chance back into the game.

Back in 2002 his contract was expiring at the end of the year, and labor negotiations with the hated Players Union were heating up. In August of that year, less than a year after the World Trade Center Towers crumpled and fell in Manhattan, Bowden said for publication that the Players Union was akin to the 9/11 terrorists. He apologized profusely, said whatever needed to be said to move on, but he had planted an important seed in the public's mind about the union.

The 2002 congressional elections were in full swing at the time and one political party in particular was wrapping itself very effectively in the flag, so MLB, Inc., did the same, looking for good PR, public sympathy, or whatever it took to corner the union and head off another failed labor negotiation like the strike in 1994. It is a recurring theme for Selig, the union. His friends have stood by the owners in the fight and that is an important measure of his friends.

The next year, after achieving no greater level of success, Bowden was fired in Cincinnati along with manager Bob Boone. There were no other phone calls; no offers were forthcoming until MLB tendered him the Washington job more than a year later.

Apart from his acumen at crafting political spin, Bowden's resume bears reading. He started in baseball as a young junior management hire with the Pittsburgh Pirates organization in 1987. Within only six years he was hired as general manager of the Cincinnati Reds at 31 years of age. Bowden was the youngest GM ever hired by a major league franchise at that time. He was the first of a wave of such young, professionally trained GMs. The trend reached its culmination when the Red Sox hired 28-year old Theo Epstein in 2003. Unlike Bowden, Epstein was able in two years to lead the Red Sox to their first World Series win since 1918. Bowden has known modest success, but nothing at that level.

Bowden's tenure in Cincinnati lasted for almost eleven years, beginning in 1993 up until he and manager Bob Boone were both fired in the middle of the 2003 season. During that run, Bowden's Reds won 830 games and lost 830 games, dead-even, a statistical anomaly worth computing. Bowden's initial teams under manager Davey Johnson were competitive and finished near the top of the National League, leading the Central Division in the strike-shortened 1994 season, and going to the play-offs as Central Division winners the next season. But there were no league championships, no trips to the World Series.

Bowden's reign stretched over the era when the current baseball economy was written into stone, where small market franchises, such as Cincinnati, were at war with the mega-bucks teams like the Yankees. Teams like Oakland and Minnesota have mastered the discipline needed to compete effectively against the moneyed teams. They have made the playoffs many times in recent years, losing out to wealthy teams like the Red Sox and the Yankees only in the championship series. Yet they have made the postseason competition each year and drawn fans to watch their underdog team compete on an even footing against the best that money can buy.

Bowden plotted a very different direction from the one that Billy Beane has publicized in Oakland. Bowden is fond of marquis players. From the beginning he held on to the legendary names he inherited in 1993, those like Barry Larkin and Jose Rijo. His last gambit was to sign Ken Griffey, Jr., to a long term and very lucrative contract in 2000, even after the concerns about Griffey's durability surfaced. Beane has made his mark by letting marquis players like Jason Giambi leave Oakland. He has traded in these high-salaried stars for draft picks and young players making the major league minimum salary of $300,000 and has somehow made it work remarkably well.

Bowden's focus on proven box office stars is easily defended. He was loyal to his fan base and Griffey and Larkin were wildly popular figures in Cincinnati. But if these moves were done wisely and with such open support from everyone, why will some other GMs not return his phone calls? Why did Cincinnati's baseball fortunes sink so low, and what does it all portend for the Washington Nationals?

The first concern is Bowden's inability to develop great pitching. The three-run homer was never missing from the Reds' equation, but he was never able to acquire or develop the staff ace, that great pitcher who could win twenty games and forestall a losing streak with a great complete game shutout. As every pundit has said, "Good pitching beats good hitting any day." Any analysis of the Washington Nationals going into the 2005 season gave them credit for their mix of young pitchers, many of whom had experienced some success at the major league level and were still in their middle twenties, young enough to push their game to the next level with proper tutelage.

Before the season is done, Bowden has traded away Zach Day, Tomo Ohka, Sun Woo Kim and he has waived Claudio Vargas: four young and potentially potent arms. In return he has Preston Wilson, who is a free agent at the end of the season, and Junior Spivey, obtained from Milwaukee for Tomo Ohka. Spivey's athleticism at second base is fun to watch but offensively he is inconsistent. More importantly, the Nationals have Jose Vidro to play second base; Vidro is a better offensive player and someone who stayed with the Expos when all others bailed. Loyalty should be worth something.

Now Ohka and Vargas are experiencing success with their new teams and each is a regular member of the pitching rotation. Day remains hurt, but many believe will fit well with the Rockies. So, on one side of the equation Bowden has dealt three young major league pitchers who are likely to be with their teams again next year filling valuable rotation spots at minimal cost. To show for it, the Nationals will have only a redundant part in second baseman Junior Spivey and a slugger who can go elsewhere at the end of the season. They received in none of these deals any of the famous "players to be named later"; no minor league talent of any kind accompanied the major league ready players Bowden obtained.

Bowden has filled the holes as they have occurred during an important year for building fan support for the Washington team, but it is fair to look back at Bowden's prior tenure in Cincinnati and wonder what it portends. Could he have gotten more for Ohka than Spivey, and could he have kept Vargas in the bullpen long enough to trade him for help somewhere down the road? Vargas has never been demoted by the Diamondbacks. He has remained in their rotation and, after a brief period of adjustment, has been consistently strong. There is an impetuous quality to many of these moves by Bowden. With the exception of the Preston Wilson trade they were done quickly, whereas most trades take months to germinate and reach fruition.

Peter Gammons wrote in the middle of July for *ESPN* magazine about the importance of developing a robust minor league system. Any major league team that wishes to compete effectively must have one, and Gammons evaluated how various teams perform the task. In the article, he highlighted Brian Cashman, the GM of the Yankees, who has brought up several young players to fit among the giants of baseball now playing for New York. Robinson Cano starts at second base for New York and, until recently, Chien Wang was a starting pitcher. Neither of these two had ever played in the majors. Gammons quoted Theo Epstein in the article as saying about Cashman, "Here he is without a contract, and he's putting the long-term good of the New York Yankees ahead of his own job security."

Can the same be said of Jim Bowden? Is trading away three young pitchers to fill short term holes in the roster in the interest of the team, or is it done more in the interest of Bowden's claim to be the wizard behind the screen pulling the levers that control the success of the Washington team? If the Nationals fail to make the play-offs this year, all of the fans will be disappointed, but if the team is a doormat for the National League for years to come, is that not worse for the team over the long term? Does that not spell shrinking attendance and all of the ills that have followed other Washington sports teams?

Bowden said very early in the season that he would emphasize veteran talent in 2005. He stated that the weakness of the 2004 Expos was the preponderance of young and unproven players. In 2005 that has meant only the difference between Carlos Baerga and Brendan Harris, between Wil Cordero and Matt Cepicky. Baerga has certainly gotten key hits for Washington and it is endlessly entertaining to watch him pump his short little legs going around the bases. But in the end, Cepicky and Harris are more likely to remain in 2006 than either Baerga or Cordero, both of whom are well beyond their prime but must be paid veteran salaries. Is it in the Nationals' interest to develop younger players like Cepicky, or at least see them swing the bat at the major league level and, if so, why not Bowden's? Why the love affair with veterans whose careers are dimming faster than "Cool Papa" Bell's famous lightbulb?

In 2005 the Nationals roster features no future Hall-of-Famers, only every day major leaguers putting their best into each game. Washington fans love this version of baseball. Perhaps there is a reason a team of hard nosed ballplayers who seem to leave it all on the field every game is preferable if the only other variation is a game played *by* millionaires *for* millionaires, where the greatest concern is the bottom line. The 2005 Nationals are about love of the game, playing hard, and winning the appreciation of the fans.

Bowden is owed a debt of thanks by all for putting a competitive team on the field when it was difficult to convince players and anyone else that there would be a team in Washington, Montreal or anywhere else. Yet he is not Frank Robinson. He has not seen this team through its worst days in Montreal. He was just brought in to clean up the mess the owners had made. His record with Cincinnati speaks for itself and the assessment of his trades for the Nationals yields a handful of glitter, fools gold that will blow away in the smallest breeze. If he leaves the franchise for another at the end of the season or if he stays, Washington will have almost nothing to show for his efforts here.

Bowden likely will campaign hard to remain with the team unless other offers are forthcoming. He will say he needs to complete the "miracle" that he has wrought. Buying this line will be a huge mistake for the new owners. Bud Selig will work hard behind the scenes to keep the management team in place that he brought to town. Control is hard to give up for some. Bowden is just another string for Selig to pull in D.C. Regardless of which side of the aisle the new owners sit, left or right, a clean break with the regime that the Commissioner has put in place would be refreshing and give Washington's long-suffering fans a chance to develop their own team, with its own unique Washington signature, whatever that may be. It should be one that will endure, not one that is just here for the show.

## The Great American Ballpark

The new ballpark in Cincinnati, gleaming red and white, with tugs and barges plying the Ohio River in the background, opened in 2003, the last year Jim Bowden was GM for the Reds. The park was designed by HOK, the architectural firm from Missouri that has designed many of the new stadiums. The stadium's name, the Great American Ballpark (the GAB), evokes the era of baseball it seeks to capture, when the ballpark was as American as Lassie riding in the back of a Ford pickup truck. HOK designed Camden Yards in Baltimore, and the success of that park has led to many other commissions for the firm. HOK has been awarded the contract to build the new stadium for the Nationals, targeted to open in 2008. Most fans smile and roll their eyes skyward at the thought of its optimistic schedule.

The GAB hosts smaller crowds than its predecessor along the river, Riverfront Stadium, which is famous for being inundated by the Ohio River floods in the 1970s. Bowden and the new owners brought Ken Griffey, Jr., back to re-create the magic of the great Reds teams from the mid-seventies when Sparky Anderson led the team to four League Championships and his successor, John McNamara, won another before the end of the decade. The current Reds pitching coach, Don Gullett, led the staff of several of those teams, but he has had no luck coaching the modern Reds pitchers. They are the worst in the National League, a more hapless bunch of starters cannot be found and the luck holds for the bullpen crew. On the day the Nationals arrive in town for the three game series, the Reds announce that they have released their All-Star reliever, Danny Graves. He has been a fixture on the team for a half dozen years and has only run into troubles recently.

Graves flipped off the fans booing his failure to bring home the win two days previously. Like Jose Guillen's similar incident in Anaheim that led to his suspension and ticket out of town, Graves is perceived to have crossed a line that begs a high price. The incident with Graves is reported to be part of a larger malaise with the team whose record is among the worst in baseball. The Nationals seem to have arrived at a perfect time. They are battling injury after injury and need a struggling team against which to get well.

This plan goes poorly on the first night out. Loaiza, the Mexican don who has pitched remarkably well all season, does not have his good stuff. Eric Milton, the former University of Maryland All-American, is allowing more than seven runs per nine innings and this looks especially inviting to a Nationals lineup that has been scoring fewer than four in the past few weeks. Baseball is a study in the play of probabilities, of random occurrences where sure things disappear from view like yesterday's newspaper, and some nights, maybe most nights, expectations can be thrown out the window.

Milton pitches a fine game that recalls the many excellent nights he has had in the past half dozen years when he has been healthy. Those nights however, are balanced against the too frequent outings on the other side of the scale. Ron Darling says on TV that he is pitching backwards, starting the hitters with his slow stuff and curveball and finishing them with his fastball late. Pitchers whose fastball is their best pitch use it almost exclusively in the early innings to get loose and limber, when their control and feel for the ball is tentative and they want to go with their best stuff. Then, on the second time through the batting order, they go more to their off pitches, changeups, sliders and curves as hitters begin to time the fastball more effectively. At his best, Milton had a great fastball, especially for a lefty, but it is not there anymore, at least not often. He may be developing into the prototypical crafty lefty.

Loaiza gets hit by every player in the lineup except Ken Griffey, Jr., and a young second baseman who does not look old enough to be out this late. Even Eric Milton gets his hits and drives in a run with a deep double to center field that one-hops the wall in the deepest part of the Great American Ballpark. The Reds collect eleven hits in five innings and Loaiza limits the damage to only five runs. It is enough for them to win. Milton holds on and, despite a late home run that brings the Nationals to within two at 5-3, there is no further excitement and Washington loses its 21st game against 24 wins.

Hammonds has been placed on the disabled list with a hamstring pull at the end of the Toronto series. Brendan Harris is a 24-year-old minor leaguer called up from New Orleans where he played second and third base. He may be the only middle infielder the Nationals have who is ready for the majors, but it is not certain that he has the athleticism to play second base or that he can hit with enough power to play third. In 2004 he was one of many young players who were called up by the Expos and struggled mightily under Frank Robinson's tutelage. He has shown patience at the plate during his minor league development with the Expos. At present he is the kind of question mark that Bowden has been trying to avoid by playing Baerga, but Harris has reached a plateau in the minors. He is as ready as he will ever be and the team certainly does not need to learn what Baerga can do, but Bowden is nervous without "veteran" players. Harris's two run homer in the eighth inning the night before is a good sign.

Harris is not in the lineup for the second game of the Cincinnati season when Livan Hernandez is the starting pitcher. Ryan Church starts, even though he is a left-handed bat against Brandon Claussen, the young Reds left-handed pitcher. The platoon with Marlon Byrd is discarded for an evening. Church strikes out in the top of the first inning after Castilla doubles in the first run and gives the Nationals a 1-0 lead before Hernandez even takes the mound.

In the early innings, Hernandez's knee is clearly bothering him as he limps to first base after a bunt in the 4th inning. Whether it is the knee or something else, Hernandez cannot control his pitches in the first inning and his velocity is noticeably off. He walks one, hits a batter and gives up a three run double to Austin Kearns, one of the Reds' young sluggers. Hernandez settles down in the second and third innings and he has more zip on his fastball. The Nationals are still down 3-1 despite loading the bases and having runners on base in every inning. They cannot score because the middle of the lineup is so thin. Nick Johnson and Jamey Carroll get on base but the Reds pitch around Castilla, who is the leading RBI threat in the lineup. They limit the damage to a single run in the fifth to maintain a 3-2 lead.

In the end, the Nationals make the Cincinnati pitchers look overpowering. Brandon Claussen pitches backwards, just like Eric Milton and the lack of predictable fastballs to hit, and the Nationals flail at pitch after pitch. The Nationals come back in the late innings and score the tying run in the ninth, but they cannot score in key situations with Ryan Church and Jose Guillen leaving men on base when nothing more than a fly ball would produce a run. It is easy to understand why Robinson loses confidence in the team and looks for different ways to score runs. After fourteen innings they lose painfully 4-3.

The day game on Thursday, May 25, goes even worse. They have lost two games to the worst team in the National League and send Claudio Vargas out for the rubber game. Vargas has been hit hard every time he has pitched after his first start went well and raised hopes. He is gone by the end of the second inning again, but this time he gives up only three runs and the game is still within reach. Rauch relieves him and keeps the game alive for a while but gives up three in the fifth inning to make the score 6-1 after the Nationals score a run in the fourth on a Guillen double and a Church single. Guillen accounts for all of the scoring as he goes on to hit two solo home runs. But the rest of the team cannot demystify the Reds bullpen that was woeful until they met the Nationals hitters.

Robinson is second-guessed after the sweep to a team as bad as the Reds. He bunts players over whenever the chance presents itself and the writers question why, without going into the many opportunities to score runs that have been lost to the failure to move runners at key junctures. Robinson's moves are sometimes inexplicable, but it is the team that is no longer playing sound fundamental baseball. Wilkerson, who came into the season with a decent on-base percentage, has lost his patience at the plate. Guillen is pressing in key situations. The team still has a winning record, but the road trip continues on to St. Louis against the team with the best record in the National League. After the weekend Atlanta comes back to Washington to face a team very different from the one that beat them at home in April.

There is more bad news on the off day Thursday as the team puts John Patterson on the disabled list with back spasms that have not subsided for two weeks. He is the eleventh Nationals player out of action, and no other team in the major leagues can even come close to this level of misery. Keeping this team stitched together will take more than mirrors. Bowden does not announce whom he will call up. He has Sun Woo-Kim pitching well in New Orleans. Kim pitched better than Vargas in 2004, but he is just one more unproven 27-year-old who was part of the 2004 Expos. Bowden is looking for something more, he wants to shop for players at Saks, not at Filene's basement. When will the Yankees call? The Nationals need something else completely, but Bowden doesn't seem to have any more patience than Endy Chavez.

## Everybody Is a Star

The All-Star ballots are available at the game, neatly stacked in metal racks that can be picked up as fans enter RFK through the yawning gates behind home plate. Young boys grab fistfuls and begin going through them, punching holes next to the names of their favorite Nationals players and other box score wonders that they look for every morning before going to school. Such time honored procedures are essential to forging lifelong fans. Kids watch the box scores for the favorites, buy their baseball cards, and hopefully seeing them at the All-star game—or, better yet, the World Series.

It is hard to see who on the Nationals qualifies as an All-Star. Livan Hernandez leads the National League, along with D-Train, in wins at 7. Yet, Hernandez is not in the top ten in ERA or strikeouts, two categories where the truly dominant pitchers' names can be found. Roger Clemens, the future Hall of Famer, and D-Train allow the fewest runs per nine innings—ERA—and Clemens also is near the top in strikeouts. Hernandez leads in only one category, innings pitched.

Hernandez is starting to take on heroic qualities, trudging to the mound to start the game but limping down to first base when he bats. He is banged up, but playing anyway, giving everything he has for the team. The writers ask whether it is wise for him to pitch with his knee in such bad shape, the same way that they used to ask whether Cal Ripken should rest when he was pursuing Gehrig's record. But writers then were concerned that Ripken's quest was at the expense of the team, that by playing hurt, playing below par to pursue a record was not in the best interests of the team.

Perseverance through adversity is beginning to define the Nationals, to shape the team's personality. They lose their front line players to injury, first the pitchers Eischen and Tucker, then Sledge, Vidro and now Guillen, but the team continues to win. Jamey Carroll hits almost .400 for the two weeks he fills in for Vidro, like some latter day Dal Maxvill, the great utility player for the Cardinals in the '60s and '70s. Playing a role and playing it well are what make a team something more than a sum of its parts. Like an acting ensemble that achieves great drama even though no player steps out of the cast individually, the Nationals are a team without all-stars, winning and doing it the old-fashioned way, through effort and teamwork.

The injuries are also helping to build teamwork and trust. Jamey Carroll will never win an All-Star ballot, but he will win the hearts of fans with his gutsy play that squares with his jarhead looks, and solid performance at second base while Vidro is out with an ankle sprain. His teammates can trust him to turn the double play. The pitchers know that the balls hit to him are quick outs, and they can concentrate on keeping the pitches low and breaking down so that batters pound them into the turf and into the waiting gloves of Castilla, who made fewer errors at third last year than any other third baseman in the game. Trust in the ability of everyone up and down the lineup makes for great teams. There may be few great stars on this team, no Barry Bonds, no Sammy Sosa or Miguel Tejada, but this team can play the game the way it is supposed to be played. And there may be some budding stars in players like Nick Johnson.

"He reminds me of old time ball players," says a fan.

"Yeah, until he shaved the mustache and beard, he kinda looked like one," says the other fan.

"I bet he doesn't work out with a personal trainer,"

"Doesn't look like it, does it?" says the second fan, laughing.

"I mean he does everything well," says fan one, punching a hole next to Johnson's name, "there's no hole in his game."

Johnson has reached base via a walk or hit in almost every Nationals game. He is leading the club in batting average with an average, that has been consistently over .300, and his home runs are starting to come more frequently. He has six and is second on the team to Jose Guillen, with whom he is tied for most runs batted in. He has a maturity that belies his 26 years, and his ascending status does not prevent him from signing balls and being accessible. Perhaps it is his knowledge of the game garnered from his uncle and former major league manager and player Larry Bowa that makes the game seem to come to him so naturally.

What would be unfortunate is for the media to attach too much importance to any one player, to forget the wonderful chemistry that has developed during the early part of the season. Like soldiers who fight more out of loyalty to their comrades in arms than to ideas or concepts, teams play best when they are an integrated whole. In a town known for artifice and spin, where the government is no longer trusted to tell the truth but to craft reality as a "message," keeping the Nationals real will be hard, but players like Livan Hernandez and Nick Johnson, who still seem real, still seem motivated by the love of playing, keep this team real to its fans. Whether it is appreciation of the great veterans like Castilla and Hernandez, or of the developing wonders like Guillen, Wilkerson, and Johnson, all of the Nationals are stars in Washington.

The Cardinals offer a great model for building teams. They have had great ones and the three day weekend series at the end of the month will give National fans a long distance look, as the games are finally being televised with a new cable television deal signed at the beginning of the road trip. Watching Scott Rolen, Jim Edmonds, and the best player in the game now, Albert Pujols, will offer Nationals fans a look at how much more than a single star it takes.

## LaRussa's Game

While the star of the Tony LaRussa book is ostensibly Tony LaRussa, he and Buzz Bissinger focus the spotlight on all of the players on the roster. The focus is sometimes admiring, as with Pujols, perhaps the greatest hitter in the game. At other times the book illustrates the frustration LaRussa feels with certain players, and how his expectations are sometimes completely turned on their head. The book humanizes LaRussa to a remarkable degree, especially given that it is a baseball book and character development generally takes a backseat to hero worship.

The book does not dwell on or explore in any depth one of the key roles LaRussa has played in making his team a winner. The primary ingredient is not the analytic approach he describes with Buzz Bissinger, and he admits that the moves a manager makes during a game win only a few games each year. Rather, the difference he makes on the team is his ability to draw great talent like Rolen and Edmonds, because great players respect him and want to play for him. When he came over from Oakland in 1996, great players followed out of loyalty. Mark McGwire was the first and most notable, coming to St. Louis in the middle of 1997 and hitting 70 home runs the next year. LaRussa has finished first in the NL Central Division five times in ten years and last year's team led all of baseball, winning 105 games. This year's team is also ahead of every team except the surprising White Sox.

LaRussa is there pacing in the dugout for the first game of the Cardinals series with Washington. Nick Johnson comes out of the home team dugout with a beard and goatee, going back to the look he sported when the Nationals were winning earlier in May. Baseball players are a superstitious lot, and one can imagine his decision-making to return to the winning look. The change has no demonstrable effect however, as, in the first inning of the game, Matt Morris, the Cardinals' starting pitcher, strikes out the side, including Johnson. Then, in the bottom of the first, Jim Edmunds hits a two-run home run out into the grass hill that rises over the center field wall at Busch Stadium. A fan runs out into the grass to get the ball and he wants to replace the divot the high fly ball leaves on the hill.

The Cardinals seem a juggernaut rolling down the same hill that the Nationals are struggling to climb. Then the Nationals strike in the beginning of the third inning. Guzman leads the inning off with a single and then Wilkerson doubles down the first base line to bring him home. Nick Johnson hits a long drive into the right center field alley to drive in two more and the Nationals take a 3-2 lead. Getting to Morris for three runs shows that Washington's offense still has spark.

Tony Armas is making another start and he just is not sharp. He walks five batters, one that Jim Edmunds brings in on his home run in the first, and then, after Armas walks two more in the third, Edmunds doubles them home and the Nationals are down 5-3. Morris, on the other hand, is in complete control. He bends curveball after curveball over the plate with an occasional slider or fastball inside. He has an excellent curve, but it is clear that the scouting report on Washington's hitters is that they live on the fastball. This trend to throw slow stuff to Nationals hitters seems to play a role in their offensive swoon. The batting coach talks to the press about Guzman not having a plan at the plate, but it seems the problem is more widespread than that. The team is not adjusting well to what the lead is doing in response to their quick start. They roll over on curve after curve, either failing to make contact, or hitting weak ground balls to Eckstein.

The intermittent light rain that has fallen during the night suddenly intensifies in the sixth inning and the umpires order the game suspended after five and a half innings. It is Friday night in D.C. and the bartenders across town reach up to flip the image above the bar to other sports images, to the Orioles game, where they are losing to the Tigers. Maybe there is beach volleyball somewhere on ESPN.

As the St. Louis series continues, Bowden is forced to make moves. His team is hurt and key replacements are performing poorly. The media detail the moves in the Thursday sports pages and the Friday pregame show buzzes.

"I call nine moves a pretty big shake-up," says Proctor in the run-up to the Cardinals game.

"Well, a lot of it is injuries and players who are just not performing up to the level they should," says Darling, in real world terms.

The announcers are talking about Bowden's additions to the team on the off day between the disastrous Cincinnati series and the St. Louis series that is shaping up as poorly, although for reason, at least. On Thursday, Bowden brought up Sun Woo-Kim, the Korean pitcher who has had much the same experience pitching for the Nationals in the past as Vargas and Day, as well as Tyrell Goodwin, an Endy Chavez-type, and T. J. Tucker, who pitched well in relief before an early season injury. These players replace Jon Rauch, Zach Day, and Claudio Vargas.

There is no difference in the overall level of talent before and after the moves, with one exception, C. J. Nitkowski. Nitkowski is to left handed pitcher as Baerga is to hitter. No one else will let him pitch in the major leagues any more except Bowden. He is a veteran, however. The cost of the acquisition is Claudio Vargas. Vargas is a hard throwing right-hander who showed promise in 2004. He must pass through waivers to make it back to New Orleans and he does not. Arizona claims him and promptly puts him in their rotation.

Nitkowski has a career 5.37 ERA and pitched poorly enough in a brief stint in 2004 that no one would sign him to a major league team for 2005. He was once a promising pitcher who is now nothing more than a LOOGY, a term coined supposedly by sports writer John Sickels and standing for "Left-handed,

One Out, Guy." Pitchers like Nitkowski have been made serviceable by managers like LaRussa, who match-up pitchers in the seventh and eighth innings, so that against those left-handed batters who are vulnerable to left-handed pitchers he can bring to bear the appropriate LOOGY. The game of match-up is a desperate affair that culminates in the ninth inning, when each team brings in its best and most talented reliever—the ninth inning closer.

Against LaRussa and the Cardinals, Frank Robinson, who is using the tools he has been given by Bowden, allows Nitkowski to pitch to the left-handed hitting Edmonds in the eighth. Edmonds continues his love affair with Nationals pitchers and hits one almost as far as the home run in the first inning, but this one stays in the park for a double. Mabry is the next left-handed hitter and the Cardinals give Nitkowski an out on a sacrifice that sends Edmonds to third, from where he scores the final run of the game. The Nationals lose 6-3 after the rain delay and have now lost 24 games to go with their 24 wins. They are one and a half games ahead of the Phillies, who are in last place in the NL East.

The Saturday night game gives the Nationals their best shot at the Cards. Jeff Suppan is arguably their weakest pitcher and the match-up with Loaiza works in Washington's favor. Confounding the odds, nothing works for the suddenly free-swinging Nationals. Suppan carries a no-hitter into the sixth inning, while Loaiza allows Edmonds another home run during a three run second inning. With a 3-0 lead going into the sixth inning, Suppan allows Wilkerson the first Nationals hit—a single to center. Then both Marlon Byrd and Jose Guillen get scratch singles and the bases are loaded with only one out. Nick Johnson comes to the plate. Johnson is the one Nationals hitter through this offensive drought whose approach at the plate has not changed. He is patient facing Suppan, works a full count, and fouls off several pitches before coaxing a walk that forces in the first Nationals run for a 3-1 score.

With Vinny Castilla coming to the plate, the Nationals sense a turnaround in the offing. He led the National League in runs batted in for 2004 and is a tough out in these situations. The depth of the funk into which Washington's offense has sunk is readily apparent when Castilla jumps at the first pitch and grounds weakly to shortstop Eckstein, who starts an ending inning double play. The Nationals cannot mount another threat and the game ends 3-1. The team has a losing record for the first time since April. The road trip has become a monster that will not let them go. Since winning three of four from Milwaukee in Washington in mid May, the team has lost seven of eight on the road. The last game of the trip will pit Livan Hernandez against Chris Carpenter, who, like Hernandez, has seven wins against two defeats. They are both workhorse pitchers and the final game of the road trip should be a great one.

The final game of the road trip is a great one and it showcases the talent of someone for whom Nationals fans are gaining increasing respect with every

## 8. Where's That Famous Golden Touch?

game he pitches. As the game begins, Livan Hernandez is shaky. Nationals fans are ready to change the channel, ready to watch attractive young Danica Patrick try to win the Indy 500. Pesky little David Eckstein, the Cardinals' diminutive shortstop, spanks the ball to deep right center and before Wilkerson can get the ball back in he parks his five-foot-eight frame on third base with a triple. Eckstein is the spark plug player whose grit and clutch play defined the 2002 Anaheim Angels team that won the World Series, the year that he led the majors remarkably enough with three grand slam home runs. Now he is trying to spark the Cardinals to a sweep that will cap a horribly depressing road trip.

Nunez singles in Epstein with the first run and the Cardinals lead 1-0 immediately. Hernandez gives up a walk but limits the damage. Then in the third, archfiend of high fastballs Jim Edmonds hits his third home run in as many days to give the Cardinals a 2-0 lead, and the slow methodical carving away of the Nationals seems unstoppable. But Hernandez pitches carefully and craftily out of jams and in the fifth inning the Nationals mount a rally against Cardinals pitcher Chris Carpenter. Carpenter is bending the big 12-to-6 curveball over the plate, but Marlon Byrd, getting a chance to play against a right-handed pitcher, comes through with a solid single to center. Schneider takes a curve off the plate to the opposite field for a single, an approach that only Johnson has been using during the two-week slump. With one out and Schneider and Byrd aboard, Hernandez lays down a perfect sacrifice and with two out there are runners on second and third.

This situation has played itself out repeatedly during the slump and whether it was Castilla, Guillen or Wilkerson, the Nationals' best hitters have not been able to deliver. But Wilkerson is hot today, and he already has two hits. He gets a pitch in the sweet part of the bat and drives the ball into deep left, where it one-hops the wall for a ground rule double. The score is tied and the Nationals players have found a hero. In their early season games there was always someone who found success at the plate, usually someone new each game. Wilkerson has not had a hot hand in weeks and it is good to see him beaming back toward the stands from second base. Carroll is cheered by his presence as well and again takes a curve off the plate and hits it like a sand wedge into left, where it falls for a single, Wilkerson flies around third and comes home before the Cardinals can muster a throw. The Nationals have a precarious 3-2 lead.

In the bottom of the inning Hernandez adds to the drama, loading the bases, but getting Mark Grudzielanek to ground out to end the threat. Then in the sixth and seventh, Livan Hernandez seems buoyed by the offensive support and pitches with greater command than ever, mixing slow stuff away with fastballs inside. For the next three innings Washington's bats are silent as well, but in the eighth inning, Hernandez stays in the dugout and turns the ball over to the bullpen. Edmonds leads off against the veteran LOOGY Nitkowski, who cannot get him out as he singles sharply and stands on first base with no one out. Robinson takes the ball from the frustrated Nitkowski and gives it to Gary Majewski, who has pitched well all season and has gained new confidence from Robinson.

Majewski shows the mettle that has impressed Robinson and he gets two fly ball outs and a pop-up to end the inning. Now the Nationals have turned the tables on LaRussa. The closer, Chad Cordero, comes in and pitches a strong ninth inning to preserve a badly needed win. The team is back at .500 and can get its breath before playing against the best two teams in the NL East, the Braves and the Marlins, back at RFK. It is sometimes a win like this one that changes the course of the season, or changes the flow for a while. Beating the Cardinals in St. Louis, against a great team and one of the best managers in the game, will keep the Nationals smiling on the trip back to D.C.

# 9

# There's No Place Like Home

"Dad, do you think home field advantage is best in baseball? asks an 11-year old trying to impress his father with his budding sports acumen.

"Maybe," says his father, thinking. "But it's pretty important in basketball, too."

"What about chemistry, Dad?" asks the boy. "Is chemistry more important in baseball?"

"Yes, son, it's important," says the father, "but let's watch the game."

For the Washington Nationals there is nothing to compare with this home field advantage. Just having a home is a distinct advantage now, and after the disaster that loomed during the road trip it is good to be back at RFK. During the pregame rituals, Schneider and Byrd are wrestling playfully on third base. Everyone is all smiles standing around before the game. The take away win of the last game in St. Louis was an important emotional pick-me-up for the team.

Frank Robinson and two of the men in blue are talking by the third base coach's box. Robinson is working them quietly, like the chairman of a congressional committee working two members of the opposition before the meeting is called to order. Jerry Layne, the third base umpire, his traditional umpire's stomach extending outward from his belt like some army scout, is talking to Robinson along with Ed Montague, the crew chief who will be at second during the game. It is an amiable discussion and the three men part company as an honor guard comes through the center field gate for the formal Memorial Day salute to those who keep us safe and those who have died doing so.

After the last strands of the national anthem are sung by a stocky, uniformed woman, Tomo Ohka goes to the mound and the Nationals take the field. Ohka has pitched well since coming in to replace Claudio Vargas in the second inning in Milwaukee, his exile to the bullpen over quickly. He has an easy first inning despite a walk to Marcus Giles, who is erased on a double play by Cristian Guzman. In the third inning both Castilla and Carroll mishandle ground balls around Ohka's second walk. In the early games Washington's defense was a fortress, but now errors have become more commonplace. Castilla's error allows a run to score, but he bounces back and turns a nice double play several pitches later on a grounder hit up the third base line. In the fourth inning Washington rallies behind a double by Nick Johnson and a walk to Castilla.

It looks as though Atlanta is pitching around Castilla to get to Byrd, who confounds the strategy with a sinking line drive into the gap that Andruw Jones cannot come up with on a diving try. The ball skids under his glove and Johnson scores. Castilla is too slow to score even though he is running with two outs. He is stranded on third when Guzman makes the last out on a weak fly ball to left.

The Braves scratch out nothing more than a single and a walk from Ohka in the next three innings. Nick Johnson and Marlon Byrd each double again in the sixth inning and the Nationals score again, taking a 2-1 lead. Byrd repays Frank Robinson's decision to expand Byrd's half of the platoon with Ryan Church by driving in both of the Nationals' runs through six. The media report that Church is hurt, but many wonder whether Byrd's play will not keep him sitting longer than any lingering malady.

In the seventh inning, the play of the game occurs that drags Frank Robinson's amiable pregame conversation with Jerry Layne back into focus. With one out, Brian Jordan lifts a very high, lazy fly ball toward the left field corner. It seems too weakly hit to go over the wall, but it carries into the dead part of the park. Marlon Byrd goes back on the ball slowly, watching its high arcing flight, but it goes over the wall just beyond his glove, seemingly fair, which is Jerry Layne's call. The fans in the corner and the Washington bullpen begin to shout and gesture with hand signals that the ball went to the left of the foul pole. Robinson jogs slowly out to left in his warm-up jacket, where Jerry Layne is standing not really listening to Byrd protest the call.

Robinson arrives as Montague begins to walk out from behind the second base bag. Robinson seems to ask Layne to get a second opinion. He is not loud, but he convinces Layne to talk to Montague, who arrives, and suddenly it is the same threesome who were talking before play began. Then home plate umpire Tom Hallion joins the debate. Hallion may have had the best angle to see the ball, but he is also the farthest away from the play. Montague has no angle at all, but he takes an aggressive role in the discussion by the four-man crew, who walk away from Robinson to begin their deliberations in the outfield grass. They break up the parlay and Montague signals with both hands the safe sign, an apparent decision that the ball is deemed foul. The fans are not sure about the call until Atlanta Braves manager Bobby Cox charges toward Montague, whom he meets behind the pitcher's mound for a heated discussion that does nothing to overturn the call.

Television replays after the game are inconclusive because no camera angle can be found to truly track the ball against the foul pole. The Nationals score an insurance run in the eighth inning on a double by Wilkerson and an RBI single by Guillen, but in the ninth with Chad Cordero, the closer pitching and two out, Andruw Jones hits a long home run to left. Atlanta fans mockingly call the ball foul, but Washington takes the series opener 3-2 as Cordero gets catcher Estrada for the final out on a can of corn to center field.

"What's a can of corn mean, Dad?" asks the boy.

"Old grocery stores used to keep the canned goods up on high shelves. The grocer would use a long pole to pull the cans of corn off the shelf, then he would catch them when they fell, just like Wilkerson caught that fly ball," explains the father patiently, passing on the wisdom of the ages about fly balls and how home field advantage can win baseball games.

The Tuesday night game features pitchers Mike Hampton for Atlanta, and John Patterson for the Nationals.

"So Patterson and Hampton are both coming off the DL?" asks a fan, watching Patterson limber up playing long toss with Washington catcher Gary Bennett in the outfield.

"Yeah, if they are both healthy, could be a great game," says his friend.

Mike Hampton, the little bulldog who never gives in to the batter, and John Patterson, the Washington pitcher and former number one draft pick of the Arizona Diamondbacks, were both activated from the disabled list for the Tuesday night game. Hampton pitched the first game of the year between the two teams back in early April. He was dominating for eight innings, giving up only a single run, while the Atlanta offense had its way with Zach Day and Joe Horgan for eleven runs. Yet this portent has proved unreliable and Washington has played the Braves well, winning four of the six games so far.

The fans are not ready to move on yet, not ready to let go the excitement from the night before.

"Everybody in the office today says it was a fair ball," says a fan on the subway.

"From my angle, it looked fair," says the usher seating a man with his two sons near field level. "Course, it's hard to tell from here."

"Well, I say it's time we caught a break," says the Dad. "I don't think anyone really knows and we sure needed the win."

Patterson starts the game looking rusty from the two-week layoff. He cannot find the plate and after a solid single by Rafael Furcal leading off he walks Marcus Giles. With one out, Chipper Jones gets a run home on a grounder and the Braves take a 1-0 lead. Washington's tall thin pitching coach, Randy St. Clair, visits the mound. After the conference, Patterson settles down and strikes out Andruw Jones to end the inning. Hampton does not look sharp and gives up hits in every inning and exits after the fourth inning with elbow stiffness. Washington fans are relieved when Bobby Cox, the Atlanta manager, lifts Hampton, but then dismayed when Frank Robinson lifts Patterson after five. Patterson had settled in nicely after the first and had not allowed a base runner after the first inning. Robinson says that he had pitched "more than enough," and prefers a cautious approach, given the number of injuries the team has endured. Keeping Patterson healthy is an important issue for Washington's success.

After the two starters leave the game, it is a contest of bullpen pitching, and here Washington has had the edge all season long. In the sixth inning, Robinson brings in C. J. Nitkowski, the latest of Bowden's retreads, and soon the base paths are littered with runners like a highway filled with black rubber after a truck blows a tread. Chipper Jones drives in Kelly Johnson with a long double to left center. Johnson takes the ball from Nitkowski and gives it to T. J. Tucker, who has been out with injuries since April. Before he gets the final out, Tucker allows a run scoring single to 46-year-old Julio Franco to make the score 3-0. Hopes sag visibly at RFK.

Leading off the bottom of the sixth against the Braves' relief pitcher, Adam Bernero, Guillen, Johnson, and Castilla get aboard with two singles and a walk to load the bases. Marlon Byrd, whose doubles spelled victory the night before, is at the plate. This evening he is not to be the hero, however. He grounds into a double play that scores a run but empties the bases save for Nick Johnson, who stands on third with second string catcher Gary Bennett at the plate. Bennett surprises the fans, who have lapsed into lethargy again, with a solid single to left to score the second Washington run, and the lead is trimmed to 3-2.

Five twenty-somethings come in to take their seats in the bottom of the sixth inning, each carrying a long necked plastic beer bottle. As his friends fill the row from the aisle, one of the young men steps across several empty seats until he arrives at his own via the shortest possible route. His companion is less adroit and she is left perched above the final step with her beer dangled like a slipper from her hand.

"Hand me the beer," he offers gracelessly, turning his attention to the field.

"I can't do it," says the young woman pleadingly, perched on a seat two rows up.

An older gentleman holds the young woman's purse as she navigates the last shoal before reaching the friendly harbor of her date and his friends. Baseball fans are not always devout. They stray from the game and lose sight of what is important in life. The late arrivals fall into a heated discussion with a middle-aged woman seated directly behind them.

"Nahhh, *Texas Chainsaw* is the scariest movie I ever saw," says the older woman, whose daughter sitting in the adjacent seat looks like a time traveler's version of her mother.

"Have you ever seen *Candyman*?" asks the young man in the row in front of her.

"Nahh, I never saw it, but *Texas Chainsaw* is a classic."

The debate rages while Luis Ayala throws his warm-up tosses to start the seventh inning. He pitches a perfect inning for the Nationals and they come to bat in the bottom of the seventh with the momentum beginning to turn in their favor. Ryan Church pinch-hits for Ayala at the bottom of the order, and gets a single. Wilkerson almost hits into a double play, but his speed beats the throw and he is aboard when Carroll gets a single. Jose Guillen continues to hammer the ball with a run scoring single to left against Kevin Gryboski, one of the Braves' best relievers. Watching Guillen swing the bat, it is easy to understand his reputation as an "angry player." He looks to kill every pitch, and is remarkably successful with this approach that brings to mind some of the other great hitters of the game, Jim Thome of the Phillies for one, who also takes hard cuts at almost every pitch. Guillen ties the score 3-3 with his timely hit.

Nick Johnson, who is batting cleanup, shows why he is slowly developing into one of the game's best hitters as he doubles to deep right field over the hard charging Andruw Jones, who covers as much ground as anyone. When Johnson is done, Guillen and Carroll are in the dugout with two runs and the Nationals have the lead 5-3. Castilla and Byrd can do no further damage, so it is the bullpen's game to win or lose now. Robinson brings on Gary Majewski, who is pitching the eighth inning for the third straight night. He is almost perfect, striking out Furcal and Kelly Johnson and getting Chipper Jones to ground out with a runner on first. Chad Cordero comes in for the ninth inning and is confronted with Julio Franco, who singled in the sixth. Franco shows what an old man can do, he fouls off numerous offerings from Cordero before launching a monstrous drive to center field that is never in doubt as a home run.

The lead is trimmed to 5-4 and Andruw Jones, who homered against Cordero in the ninth the previous evening, comes to the plate. He singles and then Estrada singles and Washington fans are convinced that three appearances in a row are too much for their young pitcher and look to see if there is activity in the left field corner bullpen. Hector Carrasco hurriedly gets up, but the fans know there is no time to get him in before the damage is done. It is Cordero's game. Brian Jordan stands at the plate, he whose disputed fly ball the night before is still so fresh on every mind in the park. He has revenge on his mind, but all he can manage is a ground ball to Guzman, who gets an out at second. There is only one out and a man at third base. Any fly ball or deep grounder will score the tying run.

Bobby Cox, another match-up manager like LaRussa, is out of pinch hitters. His only sound player is the 23-year-old back up catcher, Brayan Pena, who has a total of only nine Major League at bats. He is clearly overmatched against Cordero. After fouling off several pitches Cordero takes it "up the ladder," and Pena flails helplessly at the high fastball for the second out. Rafael Furcal is the last batter and Cordero is throwing with confidence now. He gets Furcal looking at a called third strike and RFK lets out another collective sigh for the team that cannot win without extended drama. It is too much like watching your child play soccer, where all the games are low scoring and your child's team is always teetering on the edge.

The fans stay for the bitter end for the most part. The ramps are filled with noisy revelry from the almost 30,000 fans who started the game. They sense a turn in the team's fortunes after the losing road trip. Baseball is a cruel and fickle game. The hero one night is the goat the next, and the team that lost seven of nine on the road has won two in a row at home. The Nationals are breathing down the backs of the Braves for second place in the tough NL East. Nick Johnson, who has two hits and two runs batted in, ends the game batting .322, eighth in the National League, just behind Albert Pujols.

The long run of beautiful weather continues apace in Washington for the third game of the series against the Braves. The contest promises a stiff test for the Nationals as they face future Hall of Fame pitcher John Smoltz. He and John Patterson went nose to nose in a masterful game in April that was decided in the ninth inning when Guzman could not make the ninth inning throw across the rain drenched infield, and Atlanta won a 2-1 heartbreaker from Washington. Tony Armas is the Nationals' hurler and he is still struggling to find the promising array of pitches he showcased in his rookie season several years earlier. He is not sharp to start the game, although he gets the Braves out in order in the first inning; but he gives up a long solo home run to Johnny Estrada in the second inning to put the Atlanta on top 1-0.

Smoltz is sometimes vulnerable in the early innings before he finds his groove. New he struggles and runs into trouble in the bottom of the second inning. Nick Johnson hits a ringing double to deep right center and, one out later, Ryan Church doubles him home to tie the game. Bryan Schneider doubles in Church and after Guzman moves him to third with a grounder he scores on a Smoltz wild pitch to make the score 3-1. Armas walks the leadoff batter in the third inning and Laroche brings him home two outs later to keep the game close at 3-2.

Both pitchers settle down and the game is scoreless until the bottom of the sixth inning, when Ryan Church gets a two out double, his second of the game. The enthusiasm of the crowd sags noticeably as Cristian Guzman comes to the plate hitting a less than lusty .185. To the surprise of everyone, he gets enough wood on a low and away pitch to lift a pitching wedge over the infield, where it falls for a single and Church scampers across the plate for a 4-2 lead. As well as the Washington bullpen has pitched in many recent games, the lead looks like it can be held. Hector Carrasco comes in to pitch the seventh inning and he does a remarkable job, getting two weak pop-outs and a strikeout.

In the eighth, Carrasco is in control once again, striking out Andruw Jones to start the inning and getting a quick grounder for the second out. As quickly as a hot summer storm can blow up, the Braves strike. Langerhans doubles to left and the rookie shortstop, Wilson Betemit, filling in for the injured Rafael Furcal, comes to the plate. He lifts a long fly ball into right field. Every fly ball that has looked well hit has died in the outfield, but this one keeps carrying and eludes by inches Jose Guillen's well-timed leap. Betemit circles the bases with the tying run behind Carrasco, who watches dejectedly.

The storm continues as the Braves pinch-hit Julio Franco for Smoltz. Franco works Carrasco for a walk and Bobby Cox replaces him on the bases with Pete Orr. Orr is a compelling example of the holes in the team that Jim Bowden has assembled. Orr is a speedy base runner who is a threat to steal a base at any time. Having a tool like this on the bench gives Bobby Cox options like the one now. Frank Robinson, in sharp contrast, has the slowest team in the National League and two of his bench players, Carlos Baerga and Wil Cordero, are "veterans" whose speed left them years ago. There is no player on the Washington bench who has even moderate speed, much less the ability to steal a base in a key situation. Similarly, there is no ability to pinch-hit for the slumping Guzman late in games because the Nationals have no one other than Carroll who can play shortstop. Baerga is the only backup middle infielder, and he is woeful in the field, as past games have proven on numerous occasions. Frank Robinson is only as good as the tools in his tool chest.

Orr steals second base easily ahead of a fine throw from Schneider. T. J. Tucker is pitching in relief of Carrasco and his is slow to the plate. Marcus Giles stokes a single into left and the Braves have the lead, a lead they do not relinquish. Chris Reitsma, who has pitched well in several games against the Nationals, allows base runners but nary a run and the game ends 5-4, the same score as the previous night's game but with a different winner.

It is a gray and dreary Thursday, but the weather's turn does not dampen the turnout for the last game of the Braves series at RFK. There are again close to 30,000 fans, extending well up into the yellow seats in the top tier of the stadium. For the twenty-five years that he owned the team, Ted Turner dubbed the Braves "America's Team," because of their availability on his nationwide cable network. It was a strategy successful mostly because of the great talent the team had on display. The Braves draw well wherever they go as a result of the dozen or more years they have dominated the National League, their games watched in many smaller venues across America. Most of their

**The game conditions get worse, but play continues.**

talent is gone now, and, although Atlanta is still competitive, it is instructive how well Washington matches up with them.

The heart of the Braves' order is no more intimidating than Washington's, with unproven hitters in several locations that continue to make outs at key junctures. While the Braves have the more proven starting rotation, the Nationals' starters are capable, and their bullpen is clearly deeper and those with key roles, like Ayala and Cordero, are more talented. The key difference between the two teams is the bench and the keen mind of Bobby Cox. Although Frank Robinson is a fine manager, he has not experienced Cox's level of success. Cox has managed the Braves to first place in the National League East every year except the strike-shortened season in 1994 when time ran out with the Expos just ahead of them in first. He also was the general manager who helped create the current organization with its emphasis on building talent from within.

It is Washington's turn to send out the veteran pitcher against youth. Esteban Loaiza takes the mound against lefty Horacio Ramirez. Ramirez has been pounded two of his past three outings, and in the second inning it appears the Nationals may have as easy a time also. Nick Johnson continues his hot hitting and leads off with a single. With one out, Marlon Byrd sends a long fly ball into left, but it dies. Then Gary Bennett, starting for Schneider against the left-hander, hits one that leaves no doubt where it is going as it bounces against the padding high above the bullpen in left, and Washington takes a 2-0 lead.

Loaiza throws with his usual effortless grace, his low-nineties fastball exploding on hitters. He is striking out hitters swinging and getting the calls on cutters that run back over the plate to Chipper Jones and others, who stand dumbstruck when the umpire calls them out. Yet Washington seems unable to hold a lead and Wilson Betemit, the Braves' hero from the night before, comes up in the fifth and continues his hot hand, tripling into the gap with one out. He scores on the next out and Atlanta creeps back into the contest, down only 2-1. The bottom of the fifth inning starts with Loaiza leading off and he hits a line drive into the gap in right center. He cruises slowly into second, and Wilkerson gets him over to third with one out. Carroll lifts a fly ball to right field and Brian Jordan takes it in and whirls completely around to fire toward home plate. Loaiza is off and running and Jordan's throw sails left of the plate, allowing the slow running pitcher to touch the plate just ahead of the lunging Braves' catcher.

In the top of the sixth inning, Loaiza gives up a walk and two singles, but finishes the inning strong, striking out Andruw Jones and Brian Jordan. Loaiza leaves the game after six innings with a 3-2 lead. It is the first time he has left the game with a lead in almost a month. His is a study in frustration, winning only once despite pitching effectively into the late innings in every start except one. His ERA of 3.56 ranks him first on the team and establishes him in the top ranks of starters in the league. His command and composure make him a pleasure to watch and one wonders how someone so seemingly unfazed on the mound could have been confounded by the atmosphere of the Big Apple, where he was undone in 2004.

Frank Robinson brings in Ayala for the seventh inning, the lead still only 3-2. Ayala does his job and Washington heads into the eighth clinging to the same lead. Robinson is counting on his top three relievers to get Loaiza a win, and Gary Majewski, who has a string of sixteen innings without allowing a run, starts the eighth. Carlos Baerga is also substituted into the game for Nick Johnson, who, it is later learned, was experiencing chest pains that turned out to be only acid reflux. It is an untimely occurrence.

Majewski walks the leadoff hitter and gives up a single to put runners on first and second with no one out. Adam Laroche turns on a pitch and sends it screaming toward the right field corner, but Jose Guillen runs it down, the ball a snow cone in his glove as he careens against the wall and hurries a throw back into the cutoff man. The runner on second moves to third and scores when the next batter, Andruw Jones, hits a sacrifice fly to knot the score at 3-3. There are two outs and a runner left on first when Brian Jordan hits a grounder to Cristian Guzman, who ranges far to his left for the ball and throws a one-hopper to Carlos Baerga now playing first base. Reminiscent of the double play throw from Castilla that he let go into center field weeks earlier, he never touches the throw that skips past allowing both runners to move up. The more athletic first basemen routinely dig out one-hop throws for the out, and the worst play would be to fail to handle the ball cleanly enough to get the out. But Baerga is so inept he cannot even get leather on the ball.

After Wilson Betemit is walked intentionally, Johnny Estrada scores all three runners with a single to center. Wilkerson's throwing error allows the last run to score and puts the Braves on top 6-3. In the bottom of the eighth inning, Danny Kolb, Atlanta's one time closer, is brought in his new role as setup man. He fails this audition as well, walking Wilkerson to lead off the inning and then giving up singles to Guillen and Baerga to cut the lead to 6-4. Vinny Castilla doubles to bring in a run and Baerga, who moves to third, is lifted for a pinch runner, Blanco, so that with one out the Nationals can tie the score at 6-6 going into the ninth. Marlon Byrd is intentionally walked to get to right-handed hitting Gary Bennett, whose home run early in the game gave Washington its first lead. He delivers again, this time a stinging double to deep right field that clears the bases and gives the Nationals an 8-6 lead. He finishes the game with five of the eight runs coming in from his clutch hitting. Cordero pitches a perfect ninth against the disheartened Braves for his fourteenth save.

The win gives the Nationals their second series win against the Braves. Their record for the season to date against the best team in the National League for more than a decade stands at six wins and three losses. Atlanta is now tied with the Florida Marlins for the lead in the NL East. Washington and the New York Mets are tied only one and a half games off the pace. The 11-game home stand continues with a weekend series against Florida, where there will be no Dontrelle Willis game. No one in Washington will miss the high leg-kicking D-train.

## Summertime and the Fish Are Jumping

The three-day weekend series gets started against a threat of continued rain on Friday night after early rains have left the field wet and slippery. The game has the additional backdrop of the Marlins' domination of the Nationals during the early weeks of the season. Florida's pitcher will be Josh Beckett, who is one of the best young pitchers in the game. He is only 25, but this is his fifth season in the majors. He won the decisive game six in the 2003 World Series against the Yankees, pitching a complete game shut out against one of the great offensive teams in recent history. He shutout the Nationals in their first 2005 meeting in early April. The Nationals' ace, Livan Hernandez, takes his turn in the rotation and it is the match-up of a great veteran against the young ace, if the weather holds.

Drama builds from constant tension and Friday night's game has fans on edge from the start. In the first inning Beckett of the 100-mph fastball starts the game with a sharp breaking curve. He has heard the scouting reports and he has a good curve, too. Washington gets Marlon Byrd, filling in for Brad Wilkerson in the leadoff spot, to third base with two outs, but Beckett strikes out Nick Johnson impressively to end the early threat. Hernandez is the recipient of great defensive support in the early innings as he finds his rhythm. Jose Guillen runs down several drives and Jamey Carroll has a nice play in the outfield grass, but in the third inning the Marlins get the first two runners on base with no one out. Carlos Delgado comes to the plate.

Delgado has been one of the most feared batters in baseball over the last half dozen years or so. He was signed by Florida to complement their Venezuelan masher, Miguel Cabrera, who has tortured Washington pitching so far in 2005. Livan Hernandez seems unfazed. He never seems rattled and he gets Delgado on a foul pop-up to Vinny Castilla; then Cabrera on a hard hit ground ball back to the mound that showcases Hernandez's fielding prowess. After pitching through the worst of it, Hernandez gives up a single to Juan Encarnacion, the fill-in center fielder, to give Florida a 2-0 lead and still two outs. Damage is limited when LoDuca hits a liner into the left field corner that drops for a sure double. Encarnacion rounds third and heads for the plate, but Marlon Byrd runs the ball down quickly and fires the ball in to Cristian Guzman, whose perfect throw to Schneider nails the runner with a yard to spare. Three outs, 2-0, but Beckett is pitching.

In the fourth inning, after Beckett has been almost perfect through the order, Jose Guillen gets aboard on a swinging bunt up the third base line. Then Nick Johnson crushes a Beckett changeup into the gap in right center that rolls all the way to the wall. Encarnacion slips in the wet grass and the ball rebounds past him, allowing Guillen to score the first Washington run and Johnson to make it to third with no one out. Castilla gets him in on a ground ball to tie the score 2-2.

The two pitchers settle in. Livan Hernandez has fallen in love with the edge of the plate and uses cutters to run in across the edge of the plate and sliders to run away from the batter. He leaves nothing over the middle of the plate and the Marlins cannot get good wood on the ball consistently. The fifth inning is one-two-three for both pitchers, and then in the second the Marlins start to measure Hernandez again and two long fly balls die near the outfield wall; but the Flying Fish cannot score. In the seventh inning Beckett fans both Castilla and Church. He seems to be growing stronger. Ominously, Hernandez's pitch count is growing and he has thrown over 120 pitches by the eighth, while Beckett has only 98.

To start the top of the eighth inning, Delgado draws a walk that further extends Hernandez. He gets Cabrera on a pop fly, but Encarnacion continues to bedevil him and he lines one into the outfield where Church's diving try fails to pluck the ball before it falls in. Church chases down the ball to keep Delgado from scoring the go ahead run, but the Fish have men on second and third. Then Frank Robinson decides to load the bases rather than pitch to Paul LoDuca, the Marlins catcher. Now Hernandez will face Damian Easley, who had several good years for Detroit that seems like many years ago.

Livan works the edge of the plate again and gets two strikes on Easley, and the crowd sense the drama, rising to their feet and yelling for the strikeout. Derryl Cousins, the home plate umpire, calls one just on the edge a ball and the crowd groan in unison. Then as the next pitch seems to split the outer part of the plate, Cousins calls another ball and this time the crowd scream out in anger. On the next pitch off the plate, Easley swings anyway, but like so many of his teammates can only pop the ball up. Nick Johnson tracks it across the foul territory toward the stands and spears the ball, bending over the photographer's well for the third out.

Hernandez has thrown 138 pitches now, well beyond the limits of modern pitch count methodology that ends at 120 pitches per outing. Yet when Beckett retires the Nationals quietly in the bottom of the eighth, he returns to the mound in the ninth, still wanting that ninth win that will put him ahead

Livan Hernandez talks Frank into leaving him in to throw 150 pitches.

of A-train once again for the league lead. Mike Lowell, the Flying Fish's young slugging third baseman who came through the Yankee's organization along with Nick Johnson, pinch-hits for Beckett with one out in the ninth. He gets a solid single and stands at first with the winning run, only one out.

Jack McKeon changes the equation even further, putting in Juan Pierre, one of the fastest runners in baseball, to run for Lowell. A steal here puts the winning run in scoring position with two chances to get the speedy Pierre home. Hernandez throws over to first twice, each snap throw closer than the last. Satisfied, he turns his focus toward the top of the Marlins' order and calmly retires Castillo and Conine to end the inning. He is finished for the night, having thrown the unbelievable total of 150 pitches.

Jim Mecir replaces Beckett. The Nationals fans are briefly hopeful, but he pitches a perfect ninth inning for the Fish, striking out the side. Cordero takes the mound for the tenth and nothing is brewing when he finishes. The Marlins' recent first round pick, Nate Bump, who many had thought would quickly join the rotation, comes in for the tenth. He pitches a perfect tenth and the game begins to look like it can go on forever. The crowd thins some, but there is still an eager core making noise after Ayala replaces Cordero and dispatches the Fish quietly in the eleventh inning.

Bump starts the eleventh and gives Jamey Carroll a free pass to first. Hopes soar again until Jose Guillen pounds the ball into the ground in front of the plate and the ball bounds to Nate Bump, who whirls to throw to second to start the double play. Unexpectedly, the ball sails badly and shortstop Alex Gonzalez leaps high over the sliding Carroll but is nowhere near the throw that is caught by the second baseman backing up the play. Both runners are safe and the Fish's sloppy play has provided the Nationals a serendipitous opening, as though some leprechaun were perched on Frank Robinson's shoulder.

The crowd begins to rock as Nate Bump is lifted and Matt Perisho comes out of the bullpen for the Marlins. He pitches carefully to Nick Johnson, who fails to get good wood on anything. In the end Johnson works Bump for a walk to load the bases. There is still no one out. Earlier in the season there were situations like this and the Nationals walked away with nothing, looking dejected. But there is a palpable change in the demeanor of the team. They look about as if to see where the next miracle will come from, not with that dejected, defeated air that followed them on the road. They can sense their own luck changing.

McKeon changes pitchers again, going with young John Reidling to pitch to Castilla. Although his numbers are atrocious, Reidling gets the first out as Castilla pops out, second baseman Castillo nestling the ball carefully into his glove. The crowd groans again. Maybe this string of luck is a short one. Undeterred, the crowd's noise rises as Ryan Church steps to the plate. On the third pitch, he sends a fly ball to left. The crowd are up on their feet to see how far it has carried, to see the play at the plate. Miguel Cabrera makes the catch in medium left, not deep at all, but his throw to the plate sails well to the right and Jamey Carroll easily crosses the plate before LoDuca can make a play. The team erupts in joy to greet Carroll, smiling and forming their line at second to congratulate one another, beaming smiles all around. The game ends 3-2 and it is the biggest win for Washington yet.

Most analysts believe Florida is the most balanced team in the NL East. Their three young pitchers are all that the Cubs thought they had but lost. There are no three pitchers in baseball who can throw as hard and as well as A-Train, Beckett and A. J. Burnett. Yet the Nationals have extended them to the limits and beaten them. The win is an important one, and it puts the team on the threshold, only a half game behind Atlanta and Florida. Two games remain with the Fish, but they have beaten one of the best tonight and they can feel it. The magic is still there when you look.

The Saturday night game features Al Leiter for the Marlins. He is forty years old and came to prominence with Florida anchoring a pitching staff that included Livan Hernandez back in 1996 and '97. Together they took the Marlins to the World Series in 1997, where Leiter won game seven, perhaps his greatest memory in the game. Leiter and Hernandez were then part of a purge that would have made Stalin blush, the owners selling off almost every player on that championship team to the highest bidder. Since then Leiter has pitched with distinction for the New York Mets, returning only this year to finish out his career. Livan Hernandez still has that old magic, but Leiter has lost it and he is just hanging on. He is allowing more than six runs per game, has lost six and won only two. The match-up against Tomo Ohka gives the Nationals the only real advantage during the series and the fans are hopeful a win here will give them the series against the Fish.

It is clear from the outset, however, that *neither* pitcher has particularly good stuff. In the top of the first inning, Ohka uncorks a wild pitch that puts a runner in scoring position and Miguel Cabrera promptly obliges with a double to make the score 1-0. Ohka then hits a batter before escaping further damage.

It is never certain what is going on when bean balls start flying, but with Jamey Carroll on first with one out, Leiter hits first Jose Guillen with a pitch and then Nick Johnson. It is possible to believe that Guillen was retaliation for Ohka hitting Encarnacion. Yet hitting Johnson loads the bases and leads to big trouble for Leiter when Vinny Castilla has a solid double to deep center to clear the bases and give the Nationals a 3-1 lead.

In the second inning, Ohka continues to flirt with disaster. He gives up a single run on a double by speedster Juan Pierre, but loads the bases and only averts further harm when Miguel Cabrera's long fly ball to center dies and settles into Church's glove for the third out. Washington leads 3-2, but the Marlins come back in the third and Encarnacion leads off the inning with a solo home run to tie the score at 3-3.

When Ohka gets in trouble again in the fourth, Frank Robinson comes to get him. Ohka refuses to face the manager and stuffs the ball into Robinson's hand as he stalks off the field, obviously upset. Sun Woo-Kim comes into the game, and Ohka seeing his Korean rival warming in the bullpen may have been part of the problem. Their rivalry came to blows when they were both young pitchers in the Boston organization. Ohka settled the issue by pitching well for the Red Sox that year, while Kim continued to struggle in the minors. This day it will be Kim who lets his performance on the mound settle the old dispute, as he pitches out of Ohka's fourth inning jam and then pitches three more scoreless innings to swing the momentum back to the Nationals.

Washington scores the go ahead run in the fifth on a single by Nick Johnson. The fourth run chases Leiter and gets the Nationals into the opposing bullpen once again. From here, the advantage shifts clearly to Washington. They score a single run again in the seventh with the combination of Carroll and Johnson. The run batted in is Johnson's 33rd of the season and puts him on a pace to reach one hundred RBIs for the season, a substantial landmark for a young hitter. He will make it if he can stay healthy for the first time in his short career.

In the bottom of the eighth, the team gets what Robinson has asked for, a game with a little breathing room. They score two more runs on a triple by Church, a single by Guzman and a long double by Tony Blanco, getting a chance to play after Marlon Byrd is thrown out of the game on a controversial run-in with the umpiring crew. Byrd's dispute detracts from the 7-3 win by focusing attention not on the series win against the vaunted Flying Fish, but on whether his physical contact with Joe Brinkman was intentional. After a disputed third strike, Byrd had eyed home plate umpire Jeff Nelson as he returned to his position in center field. Nelson motions Byrd off the field and he takes off on the run for the umpire. Brinkman attempts to impede Byrd's progress and is pulled completely off his feet and falls flat on his back.

The newspapers the next morning feature pictures of Brinkman lying in the outfield grass, rather than the celebration of the win that leaves the team only a half game behind the Braves for 1st place in the NL East. Little is made of Kim's first win, his clutch pitching or Johnson's torrid pace that moves him into third among all NL hitters. No one notes that Frank Robinson could sit back and breathe for a change in the ninth inning.

By game time on Sunday afternoon, the dispute has been clarified and Byrd begins the game in center field for the still ailing Brad Wilkerson. Guillen is out, too, with a sore hand from the first inning the night before when he was hit with Leiter's pitch. The 40,000 fans talk about the incident with Byrd, like they did the foul ball call that gave them the win against Atlanta a week earlier. Controversies often have a short shelf life, though, and winning five games of the six so far on the home stand will resonate far longer if they can make it a sweep.

The winning streak has moved the Nationals into position not only to sweep a series from the Marlins, but, if Pittsburgh helps out by beating Atlanta, they can also move into first place. The Expos won only 18 games at this juncture in the 2004 season, and the last time a Washington baseball team was in first place in June was 1933. There is a rather prominent obstacle in the way. A. J. Burnett is Josh Beckett's equal as a pitcher and he will pitch the Sunday afternoon game, hoping to close off the Florida losing streak, to close out the upstart Nationals.

The Nationals have a former number one draft pick of their own pitching. It is John Patterson's turn in the rotation. He does not throw as hard as Burnett, few do, but he is limiting the opposition to fewer runs and Washington fans are hoping this is his season to turn the corner, just like Nick Johnson, just like Ryan Church. Can all of these young players respond to the crowd, to the new home, by having their break-out seasons? The fans are certainly having a break-out season, as more than 40,000 turn out for the first really hot day at RFK. Will the ball carry better in the heat? Many questions, and a long season left for the answers.

In the first inning Patterson strikes out Carlos Delgado and Miguel Cabrera with Castillo standing on second. The sign above the Marlins dugout that tracks pitch speed shows Burnett throwing fastballs at between 97 and 99 miles per hour. He shrugs off Patterson's feat at the top of the inning and has a quick one-two-three inning, with Nick Johnson striking out to end it. After more of the same in the second inning, the Marlins draw first blood at the top of the third. After striking out the pitcher, Burnett, and getting Castillo on a weak grounder, Pierre lines a pitch back over Patterson's outstretched glove and then steals second. LoDuca, moved to the third spot to take advantage of his hot bat, strokes a single to left and Florida breaks on top 1-0.

There is a scary moment in the sixth inning. After getting Delgado swinging on a high and away fastball, Patterson throws the same pitch to Miguel Cabrera. The ball runs in toward the helmet of the right-hander and he averts his face just in time to avoid serious injury. Patterson is visibly shaken and struggles, but completes the inning without Cabrera advancing. Patterson is still on a pitch count and Robinson lifts him after the sixth inning for a pinch hitter. When T. J. Tucker takes the mound in the seventh for the Nationals, the crowd begins to sag a bit. He gives up a single to Castillo and Pierre moves him over to second with one out. LoDuca grounds out and Frank Robinson begins to play his own game of match-up. He brings Nitkowski in to face the left-handed hitting Carlos Delgado and it almost works. Delgado hits a weak grounder to short but it is hit so slowly there is no play anywhere and the Marlins lead 2-0. Robinson then brings in the righty Carrasco to face Miquel Cabrera and the inning is quickly over.

Burnett is still throwing at near 100 miles per hour and the Nationals have not laid a glove on him, managing only two scratch hits and a seeing-eye-single. He gets the more experienced batters on fastballs, and the younger ones like Church with curve after curve. At the top of the seventh inning, though, the same luck begins to assert itself. Castilla hits the ball hard to start the inning but right at the left fielder. Church is almost rung up for the second out, but he holds his bat up just in time—or at least the umpire sees it that way—and Burnett loses the plate after the call, sending Church to first with a walk, his first of the day. Robinson puts on the hit and run, always risky but beautiful when it works, and Schneider executes it perfectly, grounding into the hole left by Castillo as he goes to cover second base against the advancing Church.

Tony Blanco, pressed into service with both Wilkerson and Guillen out, gets the weakest of fly ball singles to center and Church comes in with Washington's first run, cutting the lead to 2-1. Nothing has been hit hard, but there are runners at first and third base with only one out. The two old timers, McKeon and Robinson, begin a game of cat and mouse. McKeon takes out Burnett and brings in Mecir to protect the lead. Mecir was so effective in the late innings the day before, but Robinson counters, lifting Cristian Guzman and bringing in Jose Guillen to pinch-hit, and sending Ohka to run for the slow-footed Schneider. It is Ohka's chance to crawl from Robinson's doghouse. Guillen gets a solid single to right and the bases are loaded. Robinson again goes to his bench and brings in Baerga to pinch hit. Mecir throws inside and low, and Baerga cannot get out of the way. He trots down to first base, sending Ohka across the plate with the tying run. The first chants of "Sweep," can be heard in the stands as the fans sense that without Burnett the Marlins can be had. Marion Byrd, whose run-in with the umpire was the talk of the pre game, comes to the plate and manages a fly ball just deep enough to score Tony Blanco with a run to make it 3-2 Washington.

Florida does not go easy. Robinson brings in Luis Ayala to pitch the eighth inning and Mike Lowell greets the ball with a single after fouling off numerous pitches. Lenny Harris pinch-hits for Mecir and gets his record 200th pinch hit, a long double into the right center gap to score Lowell and tie the game. Ayala bears down and the Fish do not score again.

In the bottom of the eighth, John Reidling is pitching for the Marlins. Nick Johnson, of the league-leading .451 on-base percentage, works a one out walk and Vinny Castilla hits one to Damian Easley that bad hops him over his shoulder and into left field. Johnson hustles around second and makes it to third where a fly ball will score him with only one out. McKeon brings in Matt Perisho the LOOGY to face Ryan Church and Robinson cannot pinch-hit; his bench is exhausted. Church shows that he can hit left-handers by depositing Perisho's pitch into the Marlin's bullpen. The players are all smiles, glad-handing Church as he goes excitedly down the bench. The score is 6-3

The hit and run—it's always risky, but it's beautiful when it works.

and Robinson has pulled all the right levers today. McKeon's pinch hitter makes the key error of the game in the bottom of the eighth instead of Baerga, who plays second in the eighth and ninth. Some days the ball bounces your way, other days it don't.

Cordero pitches the ninth inning and nails down the victory. It is a momentous win and, coupled with Pittsburgh's 5-2 victory over Atlanta, puts Washington in sole possession of first place in the East. The *Post* carries the news the next morning that no Washington baseball team has been in first as late as June since 1933, and shows a picture of Church, Gary Bennett and Castilla high-fiving at home plate after the home run. The picture is carried on most of the baseball Web sites the next morning.

In the *New York Times* the same picture is blown up and covers half of the front sports page, the glorious red of the Nationals' home uniforms shouting out with a caption beneath that reads, "First in War, First in Peace, First in the NL East." News of the Orioles' victory that day is buried in the daily reports.

# 10

# Money Buys You Everything

There is an off day between series, as interleague play gets ready for another appearance. The media and the fans are accorded a break, and once play begins again the stakes will be reduced, the head to head match-ups with the best of the NL East will be replaced by two weaker teams from the AL West: Oakland and Seattle. The media take the off day to analyze the success of the team. After looking at the stats, they find no obvious answers.

Writers are also beginning to project who will buy the team. The *Washington Post* and others have provided profiles of the ownership groups. The modern era has seen a different role for owners. In years past, owners were more often low profile, out-of-the-spotlight types. Family ownership has been common, like the Yawkeys in Boston and the Kaufman family in Kansas City. They, like the corporate owners—LaBatts Brewery in Canada, the Wrigley Corporation in Chicago, and, recently, Disney in Los Angeles—have all been quiet partners in the operation of the teams.

Yet the more recent trend has been for the George Steinbrenners to generate almost as many headlines as the team itself. Ted Turner, Peter Angelos, Jerry Reinsdorf, and Bud Selig have been outspoken owners whose egos have sometimes gotten in the way of the team. Most fans would prefer to think less about the owners of major league baseball teams. Owners live in a world most fans never experience, their glittering luxury boxes set apart, away from the eyes of the fans. Only occasionally do the surreptitious cameras focus on them when their actions are at issue. The Washington Nationals are up for sale, and part of in the bargain is the public acclaim and notoriety that is much of the allure, much of the rationale for spending so much money on something that is only a game.

Like a Sotheby's auction, the preliminaries for sale of the Nationals are as important as the actual event, and the run-up to the sale has been in full swing since early June. No sooner does the *Washington Post* detail the groups who will bid—the presses are hardly cool—than George Soros weighs in with his $7.2 billion. Is George Soros a baseball fan? Republicans, who nervously watched him push his cool billions into the middle of the poker table during the 2004 elections, have called him many things, but now "baseball fan" must be added to the list.

The struggle between owners, their handpicked management staffs and the rest of baseball was the focus of a wonderful book several years ago by John Helyar called *Lord's of the Realm*. In the book, Helyar detailed the struggle of the baseball players to squeeze themselves out from under the collective thumbs of the owners. The history of the Baseball Players Association has been written about prodigiously and is a fascinating tale. The players are now the 800-pound gorilla that occupies the same room as the larger animal called MLB, Inc. Yet, what of the fans? Who protects their interests? At one point, the commissioner of baseball was ostensibly charged with protecting the game itself and therefore could be argued to have the same interests as that of the fans. A palace coup in 1992 hijacked the office of commissioner and it has been in the hands of the ownership group ever since.

Should fans consider creating their own organization to lobby for their interests and, if so, what would those interests be? Lower ticket prices would be a first demand, but perhaps a more enduring concern is the baseball alienation from which Washington is recovering, and that has been passed on to Montreal. The Nationals fans are grateful for their team, but they know how quickly it can be gone, and if they forget they can call their friends north of the border. In the blink of a corporate investment decision, the moving trucks arrive in the middle of the night and the stadium lights go out for decades. Fans should be protected from that.

Baseball will prosper in Washington now because the crowds at the stadium have changed. Washington is affluent and baseball has become a game watched by the affluent. Washington's wealth and its economy are insulated from the vagaries and cyclical influences felt more acutely in other cities. For example, one thriving sector of the current economy is defense and security firms dependent on dollars from the Pentagon and the Department of Homeland Security. Nowhere is there a larger concentration of these interests than in D.C., and the Maryland and Virginia suburbs. When patriotic songs are sung at RFK, there are families whose loyalties are clear; they serve their country or work in industries that do. There is a unique affluence here and baseball will benefit from it, although Bud Selig was a very long time grasping the equation.

Working-class families are not able to afford baseball anymore. As demographic analysis of our society as a whole documents, working-class families can afford less in general. It is the super-wealthy who have captured a larger part of the national wealth. It is why there are so many super-rich to bid for the Nationals, why George Soros with his $7.2 billion is only 24th on the list of the wealthiest in the country.

The less affluent baseball fan is more likely to visit the minor league stadiums across the nation, where wonderful ballparks feature carousels and moon bounces for the kids, or, like the famous Durham Bulls' HOK-designed stadium, an inflated obstacle course for children. At major league venues it is more common to see children wiggling and squirming, their mother watching them, or chasing after them while Dad watches the game, because the major league experience has become increasingly "not for children."

At a recent game, the parent of a young boy was clearly disturbed by the language of immoderate fans around him, but the ethos of major league baseball is more and more about getting the highest price, whether it is the players union getting the highest salary, or the owners moving to a city where revenue will increase. The bottom line is king in baseball. Recently a young boy watching a major league game in the outfield bleachers was tossed a ball by the right fielder. Players who regularly toss kids balls cherish a vision of helping to instill a love of the game in the young. Yet as the young fan rolled the ball around in his glove, a grown man several rows up yelled down to the boy, "Hey kid, I'll give you $20 for the ball." The boy's father urged his son to take the money and he did.

Similarly, a young boy and his father seated in the outfield in Toronto caught Tony Blanco's first home run ball and the team offered him a ball autographed by the team in exchange, hoping to give the souvenir to Blanco. The father declined, reportedly saying, "I wonder what I can get for this on Bay?" Mercenary interests have taken long had their grip on the game and that influence always has reflected the values of our society. Yet one cannot help wondering if there is not some way to stem this tide, some way to snatch the game from the grasp of money and ego that threaten to corrupt it even further. One can imagine now a Republican ownership group bidding for the Washington Nationals, and a Democratic one. The one nonpartisan experience left in this town may soon be a thing of the past. Unite, you fans of the pure game; you have nothing to lose but your season parking pass and discount coupons at the team store!

Whoever buys the Washington franchise and steps into the morass of economic tribulation and public attention that surrounds it has some important decisions to make. The economics of the team are certain, although the relationship with Baltimore that is certain to evolve and change over time may affect it. Yet the certainty of a fan base that will respond to a winning team can be seen every night at RFK and ranks well with most of the other cities in the country. However, one can hope that the new owners will be savvy enough not to tread down the road taken so recently by Peter Angelos, thinking that money will buy you everything.

Money may buy you J. D. Drew, but it will not land you the great pure talents of the game that Buzz Bissinger and Tony LaRussa were recounting in their book's discussion of Albert Pujols. Selected in the 13th round of the amateur draft, Pujols became a great player through hard work. Dedication to the game and the work to develop and put personal talent in the service of team goals is almost never for sale. The "Nationals Way," something local but akin to the ethos that developed just north of here as the "Oriole Way," is yet to be defined. So far, in 2005, the team's character has been about exactly that—team. There are no stars, only veterans. The statistics point to their capable defense, they do not give up many unearned runs. But more important than anything else has been the ability of a different player to step forward on a given night and be the hero. The Nationals might be called the 15-minutes of fame team, because each night several players get their 15 minutes. That is what is becoming the "Nationals Way." No matter how deep the pockets of the new ownership, it would be foolish to discard something so difficult to create from whole cloth—teamwork.

## The Future

As the Nationals parade Ryan Zimmerman around like a chimp on a leash, one cannot help but remember another Ryan—Ryan Minor. The Orioles trotted him out exactly as the Nationals have Zimmerman. Minor was going to be the rookie that made us forget that Cal Ripkin was leaving. Or was it that he was another Brooks Robinson? Hyperbole is so much a part of the Orioles front office. It is too bad that the Nationals are tearing a page out of that same book.

On Tuesday, with the Nationals sitting atop the NL East, all thirty MLB teams will begin a rapid-fire process of choosing talent from the ranks of the best young high school and college talent. *Baseball America*, the weekly journal that tracks baseball as it is played in the minor leagues, college, and other nonmajor league caliber venues, reports that Washington's top management have seemingly settled on a University of Virginia third baseman as their top pick in the amateur draft. Peter Gammons, ESPN's noted analyst, concurs. *BA* describes a trip by Nationals senior staff to watch Ryan Zimmerman, the UVA standout, when the Cavaliers played the perennial collegiate powerhouse, the University of Miami. Zimmerman hit a mammoth home run during the game and cemented his status with his play during the game. The Nationals have no other picks in the draft until the fourth round, but assert that the team has been active in recruiting via Latin American outlets for talent that may compensate.

Zimmerman is a fine prospect and *Baseball America's* assessment is that he is probably only a year or two away from being able to play at the major league level. The UVA Web site details a long list of accomplishments, and the school is known for smart athletes who have prospered as professionals in football and basketball. Zimmerman is also highly regarded for his maturity and character, compared by Gammons to Scott Rolen—high praise, indeed.

Another key discussion, spurred by *Moneyball*, is how frequently major league teams waste high draft picks on high school players, when college level talent—like Zimmerman—has a higher probability of major league success. Zimmerman fits the *Moneyball* mold. He has great plate discipline with a .471 on-base percentage during his senior year at UVA and has struck out only five times during his 225 at bats during his season with UVA. His command of the plate at a high level of collegiate play is indicative of considerable skill and talent. The change in the draft has been remarkable as team after team has switched its focus to more reliably projectable talent from the college ranks. High draft picks from the high school ranks were once the norm, but now that logic has been completely flipped on its head. Only the highest-graded high school talent is chosen early now.

Peter Gammons asserts that the baseball draft is very different from that of other pro sports. High school level players, and even college players, are hard to project as pros. College football players who grade out highly during pro camps generally play to the level that is indicated by their status in the draft. College basketball players also grade out fairly close, although the basketball equation has been complicated by the inclusion of high school talent. Any Washington, D.C., sports fan can tell a sports writer about the failure of "sure thing" high school basketball players as the team wasted its first pick in the 2001 draft on Kwame Brown. For the most part, however, the players highly sought after in the professional basketball draft become regular contributors to their teams, which is not necessarily so in baseball.

The analysis of the Expos last few amateur drafts reads like a graveyard of hope. There are almost no names that would be recognizable to avid fans looking down toward New Orleans or Harrisburg to see what talent is on its way up the ladder to RFK. There are only the journeymen like Baerga and Hammonds, and the few other players like Sun Woo-Kim or Brandon Harris who have had limited success in the major leagues but are unlikely to be significant contributors to rising expectations for the Nationals.

*Baseball America's* assessment of the Expos organization is not sanguine. Their note of skepticism about MLB's role in the Nationals' player development apparatus is not complimentary. Although they believe that Zimmerman is a more than a legitimate pick for the team in the draft, they note the damage done by MLB to the Expos over the past three and a half years. Not only have there been no efforts made to increase the presence of the Expos in the supplemental rounds of the draft, MLB purposefully diminished the organization's ability to compete in the amateur draft generally. The head of MLB's scouting effort for the Expos, Dana Brown, is well respected, but he was given what *BA* calls a "tiny" staff—eleven scouts total—and a miniscule signing budget. The effect was to reduce the team's ability to go after high profile position players.

There has been one notable exception. Chad Cordero signed in 2003, the last year of the Omar Minaya regime, and he has rocketed through the system with remarkable ease, arriving only a year after being drafted number one by the Expos. There is no other player even close to Cordero in the Nationals farm system. There are no recent high-level draft picks playing in New Orleans except for Josh Karp, who was chosen by the Expos in 2001 as their top pick out of UCLA. Much heralded, he has been a mysterious but total flop. Larry Broadway and Darrell Rasner, high picks from 2002, are still stuck at Double-A Harrisburg.

All of the other talent taken recently during MLB tenure is stuck at either High A Potomac, or Low A Savannah. The first round pick from 2004, Bill Bray, another Virginia college product out of William and Mary, has shown recent promise in Potomac. Edgardo Baez, Ian Desmond, and Devin Ivany are other high picks who are playing in Savannah, along with Collin Balester, a high school pitcher chosen in the fourth round in 2004. The most egregious problem is total lack of quality position players. Players like Zimmerman are much needed, and they should be easy to sign given the positive aura developing around the team. With Vinny Castilla signed only to a two-year contract, and given Castilla's age, Zimmerman has an open track to the opening day third baseman's job in 2006.

It will take far more than a single pick, however, to replenish what was for many years the best organization in baseball, picked clean under first New York art dealer Jeffrey Loria, and then MLB, Inc. Peter Gammons has an online article on ESPN in which he breaks down the origins of the 2003-2004 All-Star teams for both the American and National Leagues. What is quickly apparent is the value of international talent, players who do not originate in the United States; like many of the great players—Pedro Martinez, Vladimir Guerrero or Miguel Tejada—they are from Venezuela, the Dominican Republic or Puerto Rico. The teams that have invested in developing this talent have shown large dividends. The Expos were such a team at one point in their recent history, but those connections have been severed. It may take a long time to re-build them, although the popularity of the D.C. United soccer team shows that there is a ready market for Latin sports in the area.

New ownership will have many important decisions to make about the team. The first will be how to rebuild the infrastructure of a minor league system, a scouting system for judging not only amateur talent, but also international players. The *Washington Post* reports that the team chemistry is remarkably good, that Latin players like Vinny Castilla have good relationships with American ball players and that others report much the same. Approximately 60 percent of the team is between the ages of 24 and 28, most of whom are American born, but it also includes two Korean players and a half dozen Latin-born players important to its future. The positive impact of poverty for the Expos organization is that, by not bringing in expensive talent, position players like Wilkerson, Schneider, and Nick Johnson, and pitchers like Ohka, Kim, and John Patterson, have been allowed to develop and to develop together. This team has forged its maturity and character through the frustrations of the Expos organization as administered by MLB, Inc. It will serve them well as they head into August and September, when the fight to see who is left standing will be decided.

## Playing the *Moneyball* Team

Billy Beane's Oakland Athletics come to town to test the First Place Washington Nationals. It is a contest that showcases varying philosophies. Oakland is a team of young talent trying hard to play themselves into contention. Only Scott Hatteberg among the Oakland regulars is over 30 years of age and their pitching staff is even younger than the eight regulars on the field. Beane allowed his most gifted pitchers, Mark Mulder and Tim Hudson, to leave after 2004 because he could not afford the exceedingly large price they will bring on the open market. Mulder pitches now for St. Louis and Hudson for Atlanta, after pitching the A's to the play-offs every year except 2004. Several of the amateur draftees featured in Beane's book, *Moneyball*, are playing regularly now, including Nick Swisher and Joe Blanton, but others are first round draft choices from other recent drafts, such as Rick Harden, who most believe will be as good or better than either Hudson or Mulder.

For Tuesday night's game, the last remnant of the A's Three Aces, Barry Zito, will pitch. He is only 26 but has already won a Cy Young award. Washington counters with Tony Armas, who is also 26 and has been pitching in the majors almost as long; he illustrates just how young the Nationals team is apart from Bowden's new veterans. The weather is hotter even than it was for the weekend series with the Marlins, topping out at 92 during the afternoon. Will the heat give the ball any lift in RFK?

The answer does not come immediately. Armas starts shakily, as he has now in most of his starts. He gives up a single to Jason Kendall, the A's veteran catcher, who then steals second and scores the first run of the game on a Scott Hatteberg double to deep right. Zito protects the 1-0 lead with inning after inning of marvelous stuff. In the fourth inning Nick Johnson takes him for a double but no one can even move him to third and, after a walk, Guzman flails helplessly, looking like a schoolboy as he swings and misses at a Zito fastball up near his shoulders.

Armas is nearly as good, but his pitch count is very high and he is lifted after pitching the top of the sixth inning. In the bottom of the inning, Zito loses the strike zone and walks Jose Guillen on four straight pitches. Nick Johnson, who has been reading the pitching charts in the half inning, steps to the plate knowing that Zito will try to get a fastball over for a strike. He answers the question about the ball carrying with a line drive that seems to carry well as it lands well beyond the wall in right center field. The home run gives Washington a 2-1 lead going into the seventh inning. Castilla gets to second with no one out, but Zito strands him there without giving the Nationals the extra insurance run.

Frank Robinson goes to the plan that has worked well recently, bringing Majewski to pitch the seventh, Ayala the eighth and Cordero the ninth. Majewski does his part by getting the first two A's easily. Then he is wild and cannot find the plate, walking a batter on four straight and then going 3 and 0 on the next. Kotsay, who is a wily batter and can work the best of pitchers for a walk, is at the plate. Majewski comes back with Kotsay taking the 3-0 pitch, and gets a strike. Then after another strike he gets him on a grounder to second to end the inning.

In the eighth, with the score still 2-1, Frank Robinson is playing match-up. He starts with Carrasco, who gets a quick out facing right-handed Jason Kendal. Then Robinson brings in his LOOGY, Nitkowski, to face Eric Chavez and Hatteberg. Nitkowski has gotten out three of the seven left handed hitters he has faced, his intended opponents batting a whopping .571 when facing him. True to form Chavez lines a ball deep into the gap for a double and Hatteberg walks on five pitches. It is on Ayala to bail out the Nationals. He is equal to the task as he gets Bobby Crosby, the 2004 American League Rookie of the Year, to ground to an inning ending double play where Carroll's low throw is scooped beautifully by Nick Johnson, whose glove and bat are beginning to make a big difference for the Nationals.

Washington has even less luck against the very good Oakland bullpen. Kiko Calero and Justin Duscherer are perfect for the seventh and eighth and Oakland comes to bat in the ninth inning behind 2-1, with one last chance against Chad Cordero. "The Chief" shows Oakland no mercy, striking out Kielty, and getting Swisher on a fly ball for the second out. Then it seems like déjà vu all over again. Scutaro and Byrnes get aboard on singles and, like the seventh when Kotsay faced Majewski Cordero he is at the plate again with two men on and a chance to win the game with a hit. With the fans on their feet and every Nationals player watching from the rail along the top step of the dugout, Cordero gets a ground ball to Carroll that Carroll gloves carefully and throws to Nick Johnson.

"What do you make of Johnson?" asks the old scout, his Dale Earnhart hat perched off to the side of his head as precariously as the weather vane on an old barn.

"He's going to be as good as they always said he would be," says the young scout, clicking and unclicking his pen nervously while he looks over his notes.

## 10. Money Buys You Everything

"He could keep this team going," singsongs the old scout.

"He already is," says the young scout, pulling his sunglasses from the top of his head and hanging them off his shirt pocket as he heads for the exits with the rest of the fans.

What is apparent after the second game with Oakland is that there is something to what the little boy asked his father about chemistry and home field advantage. First, Washington has 20 wins at RFK versus nine losses, a significant advantage. Oakland has almost the exact opposite record when away from Oakland, eight wins and 20 losses. What Oakland does not have is either the veteran presence of Livan Hernandez, Esteban Loaiza, and Vinny Castilla, or the chemistry of the Nationals that has them grinning like young boys after some of their recent heart-stopping victories at RFK.

It is chemistry that the media are beginning to write about. The chemistry of the Hispanic players and the young Anglos who have spent the past few seasons suffering through perhaps the worst baseball environment ever invented. Oakland is a team whose star, Eric Chavez, is reputed to be begging for a trade, whose best pitcher, Barry Zito, is supposedly on the trading block. Their manager has little insight into the young players he is teaching, and is not accorded much respect by his general manager, Billy Beane, according to the now famous book. So it appears that the Nationals have more than home field advantage, they have chemistry. It shows in the second game.

Ryan Glynn is the pitcher for Oakland in the second game and he is up against hard-luck Loaiza. Glynn is a journeyman called up from Triple-A Sacramento to fill in for the A's injured young star, Rich Harden. He is no match for Loaiza. Loaiza looks a little shaky in the first inning and Glynn cruises through the first two innings with a 2-0 lead from a long Bobby Crosby home run over the 410 sign in to the left of dead-away centerfield. Then Ryan Church cuts the lead in half with a home run in the third inning to the left field bullpen. It is a portent of things to come.

The writers and announcers have decreed that the ball is not carrying, Mel Proctor saying every night that RFK's center field is "where home runs go to die." The ball is not carrying, they say. Now the heat of summer is on, and the ball is starting to carry.

In the fourth inning, Loaiza will get the kind of run support he has deserved all season long. The Nationals start the inning with Nick Johnson showing how the leadoff man responsibilities should be handled. He draws a walk and steals second base. Castilla grounds out, but Carlos Baerga, filling in for the injured Jamey Carroll, hits a drive to left that looks like its going out, but instead hits off the top of the wall for a ringing double. The stubby-legged Baerga little-steps his way into second base ahead of the throw, with Johnson scoring easily with the tying run. Schneider then shows how it can be done by hitting a drive over the wall in left center that is obviously a home run from the moment he hits it. Baerga scores in front of him for a 4-2 Nationals lead.

Loaiza does not squander it. He has a one-two-three top of the fifth inning and Oakland lifts Glynn for Keichi Yabu, a thirty-five-year-old Japanese pitcher who was very successful in his long career there. His first pitch sails over the catcher's head and goes all the way to the backstop. The second pitch is so far inside that Jose Guillen has no chance to get out of the way and is hit in the forearm. He takes a step toward the mound but is restrained, his notorious temper in check for now as he takes his base. Yabu regains his control and gets out of the fifth inning, but he is not so lucky in the sixth, giving up two walks before leaving the game. Ryan Church's triple scores both runners and Washington leads 6-2. It is the kind of game that manager Frank Robinson has asked for, an easy win. Before it is over, Castilla has another home run to prove the ball is indeed carrying well and the final score is 7-2.

Washington extends its lead in the NL East by a game over the competition and the fans are almost cocky riding home on the subway. Loaiza wins his second game of the season, giving up only four hits, exactly as many as Ryan Church, whose home run and three runs batted in make him the hero of the game.

On the way to the third game in the Oakland series, commuters are becoming annoyed by the team's long presence on the eleven game home stand.

"All these baseball fans are tearing up the escalators," says a middle-aged rush hour patron looking at the fans in their caps and jerseys.

"Yeah, they ought to take some of that money and fix the trains," says her companion.

"I hear one of 'em wants to buy the team's got seven billion dollars," says the first woman.

"Yeah, well, he won't miss a billion then, will he, to fix the trains?"

The fans hear not a word. They are caught in the magic and the only word they know now is "sweep." It is becoming overused in the Washington lexicon. After winning three straight from the Marlins, it seems only fair that the Nationals should win three from Oakland as well. To complete the task of sweeping their second series and winning their seventh game in a row, Livan Hernandez takes the mound. He has eight wins for the season and is clearly the team's leader, the veteran presence whom they rely on at key junctures to turn the tide. He is facing Joe Blanton, Oakland's first round draft pick, who is in his first year in the major leagues. He is good, but inexperienced.

Livan Hernandez shows Blanton what experience is all about. He does not throw a pitch harder than an occasional 88-mph fastball, but more commonly the radar gun registers 63 or 77 as his junk floats over the plate, mystifying the young Athletics, who flail at the slow offerings over the first two innings. In the third, Nick Johnson misplays a bunt by the Oakland pitcher, Blanton, to put two men aboard with no one out, but Hernandez gets one routine grounder for a double play, and another for the third out.

In the bottom of the third inning, Washington picks up where it had left off the previous evening. Livan Hernandez leads off the inning with a single, and successive hits by Church and Guillen load the bases with only one out. Nick Johnson, batting cleanup every night now, tattoos a ball into right center that goes over Kotsay's head and caroms off the padding randomly enough for all three runners to score and Johnson to end up on second base. Vinny Castilla doubles to deep center to score Johnson and the lead balloons to 4-0.

It is enough for Livan Hernandez, the way he is pitching, and he takes a shutout into the eighth inning. In that inning, however, Jason Kendall leads off with a sharply hit single, and Bobby Crosby hits a long triple to deep right field to score Kendall. They seem to have discovered a pattern to Hernandez's pitching, both of them hitting 88-mph fastballs. Livan rallies to retire the side but a sacrifice fly scores the second run and cuts the Nationals' lead to 4-2.

In the bottom of the eighth inning, there is a pure "Washington" moment in the game. With Huston "K" Street pitching—the moniker K-Street put up on the score board denoting the famous law and lobbying canyon in downtown Washington—a fan standing in the first rows of the upper deck catches a foul ball with one hand fully extended, his other clasping a cell phone snugly to his ear. He does not pump the fist, he does not exult in any way, he continues talking on the phone, calmly hands the ball to a fan in the row in front of him and never bats an eye.

What is even more of a Nationals' moment occurs in the bottom of the inning when Dan Johnson smokes a liner down the first base line. Nick Johnson leaps out to his left, his large body defying gravity for just that half a second, caught horizontal just long enough to snare Dan Johnson's drive smoothly in his glove for the third out. It is this ball as much as the score that convinces Robinson to lift Hernandez in the ninth. He has thrown 120 pitches, shy of the 150 from earlier in the week, but extending him twice might ask for trouble, so Robinson turns the ball over to "the Chief," who promptly goes to work. Swisher and Mark Ellis get singles around a strikeout and Hatteberg flies to center for the second out. The fans rise to their feet as Kendall bats, each strike drawing a noisier response than the last. Kendall hits a sharp grounder toward left, but it is right at Vinny Castilla, who gloves it easily and throws toward second for what should be the third out.

Baerga, who has been successfully hidden at second since Carroll's injury, makes his second miscue, this one more costly. The prior night he had forgotten that there was but one out and had thrown to first base, letting a base runner move to second needlessly. Tonight he loses his focus again, and the ball sails into right field, never touched by Baerga's glove as he leaps to avoid the sliding base runner, forgetting the more important issue—the ball. The fans groan collectively as Swisher crosses the plate with the third run and the runners advance to second and third before the ball can be retrieved in shallow right field. The runner on second is the go-ahead run in the 4-3 game. Cordero is in trouble, facing Bobby Crosby, whose triple scored the first run in the eighth.

Cordero bears down and pounds a 91 mph fastball past Crosby to signal that he is not giving in to anyone. Cordero stares defiantly toward the plate from under his odd-looking hat that pushes out his ears. Crosby hits the next pitch hard but it is a one hopper right at Guzman, who does not have to include Baerga as he fires across to Johnson for the third out. Sweep, the fans say again, as in sweet. Washington keeps its lead on the rest of the NL East and is eight games over .500, a landmark for the team that has not known success since 1933.

# 11

# Won't Wipe Off Your Face, No Matter How Hard You Try

A Nationals fan on his way to the game stops to talk to the homeless philosopher panhandling outside a Metro station leading to Stadium Armory, the site of RFK.

"I think it's really bringing this town together," says the smiling, slightly toothless and mostly unshaven philosopher, his blue cap with the telltale cursive W on display.

"That's pretty hard to do, don't you think?" asks the happy fan, slapping a one-dollar bill into the hand of the panhandler.

"Well, yeah, but I think it's good for ordinary people who need something to believe in," says the philosopher, catching his friend's allusion to the political realities of this very divided town, but countering with his own world.

The winning streak and the team have definitely given Washington something to believe in, something like magic.

It definitely blows the mind to think that the Washington Nationals are sitting alone atop the NL East, a one-and-a-half game lead separating them from teams like Atlanta and the rest of the pack. Sure, the Mets are beginning to put it all together, Pedro Martinez throwing like he was still 28 years old. Sure, Bobby Abreu is having a monster spring and the Phillies' young pitchers are pitching with blind abandon. But do either the Mets or the Phillies have the magic that exists for at least this two week run in June at RFK Stadium? No way.

The Nationals are not of course doing this just because it's fun, but they *are* having fun. They are on a roll and they don't want the music to stop. Can the more experienced and very talented Mets catch them? Of course, they can. Washington fans know that, and that is why every night, when "the Chief" finishes off another game with that 91 mile per hour fastball, then pumps his fist, spins three hundred and sixty degrees around and pumps again, Nats fans are gleeful but still a trifle cautious. They smile because you cannot keep from smiling when you are first in the NL East. It is like having a hit song make it to number one. It is a great ride while it lasts, and no one knows how long that will be, but you smile and pat your feet while the music plays.

The home stand will end when the historic Sunday ESPN rematch of the Red Sox and the Cubs concludes with the last joke from Jon Miller and the last baseball wisdom from Joe Morgan. Only the three game series with Ichiro and the Seattle Mariners stands between Washington and the road back to the west. The Japanese Americans of the Washington, D.C., area are in for a treat. Ichiro Suzuki is one of the finest players ever to don a uniform, regardless of his point of origin. His 262 hits in the 2004 season eclipsed one of the oldest remaining records on the books, George Sisler's 252 hits in the 1920 season. There will be no asterisk by his name in the record books. He is pure ICHIRO!!!

As the crowd slowly spills into RFK, the Japanese Americans are led by a wiry young Japanese American woman who sets up camp two rows from field level, staring straight ahead, where she has the best and closest view of her hero, Ichiro. She adjusts her opera glasses, and then gets up to drape a Japanese language poster over the right field wall for Ichiro's eyes only. She wears her Euro-shades atop a Mariners cap so that she looks amazingly like the Mariners' famous right fielder. She calls to him in Japanese, he doffs his cap. The woman's boyfriend, or husband, watches amused, trying to be supportive of this hero worship. Other Japanese American fans follow her to the right field railing during the course of the game with their own signs, their own special message for Ichiro. The spectacle brings a smile to the aged African American usher who holds the edge of the woman's sign, which cannot help but warm the hearts of other fans.

The pitcher for the Mariners, Joel Piniero, warms up beneath the right field rail with Ichiro, playing long toss, his hair dyed a golden color like that of some matinee idol. Can the women of Washington endure this onslaught of masculine appeal? The Nationals answer back with the NL Player of the Week, Nick Johnson. Johnson looks more like the neighborhood barber, chubby cheeked, blowing bubble gum bubbles like a kid. He has brought more drama than appeal to RFK in the past few weeks and character actors are what make this town go. It is the Mariners who are struggling to keep their heads above water, the Seattle management's dreams are of the Washington pitching that are "to die for."

With the crowd still sparse and still queuing for Italian sausage and chicken tenders under the stands, the game begins and Piniero goes to work on Brad Wilkerson and quickly dispatches the Nationals in the first inning. The Nationals have undergone another of GM Jim Bowden's surprising makeovers, and Sun Woo-Kim takes the mound for the Nationals rather than Tomo Ohka. Ohka has been traded to the Milwaukee Brewers, continuing his troubled path through the majors, rubbing Frank Robinson the wrong way and wearing out his welcome in yet another venue. For Ohka, the Nationals get Junior Spivey, who has been the starting second baseman for Arizona and Milwaukee in recent years.

Spivey is the middle infielder the team has desperately needed, if only to keep Carlos Baerga from doing anything more than pinch-hit. He will provide a real replacement for Jose Vidro whose ankle injury has been slow to heal and who is not due back until mid–July. Robinson's bench has been woeful. He has been forced to play Jamey Carroll every day at second and there has been no replacement at shortstop for Guzman, which might normally be Carroll's role. With Guzman struggling so mightily at the plate, opposing managers have pitched around Schneider and others late in games to get to the weak hitting Guzman, who has rewarded the strategy almost every time. Now, Robinson can pinch-hit Guzman, and Carroll can replace him more than adequately at shortstop.

There is a small problem: on Vidro's return Spivey will be asked to assume a utility role that he has seldom played. It may be a good position for him, and he brings much needed speed off the bench and to the lineup, but it will remain to be seen how the team adjusts when Vidro returns. For now Robinson has a bench that will help the team compete and give him flexibility he has not had all season long.

Washington's emergency starter, Sun Woo-Kim, has been a project of pitching coach Randy St. Claire. The two were together at Montreal's Triple-A team in Ottawa and St. Claire seemed to have a very positive effect on the young Korean. Suddenly in the spotlight, Kim struggles from the outset to spot his pitches. He breezes through the order the first time. Then in the fourth, Ichiro gets his second look at Kim and leads off with a base hit. Randy Winn and Richie Sexson follow with singles that send Suzuki home with the game's first run. Kim escapes the fourth giving up only two runs.

In the fifth inning Washington draws blood against Piniero. With one out, Brian Schneider gets a solid single to center field, and Guzman gets him to second on a grounder. Manager Robinson then goes to his bench to pinch-hit for Kim. The day's transactions by Bowden have added one other name to the roster, Rick Short. Short gets a single to score Schneider with the Nationals' first run. It is Short's first major league at bat, and he has a hit and an RBI to bring Washington to within a run, Seattle leading 2-1.

Short is profiled in the morning *Washington Post* in a wonderful article by Dave Sheinin that is reminiscent of Roger Angell's "In the Country," about a nobody named Ron Kittell playing minor league baseball in Montana because he cannot give up on the dreams of his youth, on the game he loves. His wife loves him for it and writes to Angell where that story, so similar to Short's, begins. Short is from West Virginia and has played in the minor leagues for twelve of his 32 years. He has stuck with it when it seemed hopeless, when his kids needed him; he always wanted just one more chance for the "show." He makes it in June 2005, and with everyone in his extended family alerted to his good fortune, all of them watching or listening somewhere, he gets a very big hit.

In the sixth, Richie Sexson hits one of the longest home runs of the season, which reaches the upper deck above left field, landing several rows above the section sign 446. Former Expo prospect T. J. Tucker is the victim and he puts two more men aboard, making the winning streak look precarious. Tucker wiggles off the hook and ends the inning behind only 3-1. In the bottom of the sixth, Washington continues to whittle away the lead with a double by Ryan Church and a single by Jose Guillen.

With the score 3-2, Mariners manager Mike Hargrove brings in reliever Ron Villone to pitch the seventh. Carlos Baerga works the count for a walk and Junior Spivey makes his first appearance for the Nationals as a pinch runner for Baerga. A sacrifice bunt and a grounder get him to third base, where Marlon Byrd, pinch-hitting for Tucker, gets a hustling infield single that scores the tying run, the score knotted at 3-3.

Then in the eighth inning the Seattle bullpen implodes and the Nationals have an inning they have not had since early May and the road trip wins against San Francisco. Then they scored nine runs to win the first game and came back to score eleven to win the next. Tonight, Brian Schneider gets the big hit in the eighth. With the bases loaded and one out against Seattle reliever Shigetoshi Hasegawa, Schneider hits a hard ground ball past Boone at second to score two runs, and Washington is ahead 5-3. Hasegawa gives up two more hits and a walk and leaves with the bases loaded again and the score 6-3. The new Seattle pitcher, Matt Thornton, gives up walks to Wilkerson and Church that force in two more runs. With the score 8-3 and still only one out and poor Mike Hargrove watching in horror, Thornton finally gets Guillen and Nick Johnson out, although the score runs to 9-3 in the bargain.

The most remarkable event in the inning occurs on Schneider's hit to right. Ichiro Suzuki makes a rare mistake in the field. He aggressively charges the ball, but drops it pulling it from his glove to make the throw. He is one of the best defensive outfielders in the game and has an arm to rival Jose Guillen's. The error, however, draws an element in the game that has become too prevalent in recent years. Young men run to the wall to shout and curse Ichiro. The Japanese American fans that had showered him with affection now watch in bewilderment, their emotions difficult to read. Attacks by out of control fans on players, coaches and umpires have become such a startling contrast to wonderful stories like Rick Short's. Baseball is so much more a game of relaxation at the park and so much less like the bloodlust of football that it is difficult to understand how fans can work themselves into such a state of mind, where such hatred begins.

The win is a remarkable eighth in a row for the Nationals. It is another amazing comeback that goes in the books along with the Rick Short story, and a first trip to Washington by one of the great players of the game, Ichiro Suzuki. At the end of the game, as fans head out, the old African American usher who had helped the Japanese woman with her sign shakes his head slowly, the drunks still cavorting near the rail in right field. The game is like his life, it has been long and full, but it has also seen much ugliness, enough to mar the best of times and make bittersweet its moments of triumph.

## A Look to the Future

Pitching, pitching, and more pitching. As the saying goes, good pitching beats good hitting any day. It is the root maxim of successful baseball teams and John Patterson, Washington's young starting pitcher, may be to the young Nationals team even more important than Nick Johnson, and perhaps as talented. With sweat pouring down his neck in the heat at RFK, women in the stands seeking relief from the stultifying heat with small paper fans, Patterson's 93 mile per hour fastball cuts through the thick air like a knife to start the second game against Seattle at RFK.

Patterson also has a big sweeping curve and his pitches overall are as impressive as many of the talented young pitchers the Nationals have faced. A. J. Burnett and Josh Beckett may throw harder and both have more experience than Patterson, though they are much the same age, and Dontrelle Willis may be the best pitcher in the National League, but Patterson is a very good young pitcher and might continue to develop into something special. He is a sharp contrast to Jaime Moyer, the crafty left for Seattle, who at forty years of age is so much older than Patterson in baseball years, his pitches so very different, so very, very slow.

It is Saturday afternoon and the temperature is receding to just below 90 degrees, but the humidity makes it seem hotter still. Patterson follows one fastball with another and continues moving the pitch around the plate, up and down, in and out. Ichiro pops out weakly for the first out. He throws the fastball past Beltre and Sexson to end the inning. Moyer pitches more like Livan Hernandez, hitting his spots and changing speeds from slow to slower, with an occasional fastball off the plate to keep hitters honest. He bends the ball across the strike zone from left to right and works away to most hitters like Hernandez often does.

In the first inning Moyer pitches Wilkerson inside twice and the second pitch hits him. He steals second base easily and Guillen walks to bring Nick Johnson to the plate. Johnson is hitting .340, well enough for second in the league, and he has been hot for weeks, but he bounces one to Boone, who turns it into a quick double play to end the first inning.

Patterson and Moyer have little trouble in the early going, except occasional warning track pitches that RFK holds easily. Patterson starts the third by striking out Ichiro but Randy Winn gets his second hit, spanking a ball into the gap for a double. With runners on second and third with two out, Beltre pops weakly to second to end the threat. In the fourth inning Patterson strikes out Sexson, and then Boone watches a curve bend down across the plate, a called third strike to end the fourth. But in the fifth each pitcher gives up an innocuous run, Ichiro driving in a run for Seattle with a single, and Guzman seeming to have found a pitcher he can handle. He drives a ball deep to center over Randy Winn and the ball one hops over the wall for a double. Marlon Byrd brings him home with a triple down the right field line that caroms off the wall past Ichiro, who cannot get the ball in until Byrd is at third base.

The game remains knotted at 1-1 when the Mariners pinchhit for Moyer and send J. J. Putz out to start the bottom of the seventh inning. Carlos Baerga pinch-hits for Patterson and gets a solid single to center. His demeanor on the bases is a treat for fans and his teammates as well. His torso is larger than his legs and his gait is marked by smaller steps usually seen in a man his size. His short legs carry him around the first base bag hopefully, but he retreats, wisely.

Frank Robinson sends in Tony Blanco to run for Baerga and Wilkerson works a walk to put two men aboard with no outs. Ryan Church pinch-hits for Byrd against the right-handed throwing Putz. He walks to load the bases, Blanco standing on third. Putz finds the plate against Guillen and seems to have the better of him, but Jose bears down and tomahawks a high fastball into center field for a single that scores Blanco. Nick Johnson cannot deliver another hit and grounds into a double play, but Washington leads 2-1.

The Washington bullpen, the strong force, proves better than Seattle's as Ayala and Cordero pitch a perfect eighth and ninth inning, saving the win for Patterson, who was so impressive through the first seven innings of work. It is the ninth win in a row for the Nationals and everywhere in the media the streak is being followed. During the game, the team announces it has passed the one million mark in home attendance, and the fan that stepped through the turnstile to mark the moment is highlighted on the Jumbotron. No one is sure what is happening in Washington, but Peter Angelos will be smart to reconsider his approach if he believes he can derail the future of baseball in D.C. The presence down the Baltimore Washington Turnpike is all he had feared and so much more.

## 11. Won't Wipe Off Your Face, No Matter How Hard You Try 133

**Chad Cordero, the Chief, saves Patterson's win.**

The final game of the series follows a worn script. Tony Armas pitches well, though he is in trouble in every inning. Somehow, Ichiro cannot deliver the fatal hit. He has several chances, as does slugger Richie Sexson, but none of the Mariners can swim against the tide of Washington's mojo. Armas strikes out Sexson twice and Ichiro does not get a hit all day. Armas is lifted after throwing over a hundred pitches in five innings, but he leaves with the lead and the score 3-0. The telling blow is a Junior Spivey home run in the second inning off the mural above the bullpen in left field. It scores Nick Johnson.

Frank Robinson is being given kudos in interviews that span the spectrum of national sports shows. He revels in the well-deserved praise after years of frustration in the task that no one wanted two years earlier in Montreal. Robinson's cagey moves were apparent in the Seattle series. He got Hargrove to pitch to Carroll with the pitcher due up and Carroll delivers the key hit. He puts Blanco in the on-deck circle to signal that he will lift the pitcher and Carroll doinks a shot over the shortstop's head into left field to score the third and winning run.

His move at the end of the game saves it—with help from Cordero. In the ninth Robinson lifts Jamey Carroll, who has played the entire game at shortstop. The timing is impeccable. Cristian Guzman is the better defensive shortstop, with wider range and a better arm. In the ninth inning it is his excellent play on a ground ball from Sexson's bat behind second base, his long throw across the diamond, that gets the final out.

After the 3-2 win, the team engages in its usual postgame celebrations on the infield, fist bumping and trying out several new moves like teenage girls. But as they begin to head back to the dugout, they realize that many of the 37,000 fans at the game remain and are still standing, still applauding their record 10th win in a row.

"It gave me goosebumps. I've never experienced anything like that before," reports Ryan Church in Dave Sheinin's article the next day in the *Washington Post*.

"To walk off and know they recognize what we do is just a great feeling," Brad Wilkerson is quoted as saying in the *New York Times*.

The coverage of the team is growing, as everyone is beginning to stand up and take notice of the miracle at RFK. The win keeps the Nationals ahead of the Philadelphia Phillies, who are also on a home stand winning streak. The two teams have opened up some room between themselves and Atlanta, Florida and the Mets, the darlings of the sports pundits. Pedro Martinez pitches well over the weekend, but the Mets fail to win their weekend series, disappointing those who continue to see them as the class of the division.

The baseball season is a long marathon and there is no rest until its end. The Nationals have a long nine-game road trip out west. Their first road trip to Los Angeles was a watershed for the team, proving that they *could* play well on the road. Yet the last trip was a tough one, and it remains to be seen whether they can compete against the American League teams on their terms, with a DH that stacks the lineup and wears down the best of pitchers. The first games will not start until late in the Washington night. The Nationals are in Los Angeles again, but this time against the Angels. The American League West leaders feature Vladimir Guerrero, once the franchise player for the Expos until pirated by MLB, Inc. And there is Orlando Cabrera, who with Vidro was the very talented double play combination when the Montreal team had a markedly Latin flavor and hopes as bright as Carnivale.

# On the Road Again

There are so many songs, so many books about the road, its magic, its mystique, and finally, sometimes, the tragedy. Yet there is little prose or poetry to mark the concerns of those left behind. A wonderful book in the late eighties by the wife of Beat Generation celebrity Jack Cassidy, whose life on the road with Keroac and Ginsburg defines the archetype, wrote a wonderful expose of what it meant to always be left behind with the mundane tasks of keeping a household together for those engaged in walking on the wild side. Washington fans are in much the same position.

Do the Washington players on the coast write or send postcards to the fans? No, they do not. We see them on TV, but is there the slightest wave to the camera, even a terse onscreen interview that says, "I'd like to say hello to all of our wonderful fans back in D.C., sorry we lost the opener to Vlad the Impaler?" The answer is no again. The pain of loss is a shared one, and after 10 wins in a row, there is a period of adjustment for everyone.

The first game against the Angels showcases the talent of Vladimir Guerrero, who seems to draw satisfaction from ripping the mystery cloak from the visitors from Washington, as if to say, "I know these guys, they don't belong in First Place. They cannot win ten games in a row, who do they think they are?"

Guerrero played for Montreal from his first major league appearance in 1996 until he signed to play with the Anaheim Angels for the 2003 season. He saw the attendance in Montreal go below one million fans after the 1997 season—the last time the team was competitive. He watched the brief flurry of hope when Jeffrey Loria bought the team and pumped new money into it only to see hope fade and attendance fall to a low mark of less than 650,000 fans. There were often less than 5,000 fans at games that year, not enough to scare a cat.

In 2005, interleague play will not allow the Angels to visit Washington, but if Guerrero plays long enough, he will see at RFK something he never saw in Montreal, thirty and forty thousand fans whooping and jumping when his former teammates circle the bases, one flap down. He will see Livan Hernandez and Brad Wilkerson in an element he never thought could exist for his old teammates. He may want to bring them down to earth a bit, but he will be happy to see the difference in circumstances for his old friends from Canada.

The series starts poorly indeed, as Esteban Loaiza is roughed up in three plus innings of work. Darin Erstad gets on base, and Vladimir Guerrero brings him home to score each time, with the final blow a home run in the sixth. It was actually the fourth inning, when Loaiza could get no one out, which was the effective end of the game. He leaves the task to Sun Woo-Kim, who struggles as well and at the end of the inning, Washington is behind 7-1. In the sixth inning Frank Robinson sends Carlos Baerga in to play third base, Wil Cordero to play first, and T. J. Tucker to pitch. It is the second game of the season when Robinson seems to wave the white flag well before the final out is recorded, when his frustration gets the best of him.

It is hard to argue with his logic, however. Some nights you have it, and after the five-hour flight from Washington, the Nationals do not seem to have it in Los Angeles for the first game. The game ends an 11-1 laugher and Robinson says in the postgame interview, "It's ... just the end of a ten-game win streak. We'll be back tomorrow."

The media are talking about Frank Robinson again in Los Angeles. If he is staying up late looking for ways to fire up his team, pacing the floor is certainly working. He finds a beautiful opening to shift the momentum, to refocus his players on something other than the drubbing the night before. The wily old veteran steals a game with all the aplomb he used for Brian Jordan's long foul ball at RFK.

Livan Hernandez does his part first. He establishes that the Washington pitching staff can pitch to Vladimir Guerrero, and the rest of the Angels lineup as well. Guerrero comes up in the first inning with two runners already on base and no one out. It is easy to project another multi-run inning and a game lost before it starts. Yet Hernandez knows his old teammate, knows Guerrero loves to swing the bat as much as he loves to eat, so he leaves pitch after pitch on the outside part of the plate until "Vlad" bites. Once he has got him, he reels him in with two foul ball strikes and a fastball in under his hands for a called third strike. Guerrero's face falls like an iron anvil in a Wile E. Coyote cartoon and there is hope in Mudville again.

For the third out Livan reverses the formula to Steve Finley. He busts him in, in, in, and then for the third strike a slow pitch on the outside corner. It is vintage Livan Hernandez, the ace who keeps Washington's train from jumping the tracks, this time in Los Angeles.

The Angels pitcher is a promising rookie, Ervin Santana from the Dominican Republic, who stands tall and skinny on the mound, looking remarkably like Daniel Cabrera, who pitches for Baltimore. Santana's fastball clocks at 97 miles per hour and his record in the minor leagues is an impressive one. He betters the soft-tossing Hernandez on this evening, pitching into the seventh inning and allowing only a single run. Livan Hernandez establishes the Nationals' bona fides, but the Angels wear him down in the fifth and sixth innings, getting to him for three runs. Frank Robinson turns the game over to the bullpen. Washington is behind 3-1 and Robinson wonders how to change the frame of reference for his team.

He gets his opportunity in the seventh inning, and it is clear he has been like a cat waiting for the mouse to venture forth. With Nationals batting, and with one out and a runner on base in the seventh inning, Angels manager Mike Scioscia takes Irvin Santana out of the game. He stands on the mound and motions to the bullpen for Brendan Donnelly, one of his top relievers. The camera pans to the bullpen gate opening and Donnelly starts in from the bullpen. But as soon as he does Frank Robinson comes up out of the dugout, clearly on a mission of some urgency. He walks toward the umpire in charge, Dale Scott, who after a discussion with Robinson, walks toward a totally befuddled Donnelly and inspects his glove. He motions Donnelly out of the game, takes Donnelly's glove and hands it to stadium personnel for safe keeping.

## 11. Won't Wipe Off Your Face, No Matter How Hard You Try

Scioscia erupts from the Angels dugout, his arms flailing above his head like a circus clown, but he is deadly serious. He confronts Robinson in a heated exchange and first Nationals players and then Angels players all spill forth in a male display of aggression that might work better on the Nature Channel. Most vocal is Jose Guillen. He is physically restrained from a physical confrontation with Mike Scioscia. It was Scioscia whose malignant relationship with Guillen at the end of 2004 led to Guillen's exile from the team, one that left his otherwise gifted season tinged with a notoriety that follows him still.

Guillen's teammates drag him to the dugout and order is restored. When the game resumes, Scott Shields enters the game for the Angels and retires the Nationals to end the seventh inning. But in the eighth inning, Shields hits Ryan Church, whether in retaliation or not is unclear, but the next batter is Jose Guillen. The Angels fans, over 40,000 strong, boo lustily and the stadium roars with their dislike of the batter, who calmly takes his practice cuts with catcalls echoing across the playing field.

Guillen does something he will repeat again as the year wears on, showing a new level of maturity and focus. It is the best possible response for a player in this situation to do exactly as he does now. He takes a pitch from Shields out of the park on a line to left. The shot is never in doubt and the satisfaction derived by Guillen can be tasted on every tongue in the stadium. The score is tied at 3-3 when Guillen crosses home plate, emphatically stepping on it for effect.

Guillen's blow strikes home emotionally and seems to rattle the Angels. Orlando Cabrera makes an error on a subsequent play in the inning that allows two more runs to score. Then again in the ninth, Cabrera the former Expo, misplays an easy grounder that leads to the last run and Cordero again closes the game out for a 6-3 win.

Once again, on Wednesday during the day, the sports shows are consumed with the late night story from the West Coast, as they had been when Frank argued and won the foul ball call against Atlanta. Like a Shoaling Kung Fu legend, Frank Robinson, the old master, has turned the energy of the opposition against them, carefully outmaneuvering the larger man and making him appear foolish with a minimum of effort.

"That situation got the guys going, got the adrenaline flowing, and they just became closer and more determined," Robinson is quoted the next day as saying. "They were determined that the Angels were not going to beat us tonight."

The key element in the dispute may be Jose Guillen, who many believe was the source of Frank Robinson's information about Donnelly's use of sand paper. Several sports analysts, in reviewing the incident the next day, talk about how out of control Guillen was, how clearly he wanted to take the argument to Scioscia in support of Frank Robinson. There are valid questions about his temperament, but the maturity to go out the next inning and strike where it hurts Scioscia and the Angels most is largely overlooked by the sports paparazzi.

One cannot help but remember the picture from a late inning rally several weeks earlier, Jose Guillen at Frank Robinson's elbow as the key hit falls in and the Nationals start to circle the bases with the winning runs. Guillen is shaking Robinson's arm like a small boy at the elbow of his grandfather, Robinson stoically watching the action with his typical remove. Guillen, in his comments about his intensity, cites the death of his father in 1999 as a defining moment for him as a man. It came just before his breakout season in Tampa Bay and yet Guillen attributes some of the anger to the loss of his father and it seems that his relationship with Robinson is filling some of that irreplaceable void.

As Robinson has said, Guillen plays with intensity and that makeup is what makes him a great ballplayer. The two share a keen desire to win and it is on this level that they have connected. Robinson was an intensely competitive player, and it is that makeup that motivates many of the great players in the game. So if Frank Robinson can coax this young man into believing in himself and, more importantly, into listening to those around him when they seek to quiet him, then he is a great manager indeed, for getting the best from your players is the quintessential trait of good management in any organization. They are a great act, Robinson and Guillen, perhaps not LaRussa and Pujols, but this duo is indicative of a wider bond that has formed on the team. The encore performance will be closely watched by the sports paparazzi Wednesday night.

Play begins Wednesday night with Washington ahead of the second place Philadelphia Phillies by two full games. The Phillies lose to Seattle up the coast and the two teams continue to track one another. It is only mid–June, but the mid–summer break in play for the All-Star Game is approaching, as well as the trading deadline. Sportswriters pepper Jim Bowden with questions during pregame shows about whether MLB will allow the Nationals to be active in trading for whatever is necessary to keep them competitive. Bowden replies that the fan support is providing MLB, Inc. with the revenues to support additional payroll and they will be active in trading for whatever help can be found. Tomo Ohka, the last player traded by the Nationals after being banished by Frank Robinson after a season of disagreements, pitches a nine-inning shutout for Milwaukee.

Ohka derives motivation from the trade. It helps him pitch the shutout, and the next day Ryan Drese shows how similarly motivated he is by the change in scenery, the chance to start over. He is starting the third game against the Angels for Washington after being acquired on waivers from Texas. After numerous failures to stick at the major league level, in 2004 he found a mentor in Texas pitching coach Orel Hershiser. Hershiser took Drese from a struggling journeyman to the ace of the Texas staff, who won 14 games during the season. After being the opening day pitcher for Texas in April of 2005, Drese reverts to form and there is nothing Hershiser tries that brings him out of his funk, until the team gives up and places him on waivers as a condition for sending him to the minor leagues. Someone on the Washington coaching or scouting staff believes he has something left, something in his approach to pitching, that can be fixed so that he can resume his 2004 form

Remarkably, as Drese begins the game against the Angels on Tuesday night, he looks very much like Livan Hernandez. Not that they would be mistaken for each other physically, but Drese works the plate in a manner that is quite similar to Hernandez the night before. To left handed hitters, he pitches inside with the ball tailing at the last second back over the plate for strikes, and he pitches away to many hitters. Is this a Randy St. Claire formula? Drese is a sinkerball pitcher and he is able to get ground ball outs all night long, easily handled by the excellent infield defense of the Nationals, now made more capable with the athletic Junior Spivey at second base.

His opposing number for the Angels is Bartolo Colon, who looks like a bus driver, a Ralph Kramden character with his loosely fitted shirt flapping open as though he is a late arrival from the Early Wynn School of great baseball pitchers. Colon is the ace of the Angels pitching staff and he competes with a quiet intensity. His external demeanor belies the intense makeup of one of the most effective pitchers in the American league. He has been ineffective when out of shape physically and unable to withstand the long grueling summer. It has been a good year for him so far and he has won eight games.

The game develops into a pitchers' duel with Drese matching the better-established Colon goose egg for goose egg. Colon makes only one mistake, a pitch to Brian Schneider leading off the sixth inning. Schneider puts it over the wall in right center field for a home run and gives Washington a 1-0 lead. It is the final score of the game. Drese pitches well and lasts for eight full innings, giving up only four hits. Chad Cordero makes the game characteristically tense in the ninth inning by loading the bases with no one out, but then proceeds to masterfully extricate himself from the jam he has created by striking out two of the next three batters and getting the other on a week popup.

The win marks a noteworthy turnabout in the fortunes of the team on the home stand. The team goes from the 11-1 thrashing on Monday to winning the series on Wednesday with a waiver wire acquisition, Ryan Drese, on the mound. He wins 1-0 pitching a masterpiece, as if somehow there are restorative powers in the Nationals' clubhouse. It brings the team back, restores the magic of the streak with a series win against the very strong looking Angels team.

"They may look back at that game Frank Robinson got into it with Scioscia as the turning point in the season," says a fan coming in to work the next morning, reading about the game in the *Washington Post* late edition.

"Like that game for the Red Sox last season," says the fan sitting with him at the table in Starbucks.

"I know the one, Varitek's fight," says the fan, growing more animated.

"Do you remember it?" asks the other fan.

"Absolutely, I was in a bar in New Hampshire with all these Red Sox fans," says the fan, sipping his coffee. "All of the Red Sox fans gave up on the game. They thought it was just another loss to the Yankees. But then Varitek's fight brings them all back into the bar yelling like crazy. Damn, that place got noisy. It was a great game, though, no two ways about it."

"They say it was the turning point in the Red Sox season that allowed them to go on to beat the Yankees, beating them in that game."

"Just like Robinson going toe to toe with Mike Scioscia."

"It could be. You never know."

Whether it is Ryan Drese or Sun Woo Kim, the Nationals send pitchers out who find a way to win. The team wins two of the three series on the June road trip after the Angels break the spell of the winning streak. They are on the road, and winning five out of nine games on a West Coast swing is a good trip. Yet the Nationals pitching rotation has grown noticeably thin. What has been the strength of the team so far in the season, its pitching staff, is suddenly beginning to wobble. Texas hammers them in two of the three games there to take that series. Washington bounces back and wins the Pittsburgh series but Pittsburgh scores eleven in the opener and again there are cracks in the facade. The Nationals manage to win five and lose four and they keep the great run going as they head home for a final week in June, but there are signs of the struggles the team endured on the last road trip.

During the great run—the winning streak and the wins on the road—Robinson and Bowden have sent away Ohka and Vargas for reasons that only management itself can fully understand. Both players have experienced success in their new environs, which raises questions about the decisions by Robinson and Bowden. Drese's forced exile from the Texas Rangers is equally vexing, but it is his Texas teammates who are the most puzzled, questioning the decision openly in the press. By way of contrast, the loss of Vargas and Ohka does not affect the underlying chemistry of the Nationals. It is speculative to search for reasons, but it seems as if the marriage between the team and its new surroundings and its new fans, trumps the potential sources of discord. In Texas, Kenny Rogers, the staff ace, questions the loss of Drese and several days later, in a fit of pique smashes a water cooler in the dugout and breaks a finger on his pitching hand. The injury will sideline him for weeks.

In Washington, D.C., there is no noticeable dissent, just the picture of Jose Guillen, the hothead, tugging at Frank Robinson's sleeve, coming to his defense against Mike Scioscia. There is also the picture of Livan Hernandez limping very noticeably to first base, but trudging back to the mound. There is his 150-pitch effort. It is that level of effort being put forth by all of the members of the team that makes players like Ohka, with their personal grudges against Robinson, seem smaller for their ability to be distracted from the overarching goal of the team. Ohka may have a legitimate beef with Robinson, but others have been benched when they wanted to play. The rest of the team has so far been willing to sublimate their egos, take their place on the wonderful ride on which they find themselves. For now, at least, the Nationals are a team first, individual egos second.

As important to the team, perhaps even as important as the veteran presence of Frank Robinson, is the play of Livan Hernandez. When the team announces that Loaiza and Patterson are too banged up to pitch, to take their turns in the rotation, Livan Hernandez goes back out on the mound, takes his turn, and stares down whatever adversity is thrown his way during the game or between starts. He just goes out and gets it done, no matter what it takes, no matter the small pains he must endure. Livan Hernandez seems determined to demonstrate to all in baseball his unique place as a great pitcher. His prior World Series appearances not withstanding, and certainly not detracting from the importance of the great teams in San Francisco and Florida he played for, this may prove to be his greatest season.

# Part Two

# 12

# That Little Something Extra

Livan Hernandez has turned his endurance into a star quality. His ability to outlast adversity is a lesson of importance for his teammates as they return from the road trip to California and Texas for three games with Toronto and then three more with Pittsburgh to end the month of June at RFK. They will be presented with important problems to solve before the month is out.

Thirty-seven thousand fans are in attendance for the opening game of the series against Toronto on June 24, the Quebec provincial holiday. Montreal is getting read for its jazz festival, but the *Montreal Gazette* follows the games in Washington as if they were still being played at Stade Olympique. Washington fans have baseball at its best right in front of them, however, and Esteban Loaiza does not disappoint them. He shuts down the team from Ontario for six innings and the Nationals bullpen completes the shutout of Toronto 3-0 with Loaiza driving in two runs himself on a double to deep left. The game is saved, however, when Ryan Church goes full tilt into the wall in left to preserve the lead. His shoulder is either severely bruised or dislocated and he is placed on the disabled list over the weekend, the first loss of the home stand.

For the Saturday game, more than 40,000 fans are in attendance and Livan Hernandez acknowledges in the postgame interview how much better it is to pitch for a crowd rather than the empty seats in Montreal. He earns his 10th straight win on a 5-2 victory over Ted Lilly, and sets the stage for a sweep of the series on Sunday. Tony Armas cannot deliver the win and again struggles to find the plate consistently. He gives up five runs, but surprisingly it is the bullpen that fails as Luis Ayala gives Toronto the lead on two runs in the eighth inning after the Nationals tie the score in the seventh at 5-5.

**In the second half of the season, Nationals fans learned to take the long view.**

The final score is 9-5 for Toronto, but the most ominous event of the day is Nick Johnson limping off the field after landing hard on the Toronto catcher's foot, scoring the fifth run in the seventh inning to tie. Johnson's heel and Ryan Church's shoulder add to the growing list of injuries that plague the team. The two injuries take away two of the hottest bats on the team. Johnson was having a breakout season and avoiding the kinds of injuries that will again rob him of key time. Church and Johnson are also excellent defensively and will be difficult to replace.

Again, Frank Robinson has too few pieces and too many holes in the puzzle. There is Wil Cordero, whose failure to manage a single successful plate appearance hardly recommends him as Johnson's replacement. The other option, which Robinson takes, is Carlos Baerga. Baerga has begun to hit, but his defense has been woeful at times. The bad news cannot dim what has been a remarkable month for the team. At the end of June the team's record for the month is a remarkable 20 wins against only 6 losses. They are ensconced in first place by five games, and are eighteen games over the .500 mark.

The baseball pundits dismiss the performance of the team as a freakish thing that cannot be explained. The team is last offensively in number of runs scored, has the fewest home runs, and the fewest stolen bases. What cannot be explained is best ignored and so the sports paparazzi are still talking about the Mets and the Braves as the forces to contend with, as though there is still no team in Washington.

Washington fans know that it is the pitching that wins games. Having a pitching staff that can stand on the mound with a tight lead and runners aboard, seeming no more perturbed than Cuban Relaxation itself, and just pitch, that is what makes the team click, makes it a winner. That and the bullpen that is creaking at times like an old floor; but its youth is what gives it the strength to go out night after night. Majewski, Ayala, and Cordero are the magic combination for the late innings. Majewski is in his first starring role and the East Texas pitcher, with hair to rival Johnny Damon's, is establishing himself as a premier set-up man. He looks like he would prefer to be somewhere back home in a deer stand, or a duck blind, or maybe in a fishing boat lazing away the day looking for fish, but in the heat of late June, he is bringing it.

As if to prove the point, the team goes into Chicago and Wrigley Field and sweeps three games. The pitching is superb, with Livan Hernandez leading the way once again. He wins the opener, another one-run game and a 4-3 win. The team is hitting despite the loss of Johnson and Church, with Jose Guillen is carrying much of the load but getting help from every quarter. Tony Armas has a better outing and leaves early with the lead and Cordero and the supporting cast close it out. Cordero leads the league in saves and his selection to the All-Star game is announced in the papers Sunday morning.

The Sunday game in Chicago is no less exciting and Ryan Drese has another outstanding performance, going seven scoreless innings only to have Chad Cordero blow a rare save, only his third of the season. Brian Schneider wins the game in the 12th on a home run, and Joey Eischen, back from his broken wrist, gets only his second win of the season after shutting down the Cubs. Cristian Guzman has been missing games, and the team announces that he has a hamstring pull. It is just one more injury, but Jamey Carroll is playing so well in the field and getting the occasional timely hit that Guzman's absence is hardly noticed except for the stray derogatory comment that sneaks in about his four-year contract seeming wildly exaggerated at this juncture.

The first game of the series against the Mets falls on the holiday, July 4, no small event in the nation's capital. The crowd is predictably large, yet there are empty seats as some choose the National Mall for the nation's greatest patriotic fireworks display, forgoing another drama with the "One-run Wonders," as Mel Proctor calls them several times during each broadcast. Besides, winning baseball is getting to be ho-hum in Washington.

The series against the Mets brings to the surface stress lines in the façade of the Nationals that could take on dramatic proportions. For the second time during the season injuries are so widespread that the team has difficulty fielding a respectable lineup. Carlos Baerga begins to look good at first base and Matt Cepicky, who started his career with many of the current players in the Montreal system, is called up from New Orleans where he has been the only consistent offensive spark.

Against the patched together Nationals lineup that scores no more than three runs in any game, New York wins three out of the four. The best game is a match-up between Esteban Loaiza and Pedro Martinez that Washington wins 3-1. Loaiza pitches eight marvelous innings, striking out eight and adding his fifth win for the season, clearly outclassing Martinez and making it obvious why his addition has been so important to the Nationals. Jose Vidro returns and has a run-scoring double. During the series, John Patterson and Tony Armas pitch well but get no support. Livan Hernandez loses his first game since April and it becomes obvious that even playing at home and great pitching cannot make a winner of the Nationals. They need some level of offensive punch and they are badly missing Nick Johnson behind Jose Guillen in the batting order and Ryan Church as an additional option in the outfield.

The team limps into Philadelphia for a weekend series before the All-Star break at the beginning of the next week. The Friday night game is a sloppy affair, with Ryan Drese and the Bullpen giving up seven runs, but the team makes a three-run homer by Carlos Baerga stand up and Cordero gets his league leading 31st save for an 8-7 win. Then the cloud that is gathering over the team claims another victim. In batting practice prior to the Saturday game, Junior Spivey breaks his wrist. It is much the same injury as Eischen's and will keep him out for at least two months.

Whatever evil spell, whatever vile mojo has worked its way into the Nationals clubhouse, it continues despite John Patterson pitching his best game of the year on Saturday. The team loses, although he pitches seven scoreless innings, striking out eight, and allowing only two hits. The key moment in the game comes after Gary Bennett leads off the eighth inning with a walk. The score remains tied at 0-0 and it is the top of the eighth inning with no one out and a runner on first base. Cristian Guzman, who was known during his tenure with the Twins as a good bunter and fast base runner, is in the dugout somewhere. It is a perfect opportunity to pressure the defense and the pitcher, Cory Lidle, to pitch carefully to Guzman, and the infield work to get the speedy runner at first base.

Robinson elects to send Patterson out to hit. Ostensibly the choice is about keeping him in the game to pitch the eighth inning. He has thrown only 108 pitches and could pitch another inning if needed. Patterson cannot get the bunt down and after Wilkerson and Carroll cannot manage anything off Lidle, the inning ends with Bennett still standing pathetically on first where he led off.

The surprise is that Patterson does not even start the eighth on the mound despite pitching a masterful game. The purpose of batting him at the beginning of the inning is lost on the fans. As LaRussa has opined in his book with Buzz Bissinger, at best a manager can win or lose only a few games each year; it is the players who must get it done. Yet, after Washington's 1-0 loss, the question of the role of Robinson in the loss is quietly raised at RFK. Robinson is a beloved figure, but he is not above reproach.

On Sunday the team wastes another excellent start, this time by Loaiza, as the bullpen blows the lead in the late innings and the team goes into the break with back-to-back series losses against teams in the NL East. The games show the excellence of the NL East, where each team can pitch extremely well. The other teams are deeper offensively with the exception, perhaps, of Atlanta, which is winning with a crop of youngsters who are suddenly playing very well. Can they keep up that level or will the team settle back down as they have before? The Mets and the Phillies both look like the two more well-balanced teams, but the Braves are making the latest run at the Nationals. Each of the teams in the East has gotten hot and moved up on Washington, but none has been able to surpass the amazing streak that the Nationals put together in June when they were healthy.

The season is half over. The Nationals record stands at 52 wins and 36 losses. Eighty-eight games played, and seventy-four to go. It gets serious from here on, with the heat of August and the searing pressure of the September stretch run to the finish line. There has not been a Washington team in this position since the early '30s when Joe Cronin anchored the infield and Heinie Manush and Goose Goslin roamed the Washington outfield. No matter what happens in the second half, the first Nationals team of the 21st century will go down as a memorable one. It has that "something extra," something you cannot put your finger on that makes it so much more than a sum of its parts. Whatever Livan Hernandez has found these past two seasons, whatever has brought him back from the mediocrity that overcame him in San Francisco, he has shared with his teammates. They are all thriving on it.

## First Nationals All-Star

On the 12th of July Livan Hernandez represents the new Washington Nationals at the 2005 All-Star Game. Nationals fans rightly believe others are deserving. Jose Guillen and Nick Johnson have had remarkable years. Yet Hernandez's place at the game this year at Comerica Field is the one in which they can take great pride.

The announcement on July 3 was widely anticipated, after the remarkable success he has enjoyed over the first half of the season. Washington teammate Chad Cordero, the other Nationals All-Star, is equally deserving as Hernandez. Yet Hernandez is the veteran and leader on the team. It is the 15 wins in games he has started that gave Cordero this early opportunity to line up along the foul line by the visitors' dugout, to doff his cap at the ovation at the beginning of his first all-star game.

Hernandez was named to his first All-Star game last year, in 2004. Yet his designation was more as the lone Montreal representative from a bad team. He failed to pitch a single inning in the game last year.

This year the designation is not a sop thrown to a lowly team. It is about the best season that Hernandez has had in his professional career, a season where he has been among the league leadership in wins all season and ahead of all others in total innings pitched. This year it is about being the ace on a team with the second best record in the National League, about being the leader of a pitching staff on a team in first place because of its pitching.

Hernandez, at only thirty years of age, is the old pro of the Washington Nationals. After Hernandez won his twelfth game on July 1, beating the Cubs 4-3 in Chicago, the first place Washington Nationals held an unbelievable five game lead over the Atlanta Braves and were only a game behind the St. Louis Cardinals for the best record in the National League. Hernandez's presence at the top of the rotation has been a big part of that surprising accomplishment. He has anchored the team through the long road trips to the West Coast, winning seven of his twelve games on the road. The wins have not been cheap. They have been against the best, against the Cardinals in St. Louis after Washington had lost five in a row and was beginning to fall apart. Hernandez has been the one who puts an end to losing, and or adds another game to a winning streak.

The long road to stardom has not been an easy one for him. Although still a young man, Hernandez has been an every-fifth-day pitcher in the major leagues for nine years. He has pitched for the San Francisco Giants and the Florida Marlins, and was the stalwart on World Series teams for both. In his first season of major league baseball, at the age of 22, he led Florida to the World Championship, where he was named the Most Valuable Player of the World Series, his mother—just off a plane from Cuba—smiling at his side.

Miriam Carrera, was flown in by the Marlins to see her son pitch that final game of the 1997 World Series. Three weeks of negotiations were required to get the Cuban government to acquiesce to the trip, and an emotional petition, signed by all of the Marlins, was included in the package of papers sent to the Cubans requesting her travel papers. It was a tearful son who hoisted the Series MVP trophy beside his mother during those early days in his career, and it was the same emotional player who wept when he was told that he was being traded two years later, in 1999, after only three seasons with his beloved Miami team.

Hernandez left his mother and Cuba in 1996, sneaking aboard a flight from Cuba to Venezuela to follow his half-brother Orlando Hernandez, "El Duque," who was then achieving fame and fortune pitching for the New York Yankees after leaving Cuba several years earlier. For Livan Hernandez, Miami became an important anchor. He was still very young and his family many miles away. It was with some trepidation that he left there in 1999 for San Francisco after being traded.

Dombrowski, the Marlins GM who traded him, intimated then that Livan Hernandez might find himself with his new team in San Francisco and wished him well, but according to his famous baseball brother, El Duque, he was always uneasy there, never comfortable so far from home among so many whom he did not know.

"Miami is still close to Cuba," said El Duque in an interview after the trade to San Francisco. "He had a lot of friends there and San Francisco is about as far away as you can get."

Despite his brother's concerns, Livan pitched well for the Giants in 2000 after the trade. He has said many times, "Miami will always be my home," but he won 17 games that year, which is still his career best. Yet, in 2002, with the Giants in the World Series against the Angels, Livan pitched poorly, losing two of the four games the Giants lost as the Angels walked away with the trophies and rings. After two seasons of declining performance, the Giants traded him in the off-season to the Expos for almost nothing and were glad to get anything in return.

It was in Montreal that Livan Hernandez laid claim to the reputation that eluded him in his early years. He had fine seasons in '03 and '04 and established himself at the head of the pitching staff, even when it included the young Javier Vasquez. He left behind the controversies of San Francisco, the loneliness of spending long stretches of time away from home, and his strained relationship with Dusty Baker. In Montreal he found himself not just as a baseball player, but as a human being. That process of maturation made him the old man in the clubhouse, second, of course, to Frank Robinson. Livan Hernandez knows better than any of the Nationals what it means to be playing baseball in a strange new home, wondering just what to expect from a surprising turn of events. It was a virtuoso performance that cool April evening when it all began for Livan and the Nationals. "That little something extra is missing," said Dave Dombrowski, Florida Marlins general manager, when he traded Livan Hernandez to San Francisco in December of 1999. Dombrowski was right, something *was* missing: the comfort in his new surroundings and the maturity to adapt easily.

But adversity has built Hernandez's character, given him a unique sense of ease on the mound, an unflappability that confounds his opponents as easily as his sixty mile per hour slow stuff. His teammates refer to him by the nickname "Cuban Relaxation," a description of his style both on the mound and in the clubhouse.

Livan Hernandez knew adversity in San Francisco and struggled through it. Now he has found that something extra here in Washington, D.C. He has found success and admiration that he did not know how to handle in his youth.

He has worn it well this year, and whatever the second half of the season brings in Washington, D.C., the fans will remember Livan Hernandez as their first great pitcher. Nothing can change that. It has been a magic season and when Hernandez takes the mound in Detroit for the All-Star game, he will have earned his right to be there. Whether he starts the game in Detroit or comes in late, as he takes the mound his sense of pride will stretch all the way back to D.C., to the Washington fans all sharing the moment and remembering their first all-star game, their first all-star hero.

# 13

# I Put A Spell on You

The field has lost its early season luster. The deep green is visible now only in the outfield grass. Around the infield, the grass is resodded from a different stock, or a field that has not been watered, and it is pale from the heat, the impenetrable heat. The infield has been patched as well and there is a border to the infield as the new grass extends for one row of sod into the outfield. It is still a beautiful field, but the wear and tear of the soccer season is showing.

The field's condition mirrors that of the team; like the frog prince, or Cinderella after the ball, they have seen the spell lift and have watched as their magic raiment melted away, leaving them ordinary mortals, or worse yet, the Expos from 2004. The team, like the field, is beat up and patched up. Whole new pieces have been brought in to replace what has been lost. This process may be reaching its peak. The baseball trading deadline is July 31 and the rumor mill is buzzing with the possible shifts pending for players and teams. July is to baseball trades as October is to beer festivals.

The Nationals' general manager, Jim Bowden, has been trying to trade Zach Day since early in the season. Day was the first in Frank Robinson's curious doghouse that came to include pitcher Tomo Ohka and Claudio Vargas. Bowden has been trying to acquire Preston Wilson, the Colorado center fielder who has played for the Florida Marlins as well and displayed considerable power at times in his career. After the All-Star Game, Bowden announces the trade of Day for Wilson, who will replace Nick Johnson in the cleanup spot for the Nationals and, by occupying center field, will allow Brad Wilkerson to move to first base for the injured Nick Johnson.

The trade meets the short-term needs of the team. It means that the Nationals can start the second half with a lineup that boasts much the same clout as before Johnson's injury, and after he returns the lineup should be more potent. For Frank Robinson the addition is more unsettling. He had decided on a basic pattern to his lineups, and now the addition of Preston Wilson upsets the balance like a late guest upsets the cook.

Setting the table for Wilson becomes the first order of business. Will it be Wilkerson still in the leadoff spot, or does this new element in the equation throw it all up in the air? Must the chef completely change the concept for the meal? No two lineups are the same after Wilson arrives and for the first time Wilkerson does not seem anchored to the leadoff position. He bats third in a few games, with Carroll batting leadoff. Finally, Robinson drops Wilson into Johnson's spot behind Guillen, seemingly for good.

However, it seems not to matter particularly, because, regardless of the order that is presented to the umpire before the game, Washington does not hit. They are as cold as the weather is hot. They have been in funks before and those slumps saw the team falter, but this one seems worse and confounds Frank Robinson, the team, and the critics. This time the pundits begin to look to the paranormal to explain the slide. Magic may have been the watchword of the first half, but as the second unfolds, its dark-side cousin rises in the air and floats over the team like some apparition.

The first game after the break looks like so many others in June when the team was winning. Great starting pitching, whether it is Loaiza, Hernandez or Patterson, gets the team into the late innings. They either have the lead or are poised to win the game against the other team's bullpen. But something is wrong. Although starting slowly, there is a change in how the ball is bouncing. The line drives were falling for the Nationals in June, but now they are drawn to the opposition's gloves with uncanny consistency. Conversely, the line drive outs once snagged by a leaping Jamey Carroll or a relaxed Vinny Castilla are rocketing past them into the outfield.

More confounding is the failure of the bullpen. Milwaukee is the first to beat the Nationals at their own game. John Patterson pitches a very good game, taking a 2-1 lead into the sixth inning. Preston Wilson has impressed in his first start for Washington with a solo home run in his first at bat. Patterson strikes out nine, but surrenders a convincing home run by Geoff Jenkins into the left field stands at Miller Park to tie the game at two runs apiece. Robinson takes Patterson out after almost 120 pitches and reverts to the recipe that has worked all season, bringing in Majewski, Ayala, and Cordero to pitch the last few innings.

Previously this threesome, assisted by Hector Carrasco, has been remarkably effective and many commentators attribute the success of the team to how well Robinson has used them. Livan Hernandez's yeoman work has allowed them periodic rest. Today the formula falls flat, as first Ayala, then Eischen, and finally Majewski, fail to get key outs and surrender two runs that spell defeat. Conversely, the Brewers bullpen is remarkably effective and Washington cannot mount any threat against them. Matt Wise and Derrick Turnbow pitch the last few innings, closing out a well-pitched game by Doug Davis.

There is one very important difference. Nick Johnson's timely hitting is missing. Johnson's clutch hits were not the only ones, and it is pushing the others to take up the slack. They are anxious to prove their ability to do so, but that anxiousness dooms them from the start. First it is Guillen swinging at everything and the pitchers quickly extending him out from the plate until he is striking out on pitches six inches outside the strike zone. But Preston Wilson is no better in his discipline. Now, even when the bullpen pitches well, the team is failing to score runs late, as they did in June and earlier when they were beating the other team's bullpen. Now, on those rare occasions when they score runs, the bullpen fails to hold the lead. The whole is somehow less than the sum of the parts.

The second game is scripted very similarly to game one. Livan Hernandez takes a precarious lead into the late innings, and then allows a two out home run to Derrick Lee that ties the game at three runs apiece. The Brewers score the winning run after Luis Ayala puts two runners on base in the bottom of the tenth inning. Mike Stanton, newly acquired from the same waiver heap that produced Ryan Drese, balks in the winning run in a disputed call. Drese loses game four of the series, getting his pitches up in the strike zone, and gives up five runs. The Nationals never have a chance to recover, although Sun Woo Kim pitches well in relief of Drese. The Nationals rally in the seventh against Tomo Ohka, but it is not enough and the final score is 5-3 for the Brewers.

The third game is the only one the Nationals win in the Milwaukee series and it is the only one where the first half formula holds. Esteban Loaiza pitches well, but gives up three runs in six innings. He exits the game as Robinson pinch hits for him in the bottom of the inning. Carlos Baerga is the pinch-hitter for Loaiza and it is the hit that ignites a rally to score the winning runs. Yet the whole affair looks in jeopardy when Baerga and Church are perched on second and third with only one out. Vidro cannot get either runner home with the go ahead run. It looks like just another lost opportunity in a disturbing patter when Jose Guillen delivers a single up the middle to score both runners.

Guillen's fluctuations become larger in importance without Nick Johnson. He is carrying the load in the middle of the lineup, admittedly, but he is still trying to do it all. Preston Wilson can help, but not if Guillen overplays his role in front of him. And Wilson is not the hitter Nick Johnson is or that he was during May and June. The important difference is Johnson's amazing on-base percentage of over .400. Even when he does not drive in the runs to win the game, he keeps rallies going with walks that give others further down the order chances to win the game.

**With Johnson slumping, Guilen is trying to do it all.**

Guillen is a fiery and competitive player and he chides his teammates when they refuse to play when they are hurt. The strength of the team, though, has been the camaraderie that developed early on. Guillen, like Gary Sheffield and other hotheaded players before him, will mature into a quieter leader, one who takes the walk and lets Preston Wilson win the game. For now he is a quick bat but an equally quick temper.

In May Washington took three games of the four game series at Miller Park in Milwaukee. The return engagement ends exactly the same way, with the visitors getting the best of the bargain. Milwaukee wins the final game when Tomo Ohka bests Ryan Drese 5-3. Milwaukee roughs Drese up quickly and the game is never really close. Since Drese, is in effect, pitching in Ohka's spot in the Washington rotation, his win against his former team is particularly disheartening. Drese's slide back into the same funk he left in Texas puts additional pressure on the other starters, as well as on the bullpen.

The trade for Ohka netted Junior Spivey for Washington. When Vidro's injury sapped the team of a needed offensive spark, the addition of Spivey was welcomed, but now he is out for the rest of the season with a broken wrist. The Preston Wilson trade costs the team another pitcher, Zach Day. Day has been disappointing in 2005, but he is young and was judged to have significant potential coming into the season.

Going into the season, Zach Day and Claudio Vargas were two pitching prospects who had achieved a modicum of success in short major league service with the Expos and had enough potential to be promising. Tomo Ohka was a proven quantity even though he was inconsistent and moody. Now, instead of three pitchers with potential, the Nationals have Preston Wilson, who is a free agent at the end of the year, and Junior Spivey, whose career has been on the decline for several years. Spivey's acrobatic plays at second base were a good addition to the team, but with Vidro cemented into the spot at second long-term, Spivey's role on the team is uncertain. The need for pitching is never uncertain.

In trading away Ohka and Day, the Nationals have received not a single young "player to be named later." By way of contrast, the Colorado Rockies announce another trade simultaneous with Washington's for Wilson. They trade a pitcher, Joe Kennedy, whose track record is little different from Zach Day's, and receive from Oakland a proven outfielder in Eric Byrnes, who hit 20 home runs in 2004; but more importantly they get Omar Quintinella, a young middle infielder with tremendous potential. Byrnes and Quintinella will be playing for Colorado long after Preston Wilson has moved on from Washington.

The heat rises to unbearable levels at RFK and Washington fans are starting to look for a sign from the skies, a sign that the heat will break or that the team is starting to get it back together. They are beginning to think the heat and the losing string are linked by some cosmic convergence. The sweat is dripping from fans on the concourse. Some wander the concrete like crazed evangelists talking to the sun, asking the gods to end the drought, or maybe they are just on a cell phone, it is hard to know these days. The heat is so bad it bends time and perception.

General Manager Jim Bowden and the fans are hoping that Preston Wilson has brought some mojo with him, lightning in a bottle or in his bat, anything that will lead the team from this desert of heat and despair. He is up against his old teammates, the worst team in the National League, the Colorado Rockies, who are losing their foothold on respectability.

"Ten dollars to anyone who can name four players on the Rockies," yells a fan in the men's room to general laughter.

"Didn't they get Zach Day?" asks a fan quietly at a urinal.

"Yeah, and I know Todd Helton plays for them, but after that, I couldn't name a one," says his friend.

The Rockies are hapless, especially in the field where they lead the league in errors. They are worse on the road, where they have not won a series all season and have won only seven of their forty-four road games heading into the opener with Washington. The game starts well for the home team. Although the Rockies break on top in the first inning with a single run off Tony Armas, the Nationals come back in their half of the first to score two runs off Byung-Hyun Kim. Kim's motion is one of the oddest in baseball. Not only is he a submariner, throwing the ball from a point just inches above the ground, but his clipped, staccato movements in the windup remind one of the robotic dance steps once popular among the young.

The fans and the team hope a respite is at hand, but suddenly the mojo strikes again. Tony Armas is pitching with more assurance in the second inning following a shaky first inning. But as the third inning starts he seems distracted, and after throwing two pitches in the third inning he surprisingly motions for Brian Schneider, then to the dugout. Schneider and the trainer trot to the mound and a confused conference convenes. With no warning, no outward sign of earlier distress, Armas departs for the dugout with the trainer to be treated for dizziness and dehydration. An anxious gloomy mood descends across RFK.

Joey Eischen comes in from the dugout to replace Armas and pitches remarkably well, finishing the third inning quietly and working the fourth and fifth, giving up only a single run, but the single run ties the score 2-2. The rally in the fifth is marked by an error by normally reliable Vinny Castilla. In the sixth inning, Colorado scratches out two runs aided by an error by Cristian Guzman. The fans look on in disbelief as the worst team in baseball takes a 4-2 lead into the bottom of the seventh. Washington ties the score at 4-4 using Corey Sullivan's throwing error. One team's poor play seems to invite another in a grotesque competition of futility.

The final cruel joke is on the Nationals as Vinny Castilla commits his second error of the evening and allows the winning run to score in the ninth. It is not so much that the Rockies won the game, but that they were left standing at the end, less embarrassed than the Nationals, who sneak away into the darkness as the fans file out of the stadium murmuring.

"I can understand Guzman," says one fan, still carrying a popcorn tub, "but Castilla, too? This ain't good."

"It was ugly," says another, "ugly, ugly, ugly," shaking his head and wiping his sweaty brow under his cap.

Washington's deteriorating level of play reflects the injuries to almost every player. Like Livan Hernandez, Vinny Castilla is playing with a bad knee that needs surgery. Also like Hernandez, he is postponing the surgery until after the season, although Castilla's age may make his recovery more of an issue for 2006. Jose Guillen is complaining of aches and pains and the only player who seems whole is Jamey Carroll. An ESPN column describes Carroll as one of the game's best "Grunts." The term is meant to compliment, describing that set of players who achieve a surprising level of proficiency through hustle and persistence. Grunts do not get hurt because getting hurt means losing their precarious job security.

The second Rockies game continues in the oppressive heat of the prior evening. Yet for all of the inconveniences traceable to sweltering heat, for the gloomy doubts left over from the prior evening, this game is a wonder. A fan beheads a rubber chicken in a pregame voodoo ceremony and for a night, at least, the flow is reversed, the spell lifts. Fans are resorting to craziness like rubber chickens because losing to the Mets and the Phillies was strategically damaging, but losing to the Brewers is a blow to pride, and the loss to the Rockies, who are firmly rooted in the cellar of the NL Central Division, cannot go unchallenged. If fans must look to work their own magic to help the team, now is the time to do it.

The losing streak brings out the cynics and naysayers, whose attendance has been marginal at best. These are the fans who are likely to spend the afternoon on the cell phone waving into the camera at friends, or devising bizarre betting schemes during the game because the action is insufficient to command their attention. They are the first to say, "I told you so."

"Believe, me" says a cynical young man coming up from the Metro escalator, "they're gonna lose big time in the second half."

"People said the same thing at the beginning of the season," counters the fan, less sure now that there is magic in his Nationals hat. "They'll get all their players back and start winning again, you'll see."

"I thought they already had 'em back, and they're still losing."

"Naw, wait til they get Nick Johnson back, he's the key."

"Dream on, man. They're going down," says a fan, flipping his cell phone to the ready, staring at the little screen as though descending into an alternate universe.

RFK is slow filling for the game, which begins with a sparse crowd, fans slogging through the humid air hopeful that the stadium may offer some respite. The air is still and thick. The fans sit in their seats, foot long sausage dogs and iced lemonade in hand, and the sweat quickly works its way through shirts and hats and pools around elastic bands wherever they can be found. Not the slightest breeze stirs. The spell is strong.

John Patterson seems unmoved, seems to exist in his own world on the mound, unaffected by the poor play, the zombie like offense. He is resolved to win and he retires the Rockies in order in the first inning in fewer than a dozen pitches. By the end of the fourth inning he has faced only one over the minimum, a solid hit by Eric Byrnes in the second. He is sweating, but he looks remarkably focused, unmoved by the heat, the Rockies, or anything else. He is relaxed enough to be back in East Texas chunking balls in his backyard.

The Nationals offense shows a few signs of life, getting two runners on the bases in the first inning, but Guillen fails to get a key hit. In the second

Fans got fewer chances to watch the long ball at RFK than any other baseball stadium in 2005.

inning Preston Wilson works a leadoff walk from Chacon, the Rockies pitcher, and Ryan Church's double into the right center alley gives Wilson a chance to show his speed as he flies around from first base and scores on a head first slide, reaching out for home plate like a relay racer feeling expertly for the baton. With two outs, Jamey Carroll shows why he is playing for Cristian Guzman, smacking a clutch single to right center that scores Church with the second run, giving the Nationals a 2-0 lead.

Patterson makes the lead hold. The team looks like professionals now instead of the hacks from the prior evening. Only in the fifth inning do the Rockies even murmur a threat. With two runners aboard and two outs, the Rockies pitcher, Chacon, watches four balls go by for a free pass. As Chacon trots to first, the crowd groans at the prospect of another unraveling. But Patterson is merely drenched with sweat, his hands hopelessly wet and unable to grip the ball well enough to command his normally effective curveball.

"They seem to find a way to lose," says an obese fan wearing a Harley Davidson T-shirt stretched tightly across his girth. His college aged daughter home sits next to him. Perhaps she is home from school, sharing these vanishing family moments with a parent who knows that they are fast disappearing.

"What do you mean, Dad?" she asks quietly.

"Well, they were finding little ways to win," he says, "You know, all those one run games they were winning? But now they're finding ways to lose, like walking the damn pitcher."

Despite the biker shirt, he looks more like Rutherford B. Hayes, his full gray beard hanging below his chin on his protruding stomach. He folds his arms across his barrel chest and waits for his premonition to develop, but it fails to materialize. Patterson does not destruct. Instead, he tosses over the idea of throwing the curve and throws 93 mile per hour strikes to the leadoff hitter, Corey Sullivan. Sullivan swings through the last fastball up in the zone for strike three. The biker and his daughter join the other fans on their feet, applauding loudly as the ump rings Sullivan up and Washington's lead holds.

Chacon pitches well and matches Patterson, with the 2-0 score holding until the eighth inning. In the top half of the inning, Patterson is still pounding fastballs past the hitters. He gets the first two outs in the inning on strikeouts and ends it with a weak grounder to Wilkerson, who is playing first base with remarkable aplomb.

Wilkerson starts the bottom of the eighth inning working a walk to put a runner aboard to start the inning. Guillen, Schneider, and Wilson follow with sharp singles to score Wilkerson and by the end of the inning Washington has a 4-0 lead. It is enough. Frank Robinson gives Patterson a chance at the complete game shutout, sending him out to start the ninth. But when the first batter, Aaron Miles gets a sharply hit grounder through the hole into left field, Robinson comes to the mound and makes the motion to the bullpen. The crowd stands in unison as he leaves the mound.

They applaud noisily as Patterson makes his way to the dugout and gracefully doffs his sweat-drenched cap, waving it to the crowd. Everyone at RFK knows the importance of the effort he has put forth on this miserable night made remarkable by his strong right arm. The crowd has forgotten the curse for one night—put away the rubber chickens—because Patterson's effort comes from no magic, just inspiration and desire. Chad Cordero relieves him and saves the game with a relatively quiet ninth inning and the score holding at 4-0.

The next night the superstitions are back in the minds of fans. Patterson has broken the spell, they say. Livan Hernandez is pitching and surely he can beat the lowly Rockies. But the baseball mojo is back stronger than ever. Not only does Livan Hernandez fail once again to win his 13th game—plenty of fertile ground for the superstitious in that number—but in a fit of frustration he announces at the end of the evening that he is done for the season; he will have knee surgery now rather than later. Jason Jennings pitches a better game than Hernandez, giving the Rockies the series with a 3-2 win. There is intense frustration in losing another series at home, but the idea of adding insult to injury takes on new meaning with a loss to the Rockies.

Not since the lowly Cincinnati Reds swept the Nationals in May has Washington's new team hit a lower point. The talk of a curse, bad Karma, and voodoo extends to the mainstream media, and the local news writers play it prominently in the articles about the game. Yet it may be more reasonable to attribute the run of bad luck to injuries.

Injuries are a plague unto themselves, and the Nationals have had far more of them than other teams at this juncture in the season. It is hard to find a reason and no one offers one up. Both their young players and aging veterans are hurt. Older players are more prone to injury and the additional scrutiny in 2005 of chemical additives that once helped older players bounce back from injury is another reason that aging players may have more difficulty with the long 2005 season. Yet Nationals like Wilkerson have similarly been nursing wounds all season long. Vidro is a crazy quilt of soreness and muscle strains. The weakness of the many puts pressures on the few who are heathly, and as the struggle to provide a little something extra they go down as well.

Houston Street, the very promising young pitcher for the Oakland Athletics, is publishing an online journal of his first season's experiences. It is appearing on ESPN's Web site. He recounts there how surprised he is by the rigors of traveling from one city to the next to play each series, how even the longest periods of the season spent in Oakland are not enough to offset the seemingly endless flow of three game series followed by another late night plane flight, another early morning warm up session when it is hard to even identify the city.

Street also recounts in his journal how many players are affected by injuries and how much it detracts from their level of play. He says that fans and sports writers do not understand the close link between poor performance on the field and the small injuries that do not disable players but leave them hurt and bruised, unable to play their best. His article on "playing through" pain highlights how little fans see of these hurts. It is easy to project from these insights an explanation for the Nationals sudden decline. Their young players have a propensity for injury that comes less from voodoo and more from inexperience coping with the demands of the season. Real injuries do not respond to decapitated chicken heads for very long, either.

The absence of Nick Johnson is an injury of strategic importance; but it is the ongoing pain afflicting Wilkerson, Hernandez, Castilla, Church, and Guillen that has done much to silence their bats. Schneider takes a pounding on many nights and the swings in his batting average are attributed to whether he is "seeing the ball" better. But his seeing may be more effectively tied to being at least somewhat pain free in the batter's box. The old men in Nationals uniforms suffer aches and pains, but so do younger ones. Getting them well requires a solid bench with young players waiting for a chance. Atlanta has that youth movement waiting in the wings, Washington has only more old men, like the popular Carlos Baerga, who is playing his heart out, but his little legs do not run as fast as they once did. They provide entertainment to his teammates and to the fans, but they do not go from first to third like they once did.

Whether it is the heat, the mojo, or the hospital ward, the Nationals' first game against Houston continues the long July slide. They start the series tied with Atlanta for first place in the NL East. Atlanta provides an interesting contrast for Washington fans. Atlanta's marquis player, Chipper Jones, is hurt and has missed many weeks, and pitchers like Mike Hampton have also been out for long stretches. But they are playing better than ever, and all of baseball is talking about the genius of Bobby Cox and the Atlanta brain trust. They are recognized not only for having great young talent available to replace their key players as they go down, but also for knowing how to integrate them into Major League action at the right time.

For the Houston game, Carlos Baerga is in the lineup to rest Vinny Castilla at third base, whose pain in his knees is getting worse, not better. Bowden finally designates Wil Cordero for assignment at the beginning of the Houston series. Cordero has had over fifty at bats, mostly as a pinch hitter. He has gotten only six hits while being paid $600,000 annually, which works out to exactly $100,000 per hit, hardly the kind of offensive efficiency a winning team can afford.

To replace Cordero, Bowden picks up Kenny Kelly on waivers, the same way he picked up Drese. Kelly has remarkable speed, but has failed his prior auditions with Tampa Bay, Seattle and Cincinnati. Although once highly touted as a prospect, he has never stuck on a major league roster. He cannot hit and was demoted to Double A by the Reds in 2004 because of his struggles with their Triple A team. The only logic in the move is some hope by Bowden that Kelly can show up the Reds by performing well for Washington. The one thing the Nationals do not need is another outfielder, even if he can run.

The Braves are using their minor league talent to fill holes. They are plugging in pieces of the puzzle to see if they fit for the long term. Good organizations make these kinds of assessments. Jim Bowden, like Annie Hall, is still shopping in the bargain bins, and it is sometimes hard to find the formula he is using to build a successful franchise in Washington, D.C.

The first two games against Houston provide wonderful pitching match-ups. Roy Oswalt will go for Houston against Esteban Loaiza. Oswalt, at 27, stands on the threshold of rare success that others have tried to cross and failed. Many think Oswalt may get there, although it may not happen if he stays with Houston. Loaiza seemed poised on the same threshold several seasons ago in Chicago, but could not take the next step in New York.

Houston comes into the series on a winning streak. They are in second place behind the Cardinals and now have a legitimate chance at the wild card slot in the play-offs. With the Nationals dropping games at their current pace, the wild card race is getting tighter, and of course it is still early.

The heat is fierce, but the Nationals are anything but torrid. Oswalt dominates the Nationals hitters and after eight innings leaves the game with a shutout, ahead 3-0. Esteban Loaiza has not had a dominating outing in weeks, still does not have his best stuff, and allows three runs over seven innings. Preston Wilson hits a two-run home run in the ninth inning to make the final score close, but the game is never really in doubt, finishing at 3-2 for Houston.

The second game of the series showcases the greatest pitcher in the game in many decades, perhaps since Nolan Ryan retired. Roger Clemens is 42 years old and still as dominating as Ryan was at a similar age. His earned run average is below two runs per game, a threshold of excellence very few pitchers achieve even in their prime. Tickets for the game have been selling briskly because it may be the last time he will pitch in Washington and he is everything anyone might have expected. He shuts down the Nationals hitters as effectively as Oswalt. Houston hammers Ryan Drese and Sun Woo Kim for fourteen runs. The game, an embarrassment, is over before it is halfway complete, a 14-1 drubbing.

Still, the team is in first place as Atlanta loses too. The NL East is starting to bunch again. The Phillies and the Mets are beginning to play better baseball and moving up. Washington has seen the best pitchers that Houston can throw at them. In the third game, Brandon Backe takes the hill for Houston. Used as a reliever as a rookie, he is the same age as Oswalt, but in his first season as a starter in the major leagues. Tony Armas is also 27, and was once thought to have promise like Oswalt's. He has not shown it consistently since his rookie year, but it will be on display for the third game against Houston.

The heat lifts just a bit on Saturday. The game time temperature is only 80 degrees, whereas for the prior games it has hovered around 90. The humidity drops almost 20 points and the air is breathable, the night clear, crisp and clean. Armas, who had been unable to bear the heat on Tuesday, takes advantage of the change in weather and pitches one of his best games of the season.

Luck seems to follow the trends in the weather, as the Nationals get a huge break in the first inning. The Nationals load the bases with two outs and Carlos Baerga at bat. He lunges for a ball on the outer half of the plate and pokes it toward center. The ball is not hard hit, but Astro's rookie center fielder, Willy Tavares, reacts to the swing and comes in on the ball only to see it carrying over his head. He is unable to correct his mistake and the ball falls in for a double, all three runs scoring. Brian Schneider follows with a hit to drive in Baerga, who scores on a beautiful slide around the catcher's tag, and the Nationals take a 4-0 lead.

**Scoring runs against Houston proved difficult thanks to the heat.**

Armas makes the lead stand up, taking a no-hitter into the sixth inning. Then, with a runner aboard, Lance Berkman hits a long home run into right field, and suddenly the score is 4-2. Armas closes out the inning without further damage and pitches seven innings of one-hit ball. This time the bullpen holds and closes out the game at 4-2. It is only the team's fifth win since July 3 when they swept Chicago to start the month, and when Nick Johnson was placed on the disabled list officially. Still, the Nationals cling to first place, tied with Atlanta.

The last game on Sunday showcases the other great young Washington pitcher, John Patterson. Patterson has become the team's third starter and, if they make it to the play-offs, will give Washington a formidable pitching trio. His earned run average and strikeout totals are among the league leaders. As was the case with Esteban Loaiza earlier in the season, the team shows a remarkable ability to score fewer runs than he allows. On this Sunday he allows only a single run, and his teammates collect the same. He pitches eight full innings and strikes out 10 with 94 mile an hour fastballs.

He watches from the dugout as, in the bottom of the eighth, the Astros try to throw the game away. Byrd starts the inning with a walk and Bennett's poorly struck bunt gives the second baseman a chance to get Byrd at second base. Instead he throws the ball away and Byrd goes to third. With the go ahead run on third and no one out, it seems as though lady luck has once again smiled on the struggling Nats. But given the opportunity, the team squanders it miserably. Patterson looks on with both hands clutching the top of his head as though he is in pain, as first Schneider, then Church and finally Wilkerson cannot get the ball out of the infield to score the run. The bullpen gives the team five more chances to score the winning run as the tied game stretches into the fourteenth inning, when Houston mercifully ends it on another home run.

The team and the news media are convinced that RFK is not friendly to home runs. The *Washington Post* measures the distances and then the team surveys them to find that the gaps to left and right center are longer than advertised by as much as 15 feet. Yet in the four-game series, Houston manages five home runs over the wall, including Ensberg's to dead center where the dead area of the stadium is rumored to be at its worst. The ball lands well up on the wall above center field, with the Nationals, Castilla, Guillen and others who feel cheated by their home field watching it go. Yet somehow, despite the frustration, the pitiful offensive production, and the inability to win a single series in the month since Chicago, the Nationals remain tied with Atlanta for the lead in the NL East. Washington travels to Atlanta for a three game series that will decide who will lead the division going into August.

# 14

# Head to Head at the Ted

It is the last week in July, and Atlanta and Washington, tied for the lead in the NL East, meet at Ted Turner Field, affectionately known to baseball fans in Atlanta as "the Ted." The teams will meet again in August and September, so this is but the first of meetings that will do much to decide who will win the NL East in 2005. Perhaps the surging Marlins or the Mets will make these meetings meaningless, but for now the atmosphere has the trappings of a pennant race, and for the Nationals the stress shows.

The Nationals have players who have been in this position before. Livan Hernandez, who is starting the first game of the series, has more play-off and World Series experience than most, and in 2002 Omar Minaya tried to maneuver the Expos team into position to make a stretch run in August, but it did not work, though Wilkerson, Vidro, and several others were there for the attempt. Jose Guillen was there coming down the stretch with the Angels in 2004, but that is when his temper finally got the best of him. Cristian Guzman has been to the play-offs with the Twins, but they have seldom won. There is a world of experience, but a lot of it is in futility and the team as a unit has not been in this position before.

John Smoltz has seen all of this fanfare many times. He has seen many stretch runs begin and watched them carry his team into the play-offs and beyond. He has an outstanding record in play-off games both as a starter and reliever. He and Livan Hernandez match-up well for the first game, and they do not disappoint the fans hoping for a great game. Hernandez's pitches his usual game, allowing base runners in almost every inning, bending here and ready to break there, but never giving in, never succumbing to the Braves hitters. Hernandez pitches are frustratingly slow at times, but he controls the outside edge and the inside corner under the hands. As the game progresses, Ron Darling says to Mel Proctor on the TV broadcast:

"Did you know Livan Hernandez was this good? Because I did not realize just how good he is. He is really marvelous to watch."

Indeed he is, but Proctor is too wrapped up in the play by play to respond, the endless litany of statistical analysis about how this Brave has hit. Proctor has been ready since the beginning of the season to emcee the funeral of the Nationals. Many fans seem to prefer his skeptical approach to Darling's, but it may tap a reservoir of doubt that lies beneath the surface of even the staunchest Washington fans. But Darling is no homer, Hernandez is *that* good.

He pitches the better game, besting Smoltz easily. Smoltz is also known as a decent hitting pitcher, but Livan proves the better stick man as well. In both of the early rallies by the Nationals, Hernandez plays a part. He moves Schneider into scoring position in the third inning, from where Wilkerson singles him in. With the Nationals leading 1-0 in the fifth, Livan leads off the inning with a sharp single. Wilkerson moves him to second with his third hit of the game. Vidro grounds into a double play, but Hernandez moves to third where Jose Guillen gets the second clutch hit to bring him in.

The score is 2-0 and Hernandez is getting in complete control heading into the bottom of the seventh inning, until Adam LaRoche hits a long home run to bring Atlanta to within a run at 2-1. It is the first of several balls hit during the inning that are hit hard, hammered into the outfield. One long fly ball sends Wilkerson all the way back to the warning track, his hand feeling for the wall behind him in left. Eyes glued on the descending white spot in the sky, he times his leap perfectly and plucks the ball from the top of the wall, bringing it back into the park. The replays show it clearly carrying into the stands for a home run, but Wilkerson, thankfully, is playing left field for this game to rest him from the demands of center field. He keeps Washington in the lead for another inning.

The level of play throughout the game is outstanding and it is clear that both teams recognize its importance, playing all out on every play. Hernandez comes out of the game at the end of the eighth inning with the lead, only three batters to go and the Nationals are back in first place, maybe back in command of their destiny once again.

Cordero starts the bottom of the ninth ahead 2-1. Yet the Braves seem to have scouted Cordero amazingly well. He has faltered at times, put men on base in the ninth, but he manages to wrestle wins from disaster every time. For this game, though, the Braves have a formula for success that others have overlooked. Cordero is using his fastball as the first pitch to each Atlanta batter and they are clearly looking for it. Each swings at the first pitch; it is the heart of the Braves order, the Jones boys, and first pitch fastballs to aggressive hitters like Andruw Jones can be a problem.

The first Jones lines Cordero's first offering well out into the green open spaces in right center field, where it bounces against the wall. He coasts into second base with a double. Chipper Jones hits the very next pitch for a single that sends Andrew Jones to third with no one out. The tying run seems certain to score.

Adam LaRoche, whose home run is the only Atlanta run so far, is again sitting on ready, waiting for Cordero's first pitch, and he hits hard, but not hard enough. It is only a long fly ball out. But it carries almost to the wall and Andruw Jones comes home easily with the tying run. The starch goes out of the Nationals fans, who sag noticeably. After another single, Brian Schneider throws out a runner trying to steal and Cordero gets the third out. The damage has been done, though. Livan Hernandez's fine effort has been in vain.

The team is not winning these games anymore. They do not have the same strut as when they won extra inning games back in May. Mike Stanton relieves Hernandez and pitches the tenth inning. He gives up a single and after a sacrifice moves the runner to second, he intentionally walks Rafael Furcal. With two outs Luis Ayala comes in to face the right-handed hitting Marcus Giles. It is a good percentage move and Ayala has been rock solid much of the year, but he looks undone by the stress of the situation and he cannot get the ball over the plate. He hits the first batter on a wild pitch inside to load the bases. Then, on four straight balls, failing to get a single strike, he walks in the winning run.

Ayala's performance starts a run of sloppy play. Maybe it can be explained by the stress of the situation, the heat, or any number of causes, but in truth it is so similar in nature to many recent game, that it is hard to distinguish from losses in Colorado or Houston. Like the biker with the long beard said, watching the team blow the lead to the Rockies, "They seem to find ways to lose, where once they found them to win."

The second game in Atlanta starts with the Nationals in second place for the first time since June 6, when the *New York Times* recognized the historic climb of the fledgling Washington team to 1st place in the NL East. The long run at the top has lasted for over six weeks, but its end has seemed a foregone conclusion for weeks. The actuality of losing first place does not sit well with the team. The level of play that has endured at high levels through all of the frustrating losses begins to deteriorate.

Atlanta jumps out to a quick lead in the second game. Despite closing the gap, the Nationals effort is ugly and no one would argue that the better team won, despite the apparent closeness of the final 4-3 score. Washington lets two shallow pop flies fall without a play being made on either of them. Errant throws, wild pitches, and a general sloppiness by the team prompts a postgame tirade by Frank Robinson in a closed team meeting after the game. It is not without reason that frustration would boil over.

The meeting produces no noticeable effect the following evening. Defensive standout Brian Schneider throws a ball into right field on a sacrifice in the early innings to bring in the first run. The lack of any identifiable offense dooms the team, even though play improves slightly after Schneider's blunder. Tim Hudson pitches a better game than Esteban Loaiza, whose effort is credible, perhaps good enough to win with a better team behind him, but that is not the case on Wednesday in Atlanta. Another late rally falls short and Atlanta sweeps the three game series. The head-to-head match-up at the Ted, instead of being a focal point for two teams battling for first place, becomes a showcase for all of the problems of a young team that has never been there before, that has never come up against the tough heat of August and walked through it successfully. Washington heads to Florida with trepidation, for there another great pitching staff awaits them, another team playing good baseball and winning games and waiting for the wonders of June to arrive.

Miami is just another city in the grip of relentless summer heat. Ron Darling reports that at least in Miami the wind off the Gulf stirs the heat and makes it more bearable than in Atlanta. The heat may be better, but the pitching match-up in game one of the series is not. Josh Beckett will pitch for Florida against the Nationals' Tony Armas. Beckett shut out the Nationals in Miami for Washington's first loss, and then pitched well against the Nationals in early June when Washington swept the Marlins to take over the lead in the NL East. Armas's great outing in his prior start is the Nationals last win, but away from RFK he has been horrid, allowing almost eight runs per game.

Armas is as handsome on the mound as a young Brando, but lacks Brando's intensity. His face is full of questions and for the Marlins he has few answers. He starts the game by allowing three of the first four batters to reach base. With the bases loaded, Paul LoDuca hits a long double that scores all three runners. Armas is saved only by a nifty piece of fielding by Vinny Castilla to end the inning after he gives up another hit and plunks weak hitting Mike Lowell. The Marlins lead 3-0 with Josh Beckett pitching.

True to form, Beckett is almost untouchable in the early innings. Brian Schneider manages a home run in the third to tighten the score at 3-1, but going into the sixth inning Washington has managed only one other hit and trails 4-1. Then, like games earlier in the season, the Nationals come alive in the late innings. Jose Guillen leads off the seventh with a single and then Preston Wilson and Vinny Castilla get consecutive singles to score Washington's second run and chase Beckett from the game. Brian Schneider greets the new pitcher, Jim Mecir, with a solid single to score Preston Wilson with the third run. The Nationals are once again on the threshold, Castilla sitting on second base with the tying run and only one out.

In May and June the team was able to find that extra hit. Nick Johnson is back, but his bat has no key hits to offer, its magic lost. Baerga, whose play has improved steadily as the season has worn its way into July, pinch-hits for the hapless Cristian Guzman. He grounds weakly to Conine at first. Then Ryan Church strikes out. The chance squandered, the air out of the balloon once again, the Nationals go meekly in the eighth and ninth innings, losing the opener of the series 4-3.

The second game offers no relief from either the spate of top pitchers or the heat. A. J. Burnett, who has been the constant subject of July trade rumors, will pitch for the Marlins, who have decided against trading him because they are still in the thick of contention in the NL East. Burnett rewards their faith with a stellar performance in the second game. He pitches seven strong innings, giving up only 4 hits and no runs. He combines with the bullpen to shut out the Nationals 3-0. John Patterson pitches well for Washington, although he struggles with his curve again in the heat. The loss leaves the team with a precarious hold on second place in the NL East and on the wild card spot in the play-offs, to which Houston is staking a firm claim.

Going into the last game of July, the team's record for the month stands at eight wins and 18 losses. The second loss to Florida is the sixth in a row. This streak of misfortune exceeds the earlier stretch in May that saw the Nationals lose five in a row to Cincinnati and St. Louis. The hapless play of August and July exceeds expectations, except for those of the scouts. It took longer to materialize, but the wisdom of the skeptics is winning out. There is one very notable exception. The fans are still there. The team won only the first series in the month against the Cubs, losing every set of games, and getting swept in the crucial series against Atlanta.

The losing streak in May seems long ago, but it is easy to remember how well it set the stage for Washington's wonderful June run. The May road trip in St. Louis was salvaged by a great performance by Livan Hernandez against the Cardinals' best, Chris Carpenter. Hernandez has pitched remarkably well through the horrible heat and disappointments of July, but he has not won that crucial game to turn the tide. But now he is not up against a John Smoltz, or a Dontrelle Willis. It is Brian Moehler, the Marlins' lowly fifth starter, who goes against the Nationals' ace.

Hernandez continues to offer the Nationals every chance to beat the odds. He pitches his usual game, giving up a single here, a walk there, but never yielding the big inning, no crooked numbers on the scoreboard. The Marlins scratch out a run in the first and take a 1-0 lead. The first telling moment in the game comes in the third inning. Ryan Church has a solid single through the middle to center field. Jose Guillen pops weakly to second, bringing Nick Johnson to the plate with two out and a runner on first. Moehler gets two strikes and the inning seems over, but on the next pitch, with Church running, Johnson pulls the pitch down the right field line. It bounces into the corner and scores Church all the way from first, Johnson going into second with a double.

It is the kind of situation where, in recent weeks, the Nationals seem not to even bother. When Guillen has failed to deliver, the team has failed. Johnson's clutch hits have been a key to the team all year, yet this is one of his first since his return to the lineup. It sends a murmur through the team. The inning ends with Johnson still on second base, but the Nationals are cheered to be back in the game, 1-1.

Hernandez continues to weave his way through the batting order without allowing further damage. In the fifth, Jose Guillen leads off the inning with a sharp liner into the gap in right center for a double. Johnson moves him to third base with only one out, but Preston Wilson, who has not hit well since coming over in the trade for Zach Day, strikes out, leaving Guillen at third. The last hope is Carlos Baerga, who made a nice play in the third inning on a grounder down the line.

After the graceful play in the field, his teammates' razzing draws a big Carlito smile. The cheerful, round-faced elder statesman has something to smile about again as he singles into right field to score Guillen with the go-ahead run. Gary Bennett follows with a double, but Miguel Cabrera plays the ball back in quickly, holding Baerga at third. The Marlins manager, Jack McKeon, clearly wants to take Moehler out, but he settles on a different strategy. With Cristian Guzman batting, many teams have taken their chances with his .180 batting average, but he has been hitting the ball hard in the series, so McKeon takes no chances with Livan Hernandez standing in the on-deck circle. Moehler walks Guzman intentionally to face Hernandez with the bases loaded. Hernandez is swinging at the first pitch. He gets good wood on it, but fouls it back to the screen. He nails the second pitch squarely and laces it into right field, scoring Baerga and gaining a 3-1 cushion going into the bottom of the fifth.

The Marlins mount an immediate rally. With two out and runners on first and second, Miguel Cabrera comes to the plate. He is the reigning player of the week and on a hot streak that has been cut short by the series with Washington. The Nationals have pitched around him at times. He has gotten his hits, but not hurt them badly. Hernandez cannot pitch around him, but keeps him off balance with slow curves on the corners and he skies to center field to end the inning.

In the sixth inning, the Marlins cut the lead to 3-2 on a double by Mike Lowell and a run scoring single by LoDuca. Then, in the seventh inning, it is Cabrera's chance again. With one runner aboard and two outs Hernandez faces Cabrera, the lead precarious at 3-2. Hernandez blows a third strike past the hard swinging, 22-year-old slugger. Cabrera eyes Livan as he walks off the mound, and Hernandez returns the stare, a small smile forming on his lips that seems to say, "You did not think I had a ninety mile an hour fast ball in me, did you, son?"

Cabrera has many years to learn about crafty old pitchers like Hernandez. Maybe he will win the next battle, but Hernandez has won this one, and it is an important moment in the game. He continues to pitch until the end of the eighth inning. He throws the outrageous sum of 145 pitches, just a few below the record he established earlier in the season. It appears that Cordero will come on to finish the game with a single run lead, just like the key win he blew for Hernandez in Atlanta. But fate is changing, and in the top of the inning, with one out, Nick Johnson hits a long, long home run into the center field stands. It measures over 425 feet, and gives the Nationals an extra margin for Cordero.

The fish have not scouted Cordero like the Braves. They let him get the first pitch strikes and gets three ground ball outs to end the game. The team and the fans breath a sigh of relief. Hernandez has been unable to get his thirteenth victory over a span of almost a month. He last won on July 1 in Chicago, so his wins account for two of the team's rather pathetic total of only nine for the month. But it is not the pitching that has spelled defeat in most of those games, but the lack of offense. Nick Johnson's clutch double and important ninth inning home run, may do more to lift the spirits of the team and turn their fortunes around than any voodoo hexes can accomplish.

Chad Cordero's ability to close the sale is similarly reestablished with the win. None of these changes in direction may hold like they did in May. They may be lost in the trade winds that blow across the Gulf, but it seems that once again things might fall into place and get the team back to the point where it was before June, when it could put together stretches of very good baseball. They may not win ten in a row again, because teams are preparing for them.

Like Atlanta, teams that want to win are going into each series with a plan of attack against the key elements in the Nationals' arsenal, whether it is Johnson, Cordero, or Hernandez. Teams that beat these three put added pressure on the rest of the team and it has not responded well. But in Miami, Washington rediscovered their winning combination and that is a first step. It may not have as much significance as beating the Cardinals in St. Louis, beating their best pitcher as Hernandez did in May, but it is an important turnaround as the team heads back to RFK to play two series against West Coast teams.

# 15

# It Takes a Worried Mind

The news on every fan's lips before the game is the story of popular Orioles star Rafael Palmiero, who has been suspended for testing positive for steroid use. Palmiero testified before Congress during the off-season after Jose Canseco identified players who he believed were users. Palmiero testified before Congress that he had never used steroids, but now he has tested positive for two different chemical steroids used by other athletes, including the Olympic sprinter Michael Johnson, whose disqualification from competition caused such an uproar during the 1990s. The prevailing sentiment is one of betrayal at the perfidy by one who was so widely perceived as the genuine article.

"He sure doesn't look like he uses them," says one fan of Palmiero.

"That's why everybody believed him last summer," says his friend.

"Right, just like Clinton looking into the camera saying, 'I never had sex with that woman,'" says the fan, his face a show of mock sincerity.

The betrayal of public trust sadly has become commonplace in American culture, but Palmiero was more widely believed because the physical evidence, his physique, seemed to deny the charge so effectively.

"I guess I was still willing to believe it was just some mix-up, like it was really just some cough medicine he was taking, but I heard it on the radio on the way out here, it was steroids, no question about it."

Washington fans make no attempt to pawn the problem off on the team in Baltimore. It is larger than that, and Baltimore still counts as family even if, like some prodigal, it has strayed in its treatment of D.C. fans. For baseball, which mirrors American culture more than any other sport, the issue of family is an important one. How do kids perceive this betrayal of their very formative affection for a favorite ballplayer? A young boy peppers his father with questions about steroids.

"Why do they take them, Dad?" asks the boy

"To build their muscle mass," the father explains articulately to the bright, chatty lad whose dark hair and slightly swarthy features mirror his father.

"What's bad about them?" asks the boy.

"Well, it's cheating," says the father.

"Yeah, but does it do anything bad to them?" asks the boy doggedly.

"Yes, it does, son. Steroids cause acne, depression, mood swings."

"What's a mood swing?" asks the boy, wondering if this is baseball talk or a psychology term.

"You know, one minute you're real happy, the next minute you're real sad, something like that. You want some lemonade?" says the very patient father, hoping that his curious son can be pointed in some other direction.

In the row in front of the father and son, two parents with somewhat older children sit quietly, perhaps listening to the chatter of the small boy behind them. The teenage girl, no more than 17, dangles her long and attractive leg out over her knee, swinging it ever so slightly in the direction of her boyfriend, who sits beside her. When she is sure her flirtation has registered, she reaches over and pulls the cap he is wearing down across his face, hiding his eyes. She laughs, playing out a game older even than baseball.

Perhaps the loss of innocence is there for each generation of American baseball fans for a reason. There, in a less intimating environment, young fans are exposed to life's vicissitudes, to its joys and the knowledge that with it comes a more complex drama, with disappointments and frustrations aplenty. It is all part of the old ball game. You learn it best by playing it, but come to understand that the lucky ones can sit back and just watch it unfold patiently, hoping their team wins more than they lose.

RFK is a unique opportunity to sample the discussion of the day's topics. Nationally known pundits like William Kristol of the *Weekly Standard*, Mark Shields from the *Jim Lehrer News Hour*, and NBC News's Tim Russert are in attendance at the game. Yet in Washington, D.C., even the young fans are uniquely glib and informed, which is easy to overlook as they jump up and down on the stands like college kids, "waving," and whooping with joy like fans everywhere. But the issue of steroids is a pleasant diversion when compared to the situation of their beloved Nationals. The fans' faces are long and worried as the game begins. Unlike the clear blue sky, marred by only a few wispy high cirrus clouds, their countenance is cloudy.

There is plenty to worry about as the Nationals take on the Dodgers for a three game series at RFK. Although the Nationals won the finale in Florida, they need stellar pitching to win here. Only intense focus to the task of keeping the other team in check has worked and any hiccup has been too much for them to overcome. Washington's offense is unable to muster enough runs to win, despite consistently good efforts from its top three pitchers, Patterson, Loaiza, and Hernandez.

The Dodgers, however, are not the team Washington traveled to the West Coast to play in early May. Injuries have taken a toll on the team as well. The loss of Eric Gagne for the season, one of the top closers in the game, has left their bullpen in complete disarray. Their excellent catcher, Paul Bako, is likewise out for the year, and J. D. Drew, one of their most potent bats, will miss the series. The team has lost ten games more than they have won, but in the NL West, where no team has a winning record, they are still in competition for the play-offs.

Esteban Loaiza, starting the game for the Nationals, begins impressively with four straight pitches for strikes to start the game. Cesar Izturis, the Dodgers shortstop, strikes out on the first three and Oscar Robles, an unknown playing third base, swings through the fourth. Yet Loaiza loses his concentration without explanation, and walks Robles. A ground ball to Cristian Guzman is quickly converted into a double play to end the inning, but a tone has been set. The following inning, Jeff Kent hits a monstrous home run into left center to start. Loaiza teeters but another double play erases the threat and the Dodgers lead only 1-0.

In the stands, the Dodgers lineup presents challenges to the fraternity of fans who keep score in their programs, or more exotically, in ledgers dedicated to such endeavors. Few are familiar with players like Oscar Robles or Dioner Navarro, the young catcher playing for LoDuca. Fans track the game as a way to remember it, to look back over previous at bats to chart player performance, or the strikeout total of their favorite pitcher. Mainly, it is knitting for the sports fan, and the collective of fans who do it might as well sit quietly together and share anecdotes about various stitches as about their favorite ballplayers. Yet it is part of the game, a way to create community where it did not exist, as one scorekeeper lends another the results from the activities while they are away from the game.

Jeff Weaver, the Dodgers pitcher, is providing interesting opportunity to consider scorekeeping variation for strikeouts. The Nationals are watching third strikes in the second inning until one fan cries out.

"Swing, Vinny, you can't hit the ball with the bat on your shoulder."

"Boy, ain't that the truth," says his colleague.

In the third inning Washington fans get something to cheer about. Brian Schneider is hit with a pitch to lead off the inning, and a rare single, hit sharply by Cristian Guzman, puts two runners aboard with no outs. Loaiza cannot bunt them over, but Brad Wilkerson sends a long, high fly ball into center field. It looks like a home run, but the fans are used to watching them die. This one eludes the lunging fielder's glove on the warning track and before it has been fired back into the infield Wilkerson is on third and two runs have scored for Washington. It is a hopeful sign, as Weaver has been

## 15. It Takes a Worried Mind

inconsistent and this outburst may give the Nationals offense a badly needed lift.

Hope melts as quickly as it arises. Vidro pops into shallow left and the fielder fires a strike to the catcher on the fly, daring Wilkerson to run. Wilkerson scrambles back to the bag and, as Guillen makes the third out, Wilkerson walks off, just the latest of lost opportunities, senselessly stranded by a Washington offense so anemic that its pulse is visible only for the briefest appearances.

For the few Dodgers fans scattered throughout the stadium, the fare is better. In the fifth inning, Jason Repko, another little known name, hammers another Loaiza offering into the far reaches of the stadium to tie the score at 2-2. Then in the seventh, the equally obscure Jason Phillips' long home run against the padding in left field costs two runs after Jeff Kent's shallow fly ball is played into a double by the nonchalance of Preston Wilson in left field. The 4-2 score is given further cushion with a leadoff home run by Hee-Seop Choi in the eighth—the fourth of the day for Los Angeles.

"Hey, Jose," yells a fan in right field at Jose Guillen, watching the ball travel well over the fence. "Do you think the ball carries at RFK?"

"Yeah, when the ball starts carrying at RFK, we are really gonna be in trouble," says his friend sarcastically.

Trailing 5-2 the Nationals offense finds itself in the bottom of the inning. The relief pitcher that starts the inning, Steve Schmoll, is a local product from the Maryland suburbs. The fans, announced at 36,000, are still in the stadium, still waiting for their team to awake. The loud noise grows as first Jose Vidro singles and then Jose Guillen slashes a hard single to left, unfazed by the sidelong slinging by Schmoll. With two runners on base and no outs, the fan's pained frustration born in the oppressive heat tempers a bit. Some in the left field bleachers try to get their cohorts jumping, but that level of enthusiasm is missing. Then an errant throw to second base on a steal attempt puts runners on second and third.

Nick Johnson seems to catch all of a pitch in the next at bat and the fans are doing the math, 5-5 if it clears the wall. But their elation is short lived as the ball hangs up, descending toward the wall but just short, caught by the center fielders on the warning track, a long sacrifice fly that makes the score 5-3. Guillen moves to third on the play, although the throw makes it close and many in the stands think Guillen is out. There is the faintest hope that the call by the ump means their luck is changing, but Castilla can only manage another sacrifice fly to make the score 5-4. Hope rises anew as Preston Wilson walks again and Brian Schneider ropes a line drive single into right field to put men on first and second. Washington needs that clutch hit once again.

After a long conference on the mound, the Dodgers leave Schmoll in to face Carlos Baerga who pinch-hits for the weak hitting Guzman. Both the fans and his teammates increasingly favor Baerga with their affections. The stadium noise rises to deafening levels, but vanishes quickly when Baerga grounds weakly to second base, ending the threat. Majewski keeps the game close in the ninth, but the erratic Yhency Brazoban, Gagne's poor replacement at closer, mystifies the Nationals, who go quietly to another close defeat, the final score 5-4.

The second game seems another great opportunity for Washington's offense, because Dodgers pitching is so thin. On the recent road trip, Frank Robinson said of the Nationals that "pitchers come off the disabled list just to get the chance to pitch against us," in reference to the steady lack of run production by the team. The Dodgers' arrival in town should be a cause for celebration by hitters, as their pitching rotation sports two starters allowing well above 5 runs per nine innings. The Nationals scored 5 runs twice and more only once for the entire month of July.

One fan offers a unique analysis.

"Did you see those women handing out that 'Vegetarian Guide to D.C.' on the way in?" asks a fan heading toward a unique analysis of the Nats' problems.

"Yeah, I hear they have Tofu Dogs over behind first base?"

"Noooo?" asks the first fan incredulously. "Did you try one?"

"No way, but I think the Nats must be eating them," he offers, laughing at his insights into Washington's anemic offense. "They need more meat in their diet."

Of the Dodger pitchers, D. J. Houlton has been the least effective during this his rookie campaign. Even against the hapless 25-year-old, Washington lends credence to Robinson's fatherly evaluation. The lineup goes quietly in the first three innings, while Nationals pitcher Tony Armas struggles with runners on base in each of three innings, capped by a long home run by Milton Bradley to give the Dodgers a thin 1-0 lead going into the fourth.

In the fourth the Nationals begin to take the measure of the Dodgers pitcher. Jose Guillen leads off with a hard single. Johnson moves him over with a grounder to the right side, but Castilla cannot bring him in. Preston Wilson, whom Jim Bowden posed as the answer to the Nationals offensive woes, strides to the plate hitting only .220 since coming to Washington from Colorado. With two out and another impotent effort by the Nationals ready for the scorekeeper's notebook, Wilson catches all of one and the crowd jumps to its feet to watch it go. The ball lands high on the padding over the center field wall just right of dead center. The Nationals grab an early inning lead for the first time in weeks.

It is a precarious lead at 2-1. Like the old comedy acts where the drunken clown on the high wire teeters along the wire, faltering, but never falling, Armas maneuvers through the lineup for five innings without surrendering the lead. In the bottom of the fifth, Robinson pinch-hits relief pitcher Ayala for Armas. Ayala responds to the odd move with a looping single that must embarrass the next three hitters, none of whom can bring him around to score.

Ayala pitches a quick sixth and seventh inning, keeping the precarious lead intact as the Nationals continue their offensive slumbers. In the top of the fourth inning, Mike Stanton replaces Ayala, but gives up a single. Robinson brings in Gary Majewski to face Jeff Kent, one of the best, if not *the* best, clutch hitters in the National League. Majewski throws first a 94, then a 96, and then finally a 97-mile an hour fastball and Kent strikes out looking at the last one. With two outs, Valentin grounds weakly to Nick Johnson to end the inning. In the bottom of the ninth, Nick Johnson hits his second home run in three games, a towering shot that, like Preston Wilson's shot, leaves little doubt as the fans jump to their feet again for something they have not seen enough of and could grow to like. With the score 3-1, Cordero gets three fly ball outs to end the game.

The tidal change is not as compelling as at the end of May, but it may be coming. During the ninth inning, as Cordero gets two strikes on the batter, fans begin jumping in earnest along the left field foul line. Nick Johnson is starting to hit, and maybe Preston Wilson is breaking out of his slump, too. Washington picks up a game on Atlanta that loses to Cincinnati, but Houston wins to keep a two game lead in the wild card race.

Washington sends out John Patterson for the rubber match with the Dodgers. Washington is going for its first series win since July 3. It has really been only a month since they swept the Cubs, but what a dreary and hopeless month of baseball it has been. A twinkle has crept back into the eyes of fans, but then they shake their heads and smile, knowing how easy it is for things to fall apart. Brad Penny is the Dodger starter and he is the best they have. A large and imposing presence on the mound, he stands six-four and is no skinny man either, listed at 250 pounds. He throws hard.

Patterson begins the game with the same amazing economy of pitches he used in his last masterpiece, when he salvaged a modicum of team pride against Colorado, winning after eight shutout innings, allowing only three hits. A strikeout, a double play and the Dodgers are gone. In contrast, the Nationals push two grounders through the middle and have Vidro and Johnson aboard when Preston Wilson muscles an inside pitch into center for a single. But Vidro cannot score, and Ryan Church hits meekly into a double play and the same scenario seems ready to play itself out.

Patterson starts the second striking out Kent on a slider away, and then gets Valentin looking to end the inning. In the fourth inning, Milton Bradley challenges Patterson with a long at bat, fouling off pitch after pitch, but Patterson hangs tough and Bradley is just another strike out, six in four innings.

The Nationals continue to show life against Penny. In the fourth inning,

Ryan Church singles through the middle and then challenges the throwing arm of young catcher Dioner Navarro, who again cannot get the throw down. Vinny Castilla rips a line drive into the left field corner where it bangs against the wall, bringing Church around to score easily and allowing the gimpy Castilla to pull up on second base, well ahead of the throw. Gary Bennett, playing for the injured Brian Schneider, moves Castilla to third with only one out. Cristian Guzman, who is showing small signs of life with the bat, pounds the ball into the ground. It flies high into the air heading toward shortstop. The Dodger shortstop has no play on Castilla, who scores to give Patterson a sumptuous 2-0 lead.

The offense grows quiet again, but Patterson seems determined to make the scant 2-0 lead hold. In the fifth inning he strikes out the side, and in the sixth, even with Preston Wilson clanking a fly ball off his glove for a weak double, Patterson does not flinch, striking out Cesar Robles, the next batter, to end the inning. Radio announcers Dave Shays and Charlie Sloes note that Preston Wilson "still looks uncomfortable in the outfield," as though he may grow accustomed to it in his second decade as a major league ball player. His real comfort is at the plate, swinging a bat. The ball does not make metallic sounds coming off of that.

Patterson is flawless in the seventh and eighth innings, getting his 12th and 13th strikeouts, and the Nationals continue to get good swings on Penny, Nick Johnson doubling against the center field wall with two out in the sixth, and two base runners in the sixth. Yet it is not until the 8th inning, that the game is truly decided. With the score still 2-0, Preston Wilson singles to chase Brad Penny. Duaner Sanchez relieves him and walks Church and then Castilla misses the strike zone badly on four straight balls. With the bases loaded, Bennett cannot deliver, but Guzman gets the weakest of liners over the head of the drawn in second baseman to score the third run. Patterson bats for himself and pops out to bring Brad Wilkerson to the plate.

The pundits have commented on Wilkerson's struggles, the injury to his ulnar nerve that keeps only one hand on the bat in the follow through and robs him of his power. The pain subsides suddenly as he hits a towering fly ball; it is only a matter of how far out it will land as the fans watch it go, until it strikes the high wall below the mezzanine seating in right. It is a grand slam, the Nationals' first ever bases loaded home run, and it gives them a 7-0 lead. The fans, pogo-ing madly in left, are smiling and laughing for the first time in weeks, the worry lines gone. The Nationals' magic quietly spills back into RFK, coming "on little cat feet," as though looking for a warm place where the glow of 36,000 happy fans allows it to settle in, if only for the night.

In the postgame interviews, Patterson says that the early lead allowed him to relax.

"It was fun," he says of his first complete game shutout. "It just all fell together."

## 15. It Takes a Worried Mind

Ron Darling asks him whether it is correct that he does not react to the batter so much as read his own stuff, see what's working and then go from there.

"Yeah, I try to get them swinging, then I put a plan together." He is smiling like a kid and he responds to questions about his father's influence on his pitching by saying, "I'll be calling my Dad tonight. Yeah, I'll be calling home."

Darling allows that Patterson's pitches were all working and indeed they were. His strikeouts came on sliders away, curveballs that froze batters in place wincing, and finally fastballs that they could not catch up to. The town is abuzz the next day with the game. For the first time, the Nationals compete favorably in the newspaper with the Redskins, who have begun training for the upcoming season.

At the opening of the San Diego series at RFK on a Friday night at the beginning of August, a large Hispanic family makes, their way into the tenth row behind third base in the field level seats. They are perhaps friends or relatives of a player who has left them tickets at the will call window. The group's progress is slowed by the deliberate pace of an old woman, who leads them down the aisle of folded seats. Likely the matriarch of this clan, she is followed by a middle aged couple and their three teenaged daughters. The others watch her patiently as she moves along clutching her large black purse to her chest. When finally seated she continues to clutch the purse close, both arms folded over it, as though she is saying of these unfamiliar surroundings that one cannot be too careful.

She sits in this position through much of the game, looking out toward the field unless her family talks to her directly. Perhaps she sees the game; perhaps she sees the son of her best friend on the field, a neighborhood boy whom she watched grow from a child, and is hopelessly lost in bittersweet memories. More of the family and their friends find their way to the third base section: young men with their girlfriends, young women with their beaus, until the extended family numbers more than a dozen, all of them noisily calling back and forth during the game, laughing across two or three rows as the family enjoys getting together at the ball park.

In the middle innings, one of the young men comes racing back to the family, pointing for the others to look toward the exit behind home plate. In excited Spanish he explains who is at the center of an entourage making its way up the middle aisle toward the exit. It is a famous African American rap star so thoroughly surrounded by his entourage that he cannot be seen in its midst. Fans in the vicinity stand and ogle the famous star.

The rich variety of life in Washington is evident at every game at RFK. Rap stars, Senators and Congresspersons, political pundits from both sides of the aisle, they are all at RFK. It is part of what is unique about baseball in Washington.

A fan sitting behind the Hispanic family during the pregame ceremonies busily logs the starting lineups into his program.

"That guy down there is doing this right, man," says the score-keeping fan's friend sitting in the adjacent seat. "He's using a *fountain* pen."

"What do you call this," asks his friend, holding up an ink pen of no special origin.

"Well, whatever it is, it's no fountain pen."

"You are just not a member of the fraternity, so you'll never understand."

"What fraternity?"

"The fraternity of baseball scorekeepers."

"What the hell are you talking about?"

"Well, see, if I get up to go get a beer, I can do so, come back and tap this guy with the fancy fountain pen on the shoulder and get him to lend me his score pad so that I can fill in what I missed. That's the fraternity of scorekeepers."

The fan with the fountain pen and the well pressed baseball attire smiles slightly as he overhears this rather bizarre discussion. He and the more plebian fans behind him, the Hispanic family, the rap star and the gathered aggregation are part of a vanishing scene in American life. They are all part of a vast mixing bowl called RFK. Over the years, the mix has become more stratified, yet in other ways it is more homogenous than ever. There is no racial segregation as one existed at old Griffith Stadium. For $40 per seat anyone can find themselves sitting next to media celebrities.

In 1983, John Sayles, the independent American filmmaker, released a film entitled *Baby It's You*. The film is about an affluent teenaged Jewish girl just who is about to graduate from her high school and go off to an Ivy League college, and the unlikely boy she encounters and falls for, an Italian dropout whose desire in life is to start as a lounge singer and work his way to stardom. Sayles said of the film that he wanted to illustrate the experience of public high schools such as the one the movie is set in. He contended that those schools are the last place that Americans experience the melting pot that is our society. College, as the movie very poignantly illustrates, becomes the great class-sorting machine that obliterates any last remaining vestiges that residential zoning has left untouched.

The film makes a compelling case. The ballpark is one of the few places that a grown-up version of Rosanna Arquette's character could bump into that boy later in life. It is one of our few remaining public places where most can get a seat and—although the seating varies widely by cost, effectively sorting classes by section, most of society is there—they rub shoulders for the three hours each night.

The San Diego Padres are a team remarkably like the Nationals. They are built on great pitching and defense, with an offense that is more of a team effort than one featuring box office stars. At the beginning of the series, San Diego has won less than half its games, but is precariously atop the NL West.

## 15. It Takes a Worried Mind

Hopes are high at RFK after the great game on Thursday and, with Livan Hernandez starting the Friday night game, fans are hoping for a turnaround, looking for any sign of life. But on this night, Hernandez does not have it and it is painfully apparent to everyone in the stadium, including Frank Robinson. The Nationals grab the lead early when Livan Hernandez singles home Preston Wilson and Cristian Guzman in the bottom of the second inning. Yet every time they have the lead, it slips away. Hernandez gives up single runs in the third, fourth and fifth and the Padres take a 4-2 lead into the bottom of the inning. The Nationals offense continues to show some life, although getting help from Padres starter Woody Williams. With the bases loaded, Williams walks Preston Wilson on a three ball, two strike count for the first run. Then Gary Bennett gets a single to right to score two more and give Washington the lead once again at 5-4.

In the sixth inning, Hernandez begins in the same way he has each of the previous innings, giving up two quick hits. He bounces back and gets two fly ball outs, but Robinson lifts his pitcher and brings in Joey Eischen. Hernandez is not happy with the manager's decision. As he nears the dugout, the fans stand applauding their pitching ace despite his mediocre performance. Hernandez flings his glove into the stands, where it lands more than a dozen rows deep. He starts down the dugout steps, but stops long enough to throw his hat into the stands, and comes back out on the steps to throw his warm-up jacket as well.

The display of pique has many fans laughing. It is quite a contrast between the angry gestures of Jose Guillen and most other ball players, for that matter. Busted water coolers and bats broken against all manner of dugout appliances and equipment are more common in exhibitions of player ire. But even in his foulest of moods, it is hard to take Livan Hernandez seriously. He is a serious man, and one who plays the game hard, with an intense competitive spirit, but there is a streak of clown that harks back to Bill "Spaceman" Lee, and others whose merriment could not be contained.

Robinson's move pays off and Hernandez's absence on the mound shuts down the Padres, as Eischen closes out the sixth, and Ayala is especially sharp in a scoreless seventh inning. Simultaneously, the Padres bullpen is unhittable, striking out seven of the ten batters they face in the sixth, seventh and eighth innings, and giving up not a single hit.

Gary Majewski does not have the overpowering fastball that he has featured so many times. He gives up a single to start the eighth inning and, although he strikes out Joe Ronda for the second out, a single by Eric Young scores the tying run. Then in the ninth, Cordero cannot hold that score as Guzman puts the leadoff batter on with an error and San Diego brings him methodically around to score. Trevor Hoffman closes the game out with a one-two-three inning.

The fans realize as they file out of the stadium that these were the games that their team was winning in May and June.

"I think it all turned sour back on July 5, when Guillen stopped Loaiza at the third base line and started yelling at him to throw at the Mets to retaliate for Pedro plunking him earlier in the game," says a perceptive fan who has clearly thought about the issue.

"Yeah, it's not good when you take that stuff to the newspapers, either," says his friend as they walk to the distant parking lot under the highway.

"Remember how he air-mailed that throw in the ninth? I think that was just to show how pissed he was. The batters have been on edge ever since," concludes the first fan.

Everyone has a theory, everyone wants to be able to e-mail in the answer, but none are forthcoming. The Nationals lose games two and three of the series, with Jake Peavy pitching a complete game shutout on Sunday showcasing a talent that balances off Patterson's, and his wonderful game from midweek. The sweep leaves fans defeated, and the team wondering as they head out for a long road trip: "What is different? what has happened to the team they were a month earlier?"

# 16

# Baby, I Always Take the Long Way Home

Like a truck on a long steep grade, the Washington Nationals have geared down, pulled over into the far right lane, and are watching others pass by. Atlanta has long passed the Nationals and now sits in its traditional position atop the NL East. Houston has passed them for fourth place and has the current claim on the Wild Card Playoff slot, and Philadelphia is steady at their heels in the NL East. As the team starts on its longest road trip of the season, two full weeks away from a return to RFK, that truck seems slower still, burdened by the extra weight of the team's many injured players. The two most disabling injuries are Vinny Castilla and Jose Vidro. Both Vidro and Castilla are nursing nagging hurts that sorely affect their play on the field and are a burden to the team.

Errors both in the field and on the base paths have plagued Castilla, almost all of which can be tied to his gimpy knee. Running the bases he has been forced to look for ways to game the system, to go halfway on a hard hit ball so that if it falls he has a chance to advance. On several occasions he has been caught in between and thrown out to end promising innings with runners aboard. Vidro has been less obvious, but the problem is basically the same. He cannot get to batted balls that any healthy second baseman could field easily. He cannot score from second base on a single, because he cannot stretch out his quadriceps that are strained and hurting. They are like many players on the team with minor injuries: the only option is to keep playing, but doing so assures that the injured parts will heal exceedingly slowly.

The first stop on the trip is Houston. Houston is playing a much better brand of baseball than earlier in the season, and their excellent pitching staff is healthy for the first time in the season. Clemens is *the* best and Roy Oswalt is reaching for that elite level. Now they are joined by Andy Pettite who is finally healthy. Washington's draw for the series opener is a lucky one, as Clemens and Oswalt have pitched in the preceding two games. It is the fifth spot in Houston's rotation and that now falls to rookie pitcher Ezequiel Astacio, who has struggled. John Patterson, Washington's starter, is by contrast the Nationals' best pitcher in the second half of the season.

Patterson is not sharp on another hot Texas night. Neither his native soil nor the red glove with "Texas" sown into a seam generates any magic as Morgan Ensberg homers against him twice. In the sixth inning Patterson cannot finish the inning, leaving with the bases loaded and two out. Cristian Guzman allows two runs to score on an error, but Ayala finishes the inning. Luck is a funny thing. Patterson, who has had so little support from his team's hitters, should have no chance to defeat Houston. Yet it is a fateful evening and it is not just Patterson whose luck changes.

The anemic offense that has become the calling card of the Nationals during their first season feasts like rampaging Goths, and it benefits Patterson. First, Brad Wilkerson hits a solo home run in the second inning. Then after the Nationals score two runs in the third inning, Brian Schneider hits a solo home run in the fourth, with Brandon Watson the rookie call-up adding his own before the inning is over. The Nationals lead 5-1 and Castilla adds yet another solo home run for a 6-1 lead before Patterson begins to fall apart. He gives up two home runs to Ensberg in the fifth and sixth innings to draw the Astros within a run at 6-5, but Washington has hit four home runs for the evening, the highest total for the year. It is good enough for a win.

The win halts the gathering momentum of the Astros for a single night. Washington draws closer in the Wild Card race, and just as in the game against San Diego at RFK, sends Livan Hernandez to the mound, seemingly a better bet than the opposition pitcher; but once again, Hernandez is disappointing. The Washington ace was wiggling off the hook in the first half of the year, putting runners on base as if to tantalize the opposition, then getting the match-up he liked and getting the key out. He cannot find the right pitch or the right match-up any longer and the Astros, like the Padres before them, hit Hernandez hard. He hits a home run and provides most of the early offense, but in the sixth inning, with the game still close, he fails to field a bunt that sets up the fateful rally and puts the game out of reach. Washington loses 7-6 after a final flurry in the ninth against Houston closer Brad Lidge, who scores two.

The rubber match is never close. Andy Pettite is outstanding, although he gives up a two-run home run to Preston Wilson in the seventh inning. Ryan Drese cannot keep the ball down and gives up six runs so that Wilson's homer doesn't even make the game close. The loss gives the Astros the series and pushes them further ahead in the race for the Wild Card spot in the playoffs.

## Purple Haze

In the long distance camera shots from the Mile High Stadium, the Rockies can be seen through the smoggy haze that plagues Denver and its citizens. In the twilight the mountains shine purple through it. The Nationals are still lost in their own fog, but they are in Denver hoping to emerge. According to Ron Darling, Frank Robinson has laid out for his team the need to win against the worst team in the National League. Colorado came to Washington in the middle of July and won two games out of three at RFK, which at the time was part of the gathering embarrassment of July's swoon. Washington has been able to win only a single series since the All-Star break. Yet that series was at the outset of August against the Dodgers, and though the signs of an awakening are scattered, they are there.

Part of Robinson's presentation to his team alluded to by Darling is the claim that the Nationals are better than Colorado, and better than they are playing. Colorado's starting pitcher in the first game of the series is a perfect example. Jamey Wright has won six games during the 2005 season and lost twelve. His record as a starter with several different major league teams is more one of inconsistency than excellence. Esteban Loaiza is the better pitcher, if he can only convince himself of that fact. Despite Loaiza's lack of success at Mile High Stadium in the past, Robinson's talk with his team seems to bear fruit, first with his struggling offense and then with his number two starter.

Wright is known for his lack of command, and clearly the Nationals attempt to exploit it from the beginning. It is a good object lesson for a team that has been pressing generally. Brandon Watson, who is batting leadoff, walks to start the game. In Watson's minor league career patience has not been a notable characteristic, but in this instance it sets the table effectively as Vidro singles him to third and Nick Johnson doubles him in for the first run. Jose Guillen, also showing a more selective approach at the plate, singles in Vidro and Johnson, and the team takes an uncharacteristic 3-0 first inning lead.

Esteban Loaiza displays a tenacity and focus that has been lacking in his recent games. Although he gives up a run scoring single to Jamey Wright in the second inning, he bounces back from a bad moment and retires nine batters in a row over the third, fourth, and fifth innings. The Nationals add to their lead in the fourth inning on a long double by Brian Schneider that allows the gimpy-legged Castilla to score all the way from first. The bullpen bails Loaiza out in the seventh inning and allows only a solo home run to close out the opener of the series with a 4-2 win.

It is a good win and Robinson can be seen smiling a bit more widely at the end of the game. Smiles have been short-lived for the Nationals, so, while getting off to a good start is important, it is the follow-up that has been lacking. In the second game Tony Armas will pitch. He has had significant difficulty pitching away from RFK and there is no more intimidating a site for pitchers than Mile High Stadium. Armas starts the game with his usual lack of confidence, giving up two singles to the first two batters. The collective groan from back in Washington can be heard as Todd Helton steps into the batter's box, the only proven hitter in the Rockies lineup. Yet the luck of the Nationals holds.

No one can remember back to the games where middle of the order hitters for the Marlins, Mets, and a dozen other teams were silenced by Washington pitchers. Yet their success has depended on it and suddenly it returns to start the second game in Colorado. Helton hits a hard ground ball, but right at Guzman who neatly turns it into a double play. Armas is off the hook; he walks the next batter as if he can't believe it himself, but it's there and, presto, he gets another right at 'em ground ball to end the inning.

Washington hitters have forgotten the approach from the prior evening and are swinging at whatever side-arming oddity Byun-yung Kim throws near the plate. It is a quiet first inning, but with two outs in the second, Brian Schneider works a walk that seems to change the flow of the game for Washington's hitters as well. Castilla follows Schneider with a long double to deep right center that rolls long enough in the far reaches of the Mile High outfield that even the very slow running Nationals catcher can score from first base. Cristian Guzman follows with a soft liner that falls just beyond the second baseman and Castilla, running on contact, brings in the second run. The remarkable pattern repeats itself for the rest of the evening. The Nationals get timely hitting and score eight runs on thirteen hits, seven of which are doubles. The Rockies fail to get anything approaching a timely hit. Though they collect thirteen hits—the same total as the Nationals—theirs yield nothing and the final score is 8-0, a margin of victory unheard of a scant week ago.

The final game of the series is a Sunday afternoon affair with John Patterson and "Texas," his orange mitt. Patterson is developing into the ace of the staff. There is no contesting Livan Hernandez as the sage veteran, but Patterson's stuff is "electric," to quote Ron Darling. It's a wonderful concept, as though Patterson's pitches are tiny electrons beaming mysteriously through space to Schneider or Bennett. There have been games where the hitters have had no more success than if that was the case, like the thirteen strikeout game against the Dodgers in early August. Against Colorado Patterson's pitches are inhabitants of a different physical universe.

The high thin air in Colorado is reputed to diminish a curveball, notably by reducing the friction of the ball biting against the tight pack of air molecules, giving it less downward thrust. The result is a flatter pitch that is easier to track across space by a batter armed with a club. Patterson seems unwilling to throw the pitch in the early innings and since it is his best strikeout weapon, he is less formidable. Nonetheless, he coasts through the Colorado lineup. He encounters a bump in the road in the third inning, but a nice turn by Guzman on a double play ends the inning without damage.

The Washington hitters' love affair with Mile High Stadium cools in the first three innings, but reestablishes itself in the fourth. In the second run through the order against Juan Acevedo, three singles by Wilkerson, Vidro, and Preston, Wilson put two runs on the scoreboard. Then in the fifth inning, singles by Guzman and Vidro, and a walk to Wilkerson are followed by a long and deep home run by Nick Johnson that clips the foul pole high in right field against the upper deck facing. Jose Guillen follows with another home run to right, this one more of a line drive several rows deep in the right field stands. The score stands at 7-0 when Patterson takes the mound, and when he leaves in the eighth, it is 9-1 after Preston Wilson and Jose Guillen add two more runs in the seventh. The final score is 9-2 and the win gives Washington its first sweep since the Cubs series before the Fourth of July. They still trail Houston and Philadelphia in the wild card race, but they are back. The fans are starting to buzz again.

Patterson's earned run average continues to dip after the performance and puts him among the league leaders. He is third behind another Texan, Roger Clemens. Houston has three of the top five pitchers in the league, Oswalt, Pettite, and Clemens. No one wants anything to do with them in the playoffs.

Ron Darling and Mel Proctor sign off their broadcast from Colorado with whimsy about Philadelphia, about the cheese steaks they will be eating, and, Darling needles Proctor, "getting on your tie." It is one of those ties with large white baseballs everywhere on it and a little cheese might help. Everyone is smiling now. The load is lighter and the team is flying as it comes down out of the mountains and even the long flight back east isn't without its rewards.

The Phillies have climbed ahead of the Nationals in the NL East race. It is a bare half game lead, but it is August 15 and the pennant race is in earnest. The teams that play with heart for the next six weeks will make it, the rest will spend the winter wondering why, thinking long about what it will take to make them the better team. For now, Washington is starting to believe that they have a pretty good mix of talent right here and now. They send their veteran ace up against the Phillies. Livan Hernandez has been struggling, unable to create solutions to the many problems he builds for himself in the course of a ballgame.

The Phillies' Bobby Abreu is not the terror he was in June, but they are still a solid team. Pat Burrell has picked up the slack and is having his best season since 2002, again leading the team in runs batted in. Chase Utley has rewarded the team for turning over the second base spot to him. His sixteen home runs put him third on the team and he is developing into the strongest offensive force in the lineup. It is the pitching that has let them down once again. Jon Lieber, brought over from the Yankees, has been disappointing at times and Brett Myers has assumed his role as ace for now. Myers is still only 24 years old and has much to learn about pitching.

Myers is scheduled to pitch in the opener on Monday evening in the Phillies' new ballpark, Citizens Bank Park. The park plays small and has given up more home runs than almost any other in the National League. That might be an omen of ill winds blowing for the Nationals, but they are moving up in the race from the bottom. The team has hit more home runs now than the lowly San Francisco Giants, who are without Barry Bonds. The team scored 21 runs in the three games in Colorado and allowed only 4, but now must face a hot team and their best pitcher.

Like the opener against Colorado, Washington gets on the scoreboard first. Brett Myers gets both Wilkerson and Vidro to start the game, but, as Mel Proctor asks the question "Is Nick Johnson still hot?" Johnson connects with a Myers fastball on the outer half and pulls it well up into the right field stands. After Jose Guillen singles hard back through the center of the infield, Preston Wilson takes much the same pitch from Myers and deposits it over the short fence in centerfield. It is 3-0 in favor of the Nationals again, and it is up to Livan Hernandez.

Hernandez looks for a brief moment like he has his good stuff to start the game, getting Jimmy Rollins on an easy grounder. Then he walks Lofton, and Utley gets a sharp single to right. He walks the bases loaded on a three-two pitch to Abreu that is not even close. Pat Burrell shows how he has been picking up the team since Abreu cooled off by slapping a grounder through the hole at shortstop for a two run single. A visibly disgusted Hernandez stomps back up onto the mound. He failed to back up home plate on the throw from Guillen to try to catch Utley scoring from second base. So out of position was he that he could only catch the ball. A visit from pitching coach Randy St. Claire is a rarity. Hernandez does not take advice well, but clearly he has been seeking it to slay whatever demons have plagued him in July and August.

The visit is like an elixir. He pitches out of the jam and ends the inning with the lead intact at 3-2. In the second, both pitchers are perfect and Hernandez is making pitches again. His cutter is catching the side of the plate and his slow curve as well. In the third inning Jose Guillen does something he has not done in a very long time. With two outs he coaxes a walk and takes it rather than trying to make something happen with pitches off the plate. His reward is getting to trot home in front of Preston Wilson, who mashes another ball, this one high and long that is touched by a fan just before seems to be it settling into the bleachers. Instead, it bounces onto the top of the outfield wall and back onto the field of play. The Phillies play the ball as though it is not a home run, but the umpire nearest the play signals with the circular motion of his finger in the air above his head that it is indeed a four-bagger. The lead is back to three runs at 5-2.

Bobby Abreu protests the call vociferously to the umpire and is joined by Phillies manager Charlie Manuel. The umpires agree to reconsider the call

## 16. Baby, I Always Take the Long Way Home

jointly, but after several minutes of discussion they break up, signaling home run. There is not a Nationals fan watching that does not remember the home run by Brian Jordan in RFK that was disputed and overturned after Frank Robinson's protest. It is difficult not to believe that luck has turned.

Livan Hernandez seems to draw strength from the growing sense of confidence the team is showing as a unit. He puts goose eggs on the scoreboard in every inning after the first until he leaves the game at the end of the eighth inning. Then, at the top of the ninth, when he is scheduled to bat and Church is announced as the pinch hitter, he takes his bats out of the rack and goes on the steps of the dugout and starts sliding them one by one across the roof of the dugout into the hands of young boys who are sitting in the first row. They are delighted, almost as much as the little boy that still lives inside Livan Hernandez.

Brian Schneider hits a solo home run in the eighth inning to give the team four for the game. Schneider is very quietly having a great year for a catcher of his defensive ability. The home run is his ninth and with his batting average hovering just below .300 he is in the upper reaches offensively as well. Also of note is the team's posting four homers in a game for the second time since August began. They have hit more in the first half of August than in the entire month of July, when they hit only 13.

The 6-3 final score puts the Nationals back in second place behind Atlanta. They are playing with heart, and they may be hitting their stride at exactly the right time, down the stretch run of August and September.

The second game of the Phillies series is rained out and it seems provident. Ryan Drese, who has not had a good game in over a month, has his start pushed back by the rain. Now, Esteban Loaiza will get pitch in the second game of this key series. He has been remarkably consistent all year, putting in solid start after solid start, even when the team has failed to score runs for him. Jon Lieber seemed destined to be the Phillies' mature ace after an excellent second half of the season for the Yankees in 2004. He starts the game for Philadelphia on Wednesday night.

Lieber has been knocked around in his June and July starts, so the outlook seems hopeful at the beginning of the game. Yet Lieber is sharp in the first. He pitches more quickly than perhaps anyone and before the inning has started it is over. Just as quickly, Loaiza is in trouble, allowing the two tablesetters for the Phils, Rollins and Lofton, to get on with solid singles. Chase Utley brings Rollins home from third base with a sacrifice fly, and Lofton scores on a long double by Pat Burrell and immediately Washington is behind 2-0. In the third inning the Nationals offense is alive again on a solo home run by Vinny Castilla and a run scoring single by Jose Vidro that scores Cristian Guzman with two out. Vidro's clutch hit ties the score and reminds the team that they *can* get these key hits in August.

With the score tied at 2-2, Loaiza puts Rollins and Lofton aboard again to start the inning, Lofton's ringing double putting runners on second and third with no outs. One out later Bobby Abreu brings them both home on a double to give the Phils a two run lead at 4-2. The two pitchers settle in, but in the sixth inning, Loaiza departs with the bases loaded and two outs, as Frank Robinson brings in Luis Ayala to pitch to pinchhitter Jason Michaels. The move shows how important this series is and Frank Robinson's recognition that it is August and a pennant race. He cannot afford to let Loaiza lose this game, and there is nothing in his performance tonight to suggest he can get the third out.

Ayala bears down and strikes Michaels out to end the inning. By pinch-hitting, the Phillies lose Lieber from the game. Ryan Madson replaces him and suddenly the Nationals are back to their strength: the match-up of their bullpen to anyone else's. Preston Wilson leads off the seventh with a single and Brian Schneider follows with a double. Castilla gets Wilson home with a sacrifice fly to make the score 4-3, but neither Carlos Baerga nor Ryan Church force across the tying run. The Nationals bullpen holds steady, but Urbina pitches well enough to survive in the eighth and Billy Wagner is untouchable in the ninth to close out the win for the Phils.

Tuesday's rainout is rescheduled as part of a Thursday doubleheader, so Ryan Drese's start cannot be pushed back further. He will start the evening game against Cory Lidle, while the first game in the afternoon will match-up two young pitchers, neither of whom has had consistent success or good health. Tony Armas for the Nationals has been as unsteady as a sailor on leave, but he has managed to survive. Vincente Padilla, a Nicaraguan, throws hard and had several good years early in his career, but injuries have slowed his progress and he has missed several starts in 2005. He has been pitching well in July and August, however, and he shows that same form to the Nationals in the afternoon game of the doubleheader.

Armas recreates his start in Colorado, where he courted disaster but was unable to commit completely. Against Philadelphia he walks six batters in five innings—an amazing feat—gives up five hits, and somehow allows only two runs. The most dramatic movement of his performance comes in the sixth inning. Armas gives up a leadoff single and the Phillies send up pinch hitter Endy Chavez, who started the season with Washington. Chavez has had several opportunities to get some manner of revenge against his old team, but has failed in each instance.

Armas throws two wicked sliders as Chavez squares to bunt at each pitch. He cannot get the bunt down and Armas has him set up for the strikeout or the double play. Suddenly, Frank Robinson jumps from the dugout steps and heads to the mound. The Philly announcers are startled. If Robinson could stand to leave Armas in for the prior five innings during the eleven base runners, why take him out with two strikes on a weak batter? Robinson motions to the bullpen and brings in Mike Stanton. Now there is a lefty-lefty match-up and the announcers mull this over while Stanton completes his warm-up tosses.

"Do hitters even after they leave the game ever really like pitchers?" asks the play-by-play man.

"I don't think so," says the color commentator, harking back to his playing days. "And I don't think Frank has ever gotten over it with pitchers, as tough a competitor as he was."

The announcers mull over Frank Robinson's motives and reasoning as Stanton takes his warm-up tosses. The abrupt change solves nothing, but is merely a picture into Robinson's managerial style and perhaps into one of his weaknesses and its origins. At the end of the day, Armas is bested by Padilla's strong outing. Although Padilla is on the ropes in the second inning, with the Nationals getting the first four batters aboard, they can scratch out only a single run. Guzman's clutch single seems to signal a big rally as the bases are loaded with no one out and a runner home. But Armas, Wilkerson, and Vidro are weak outs and it is the only threat Washington mounts during the game. Again, Billy Wagner pitches a quick ninth inning and the game goes to Philly 2-1.

The last best hope is Ryan Drese or the Nationals' bats in the second game of the double-header. A betting man would be skeptical of the situation, so when Drese is touched for runs in three of the first four innings, there is little surprise in either the fans' or Frank Robinson's faces. As the Nationals come in to bat for the top of the fifth inning, they are behind 4-0, a large hurdle that seems more likely to grow than to diminish.

Carlos Baerga, who is giving a rest to the gimpy Vinny Castilla, opens the fifth inning with a single. Jamey Carroll smacks a ball into right field for another hit and suddenly the Nationals are showing life against Corey Lidle, the Phillies starter. Frank Robinson goes to the bench early, lifting Drese and pinch-hitting Castilla. It is a move that again marks the importance of the series in Robinson's mind. Earlier in the year, he would have tried to get another inning from Drese to keep his bullpen fresh. But the time for resting is done and now it is "fish or cut bait."

Although Castilla flies out and Wilkerson fails as well, Jose Vidro continues to get good at bats. He has singled in both of his prior at bats, but Nick Johnson has uncharacteristically stranded the runners each time. Now it is up to Vidro and he does not disappoint, lining the ball into the right centerfield gap for a double that scores both Baerga and Carroll. This time Nick Johnson comes through and his double into the opposite field gap brings Vidro home to make the score 4-3.

The Nationals bullpen makes that score stand up until the eighth inning. First journeyman left-hander John Halama pitches an inning, and then Luis

Ayala has another fine game, going two quiet innings and bringing Washington to bat in the eighth still trailing by only a run. The Phillies bring in Ugueth Urbina, whom the Nationals have hit hard in the series but have left intact. Guillen greets him with a long double beyond Lofton's reach in center field. Preston Wilson singles him home and goes to second base as the throw comes through to the catcher who has no play on Guillen. Carlos Baerga, who started the rally in the fifth inning, has another key hit, singling to center. Preston Wilson can be seen flying around third base as Kenny Lofton attempts a throw. Lofton does not have a strong arm and Wilson slides home easily with the go-ahead run. The Nationals lead 5-4 on an important and very clutch rally in head-to-head competition in August.

"They had their backs against the wall," says Ron Darling, announcing the game for the fans back home. "They have struggled to get the big hit all season long, but they came through."

"Now Stanton has got to get what could be the three biggest outs of the year," adds Mel Proctor.

Stanton gets Utley, who has had so many big hits during the series on a hard comebacker to the mound. Stanton looks more like a tired athlete, if an athlete at all, but he shows remarkable athleticism to snare the ball and flip it to first for the out. He gives Abreu a good pitch to hit, a slider up, and Abreu singles sharply, bringing Robinson out of the dugout and striding across the infield grass with a purpose that he has seldom shown all season. He motions for Cordero and brings in his closer an inning early, again leaving nothing to chance in this game that can give Washington something it so badly needs—a series split with Philly. Cordero throws only three pitches before Burrell grounds harmlessly to Guzman for an inning ending double play. Cordero pitches a quiet ninth as well, getting Howard swinging hopelessly and Pratt looking to end the game.

The win muddies the wild card race, putting the Nationals in the middle of it with the Phillies and Houston. Washington's cause is helped by an old friend. Tomo Ohka beats Roger Clemens in another game on Thursday evening. The loss levels the record for Houston and Washington and puts Philadelphia only a half game ahead. It is a loss that puts them in a tie with Washington. Ohka has pitched extremely well for Milwaukee and it brings to mind the remarks made by the Philadelphia announcers mulling whether hitters like Frank Robinson ever forgive the pitchers whom they oppose so fiercely for so many years.

## A New York Frame of Mind

The New York Mets are home to Carlos Beltran, Mike Piazza, and Pedro Martinez, some of the most expensive talent in the National League. Yet they

## 16. Baby, I Always Take the Long Way Home

are looking up at the rest of the NL East like tourists craning their necks in the canyons along 5th Avenue. The distance to the top is not that great, of course, and baseball's greatest legends revolve around 1st place teams that have folded in the heat of August and September to hand some interloper the pennant. The Mets fans have not given up and they arrive early to cheer their team in that inimitable New York style.

The Mets pitcher, Jae Seo, is a 28-year-old Korean who pitched against the Nationals twice at the beginning of the season. He won the first game in New York, but at RFK he lost after going only five innings. Shortly afterwards the Mets sent him to pitch in the minors. Since getting another shot at the rotation, he has pitched extremely well. In the first inning he starts a string of scoreless innings that last until the end of the game, as he and closer Brandon Looper shut out the Nationals. John Patterson pitches very well for Washington, but is not dominating as he has been several times during the season. He gives up only a single run over seven innings and Joey Eischen and Gary Majewski give the Nationals offense every opportunity, but the game ends a 1-0 disappointment.

More discouraging still is the next game in New York. Livan Hernandez, the all-star from the first half of the season who picked the team up when it was down, is awful in the second game against Pedro Martinez. Hernandez gives up eight runs in two innings, including three home runs—two by weak hitting Ramon Hernandez and Jose Reyes. The game gives insight into how the Friday night game might have gone had the Mets taken Jae Seo out for a pinch hitter late in the game. Against the Mets bullpen Washington scores eight runs themselves. Brian Schneider and Ryan Church account for six of the runs as the offense forces a tenth inning where Gary Majewski loses the game. New bullpen addition John Halama gives the Nationals a chance to come back and win it. The game goes down as a 9-8 New York win. The Nationals' record stands at 64 wins and 59 losses. They have lost all that their magic run in June gave them, only five games over .500, but they are certain to greatly exceed the 67 wins from 2004.

In the rubber match with the Mets, Brad Wilkerson, whose average has dipped consistently since the early months of the season, sits while Ryan Church gets the start in left field. He leads off in Wilkerson's spot in the third game with a double into the right field corner. It is the first of four doubles and four singles. First Jose Guillen and Preston Wilson rope line drives into the outfield in what is another fine first inning rally for Washington. Before the inning is over, the Nationals have a six run inning as they did the night before. The Mets pitcher, Kris Benson, pitches well, but the balls are finding the gaps and the open spots in the field. The Shea Stadium mood is quickly glum when even Cristian Guzman sends a ball up against the wall in right center and is brought in to score by the pitcher, Esteban Loaiza. Benson leaves to lusty boos from the fans, who forget so quickly the many quality starts he has contributed to the Mets season.

The Nationals' bullpen was one of their strengths. Frank Robinson used it wisely throughout the season.

Ron Darling, the Nationals' announcer, who pitched in New York for many years, says of the New York crowd, "They don't forgive a thing. They get your address, your telephone number, they never let you forget a thing."

"What do you think of those glasses Juan Padilla is wearing?" asks Mel Proctor of the pitcher who comes in to replace Benson.

"When you're a pitcher in New York, you don't want to draw too much attention to yourself," offers Darling.

Esteban Loaiza goes six innings in a gutty performance, as he is pitching in the sweltering heat on only three days rest. He makes one mistake and gives up a three run homer, but with two runners aboard in the sixth, he finds in himself just one more quality pitch to strike out Ramon Castro to end the treat. The Nationals add a run and the bullpen makes the seven runs stand up. It is the seventh win on the long 13-game road trip and the resurgent offense offers hope for the remainder of the season. Preston Wilson has changed the dynamic. Now there are three bats in the middle of the order to carry the team. The return of Ryan Church should help as well.

## 16. Baby, I Always Take the Long Way Home

After the last game of 2005, the players and fans applaud one another.

The sight of a small boy standing near the rail and loudly booing Danny Graves, the pitcher for the Mets, is another unfortunate commentary on the values that fans pass on to the younger generation. Perhaps those are the values of New York, part of the city's unique character, where studies document the level of stress produces the highest incidence of heart disease in the country. In Washington, booing even the worst performers on the team, such as Cristian Guzman, is not so quick to take hold. Somehow Nationals fans are still too appreciative of all the little joys of having a team. It is hard to imagine what level of derision New Yorkers would heap on Guzman were he playing in that tough town.

Washington fans might welcome the many luxuries the Mets take for granted. Those fans are still unable to follow the developing pennant race on television because Major League Baseball failed to force Peter Angelos to relent on his claim of sole TV rights in the Mid-Atlantic area. Nationals fans must search the local media coverage for their team, because D.C. sportscasters and commentators believe that the Redskins' preseason soap opera is of greater interest than baseball as it comes down the wire, the Nationals in the thick of the race. Yet the Nationals and their fans are resilient and will not be denied. The team has shown it can bounce back after a tough loss all season long, and the fans will be there again at RFK, tailgating in the same parking lots that once hosted the Skins, pouring out of the Stadium-Armory Metro Station until they are 30,000 strong for the Tuesday game with Cincinnati. It is D.C. baseball and it has a unique style of its own, taking root quietly but growing healthily.

# 17

# Staying the Course

The heat is gone and fans at RFK sigh in relief as they file into the cool and relaxed scene for the first game of the Cincinnati series. The saxophone man is riffing on "Take Me Out to the Ballgame," and no one is hurrying, but everyone seems to remember the humiliation from May when the Reds swept the Nationals in Cincinnati.

"We got to be able to beat the bad teams if we're gonna make the playoffs," says a fan walking toward the stadium.

"Yeah, they swept us there, it's time to return the favor," says the man standing next to him.

Inside the stadium the mood is of that of the relaxed sax player. Jose Guillen welcomes his old teammates warmly in right field, giving them some love before the game, all smiles as he points toward the center field stands daring his friend, Adam Dunn, to try to hit one out in his home park that has robbed him so many times. Ken Griffey is there, too.

"Look son, it's Griffey," says the Dad to his son about the son's favorite player.

"Hey, look, it's Ken Griffey," the boy says to his 12-year old mate. The boy sports a new mitt, its leather buff-colored from lack of use.

Griffey, Dunn, Guillen, and others stand and smile in the outfield grass before the game while Tony Armas plays long toss with Brian Schneider in left, getting ready for the game. Griffey has always been a favorite of kids, perhaps because of his own boyish looks that are there even now in the waning years of his career.

There are 35,000 fans for the game, and attendance will top 2 million during the home stand, with projections of almost 2.8 million for the season. The figure is several hundred thousand better than the best attendance figures in Montreal and slightly ahead of Baltimore's average attendance for the year to date. Baseball is in D.C. to stay. Washington is wearing the game like an old glove—found tucked away in the bottom of the closet—that still fits just fine.

Tony Armas starts the game for Washington in typically inconsistent style. Both of the first two batters tee off on his pitches. Then he retires the side, striking out Ken Griffey and Adam Dunn, the two biggest threats in the Cincinnati lineup. Vinny Castilla hits a home run in the bottom of the second inning to put the Nationals on top 1-0 and the fans begin to hope that Armas will right himself.

In the third inning, the pigeons come home to roost and Cincinnati bats around. Edwin Encarnacion, whose stellar play at third base begins the second inning, hits a long home run.

"Pitchers always get relaxed after their team homers," says an older black fan.

"Always happens that way," agrees his colleague as Encarnacion circles the bases.

John Patterson, one of the Nationals' emerging stars, pitches to the Cubs.

Armas does more than relax a little as the Reds bat around. Before the inning is over, four runs score and the score is 4-1. It appears a slugfest may be in the offing. Pitcher Luke Hudson contributes a single to the rally in the third, but it is his mastery of the Nationals that is the story of the night. Each inning as the Nationals come up to bat, the scoreboard flashes the number of runs Hudson has averaged so far in the season. The figure starts at well over seven runs per nine innings, but falls steadily as Washington goes quietly inning after inning.

In the fourth inning Washington tallies a second run. Jose Guillen hits a long home run to center field that makes the score 4-2, but it is the length of the prodigious blast that is remarkable. Wilson's gesturing to center field during warm-ups comes to mind. He seems to have talked Dunn and Griffey into believing his boast, but he shows them how it can be done with a ball that hits off of the façade of the second level above the 410 sign in dead center. The ball travels at close to 500 feet and is the longest poke of the season.

After Guillen's shot, with the fans still buzzing about the home run, the next batter, Preston Wilson, hits a high, high foul ball that carries into the stands behind third base. Ken Griffey's two 12-year-old fans have every fan's fantasy playing out before their eyes. The ball is arcing high above them, but coming straight at them, falling, falling, falling. In the last few feet both boys shield their heads, deploying their gloves like hats for protection. The ball strikes one above the knee and bounces into the second one. The ball skitters off and a melee to retrieve it ensues, but the young boy is holding his leg.

An usher appears and after conferring with the boy he holds up green cards to signify that the boy is okay. It is the same system used by soccer referees holding up a yellow or red card to signify a foul. Soon a physician on call for the evening arrives and talks to the boy and takes him away to look at what may be a nasty bruise.

"Why didn't you guys catch that ball?" asks the dad of his son who was seated next to the boy.

"I was scared," he says, smiling. "That ball is hard and it was falling from way high up."

"You had your glove?" questions the dad further.

"When it came down, we ducked, but it hit us anyway," he offers as his friend rounds the corner and heads out the exit ramp.

By the time the boy returns, the game is over. It ends for all intents and purposes on a blown hit and run play, the gambit that Billy Beane says is the most counter productive play employed by veteran managers. Vinny Castilla is hit by a pitch to reach first base. Cristian Guzman manages an awkward bunt single that just eludes the pitcher, but gets the job done. There are two runners aboard, on first and second base with no one out. It is an excellent chance to even the score and change the course of the game.

Jamey Carroll, who is the best bunter on the team, comes to the plate. Instead of the bunt Robinson signals what can only be assumed to be a double steal or a botched hit and run. The base runners are off with the pitch and Carroll must make contact with the ball or a slow runner like Castilla will be easily thrown out. Conversely, a bunt allows the runners to react to what the hitter does. If the bunt is successful, an out is recorded, but the runners move up to second and third. The offense has two subsequent batters to get them home. The risk level is lower and the ultimate benefit is much the same.

Cincinnati pitcher Luke Hudson throws Carroll a ball that is more than a foot off the plate. It does not look like a pitch out, but Carroll waves hopelessly and Castilla is out by a dozen feet. The crowd groans, because now there is only Guzman on second with one out. Carroll and Ryan Church strike out and the air can be seen escaping from the balloon.

The bruised young boy comes back wearing a sheepish grin and an ice pack on his knee. More importantly he is carrying a ball given to him by the Nationals. As he sits back in his seat, his young friend eagerly looks over the ball. The young boy has something that only Jose Guillen and he can take home from the game, a great story.

Luke Hudson has a win to take away, while the Nationals have nothing but another evening in the relative familiarity of their home park. The final score is 6-2 and on the postgame show, Charlie Shays opines that it is not uncommon for a team after a long road trip to be lackluster and fatigued. He and the fans filing to their cars are certain better things are on the way.

It is up to John Patterson in the second game. Everyone is looking for someone to pick the team up after the loss the night before and Patterson seems the logical candidate. Patterson seems up to the task and also to welcome the opportunity. He comes out throwing an amazing array of quick breaking sliders and curves. But it is the location of the fastball that makes it work and he seems to be able to put it exactly where he wants it on Wednesday night at RFK. By the third inning he has struck out four of the best hitters in the league. Washington takes a quick 1-0 lead in the first inning on Ryan Church's single and a Nick Johnson double.

Cincinnati has the most dangerous offensive team in the National League, with more home runs and runs scored than any other NL team. It is their pitching that has held them back, but against the Nationals, the Reds' pitchers rise to the occasion. Patterson, conversely, fails to hold his concentration. In the third inning, Patterson's curve starts to lose its bite and he loses the ability to spot the fastball. He gives up two hits and a single run that ties the score at 1-1. Jose Guillen gets a long solo home run in the bottom of the fourth to put the Nationals back on top 2-1.

Patterson continues to struggle with his command. To get ahead of the hitters he is forced to throw fastballs down the middle of the plate. His 94-mph fastball is a good pitch, but the potent Cincinnati offense put multiple runners on base in the sixth and seventh. Though he has lost his best stuff,

Patterson gets two gutty outs with the bases loaded in the seventh. He is visibly frustrated at one point and Brian Schneider goes out to talk briefly, which seems to settle him.

Patterson's battery mate, Schneider, provides a clutch two out single to get a rally off the ground in the bottom of the seventh and Vinny Castilla follows with another bases loaded hit and suddenly Patterson has a 5-1 lead.

The change in Patterson is uncanny. With a four run cushion he is aggressive again and pitches a quick, one-two-three eighth inning. In the ninth, after 110 pitches, he blows away Sean Casey with a 93-mph fastball. But it is all he has left and against the next two batters he gives up a double and a home run. Robinson takes Patterson out and the fans give him a grateful standing ovation. He doffs his cap as he exits. Pitching with a 5-3 lead Chad Cordero strikes out the final two batters and together he and Patterson put together an impressive effort. As Ron Darling intones after the game, Patterson is maturing and showing that he wants to pitch in tough situations.

In postgame interviews, Patterson admits to *Washington Post* reporter Barry Svrluga that the pressure of pitching in such tight games is getting to him, that the need to make pitch after pitch to keep the team in the game is wearing. The apparent frustration that brought Brian Schneider to the mound in the seventh was real. It is important that Schneider pick up his battery mate in the bottom of the inning with the two-out, run-scoring single. Team building exercises go on all over Washington every day accompanied by PowerPoint slides and contractor gibberish, but Schneider's exhibition is one of the best on display anywhere.

Reporters describe Patterson as "lanky," but he is showing the team and the rest of the league that skinny kids can pitch, and more importantly he is showing the RFK faithful that this skinny kid has a huge heart. The pitching staff needs the lift, needs the gutsy performance. It is beat up, with Luis Ayala and Tony Armas hurting and Ryan Drese on the disabled list with shoulder problems. Patching together something that will get the team out of August will be a huge challenge for Frank Robinson.

After the lift of the Patterson victory and the offensive surge that accompanied it, the fans are hoping that they can salvage their pride against Cincinnati, take the series and develop the continuity at home that they had early in the season. Livan Hernandez is pitching. It is the kind of situation that so often turned the tide early in the season. A great game from Hernandez was almost money in the bank. The fans are hoping his recent struggles are an aberration, that he will find himself somehow, and the threesome of Patterson, Loaiza and Hernandez will lead them through August and September into contention on those final days of the season.

The sentiment pervades several columns in the *Washington Post* and other papers still optimistic, still hoping there is a little magic left. Wilbon of the

*Post* calls winning the post-season wild card selection, "a doable proposition." The remarkable crowd exceeds 40,000 fans for the Thursday afternoon game. They either believe Wilbon's editorial or they are there because the mild temperatures and beautiful weather are just too good for them to stay in the office. The game at RFK is too great an opportunity to enjoy the weather, and neither the federal workforce nor the K-street lawyers can be penned in their cubicles or held by secretaries in their offices. They spill out of their buildings for lunch and do not return, phoning in from the ballpark that "something has come up."

The camera crew that roams the stadium doing interviews and providing "B" roll footage during the games displays men in ties with "doctor's appointment" screened across their guilty looking grins. The faces do have that look of a teen who has snuck out the back door of the school after lunch. One of these truants passes through the turnstiles and as the laser reader scans the ticket it sends in the signal for the 2 millionth fan at RFK. There is in the cool temperatures a feeling of success when Hernandez takes the mound to start the first inning.

The mood dispels like smokers in a high school bathroom when the assistant principal enters the door. Cincinnati puts the first two runners on base and there is Ken Griffey staring out at Livan Hernandez, cranking his bat around his head waiting, waiting. Yet somehow Hernandez squeaks past Griffey and just as luckily past Adam Dunn of the 34 home runs. But he is suddenly tentative pitching to Sean Casey and Austin Kearns. He walks them both. The base on balls to Kearns forces in a run and inexplicably the Nationals are down 1-0. Hernandez bounces back to strike out the catcher, Larue, with the bases loaded and the damage is not awful.

There have been many games like this during the season. Hernandez struggles in the first inning and then rights himself to pitch a masterpiece. It is still easy for the fans to see that Livan Hernandez, and they breath easy once again. The Nationals tie the score at 1-1 in the bottom of the second inning on a clutch hit by Jamey Carroll, and Livan Hernandez follows with one of his own. Suddenly the crowd is sitting forward in their seats expectantly. But Wilkerson flies out to left to end the inning.

The Nationals have additional opportunities as they push runners to third base in the fourth and sixth innings, but cannot get a key hit. Livan Hernandez is pitching more on heart than on sound legs and his command is clearly off. He strikes out the side in the fifth inning and it looks suddenly as if he has found himself, but then an inning later he gives up a run on three hits and in the seventh cannot get out a single batter as Griffey leads off with a line drive home run to right. Then he plunks Adam Dunn with a pitch. Robinson marches to the mound and Hernandez leaves without the display of frustration. There are no gloves tossed in the stands. It is just 3-1 on a lazy day in August and too laid back for raucous emotion.

## 17. Staying the Course

**Livan Hernandez's long walk to the dugout provided drama many times during the 2005 session.**

The score runs to 5-1 before the inning is over and the 40,000 fans start heading for home or back to the office. Wilkerson hits a two run home run in the ninth inning to bring the Nationals within two runs, but by now the fans are gone, only the faithful left gathered behind the dugout to cheer as he heads to the dugout after the blow. The Nationals make the final two outs easily and there are no jumping fans, no cheering throngs leaving the stadium after the game. The Reds win the series and have an uncanny knack against the Nationals.

They brought Washington low in May, and it is just this sequence of games, three with Cincinnati followed by three with the Cardinals, that put the team below .500 for the first time after the home opener. After losing this second series to Cincinnati, Washington is headed for another emotional pit, this one in the cellar of the NL East. It has been more than two months since they ascended to the top of the league. It has been a long road to the bottom. There are no headlines. The local papers avoid drawing attention to their plight, preferring to keep up the fantasy that the team is still in the wild card race, still in contention.

On Friday night, with the Cardinals taking batting practice, the sun is fading and the air is so cool and crisp that it is hard to imagine a better night for baseball or anything else. The overcast sky is a gray overcoat with a pink lining peeking through as the sun sets somewhere in the west unseen. There are red hats and jerseys for the many Cardinal fans in attendance. Wearing Ozzie Smith or Mark McGwire jerseys they are tailgating joyfully in the parking lot, dozens gathered in around the rear of SUVs. These fans are the product of our mobile society, displaced Missouri area natives loyal to those great teams from somewhere earlier in their life.

It is hard to remember back to that Sunday in May when the game against St. Louis seemed so important, as though the whole season hung in the balance. The promising start from April and May was a precarious thread waiting to be run through the eye of a needle that led to June. The road trip to Cincinnati and St. Louis was the first real disaster of the year. The team was four games over .500 going into Cincinnati, but after losing five in a row had its first losing record. All that was left was that great Sunday game between Livan Hernandez and Chris Carpenter, the Cardinal ace, before the return home.

The Cardinal team that comes to Washington in August is not the same team. It still sports the best record in the National League, but it is a team devastated by injuries. Scott Rolen, their all-star third baseman, is out for the season after shoulder surgery. Right fielder Reggie Sanders is on the 15-day disabled list and starting second baseman Mark Grudzielanek has missed numerous games with a bum knee.

Even the weakened Cardinals are winning. Albert Pujols is still in the middle of the lineup, as is Jim Edmonds. Pesky David Eckstein is still there at the top of the order to confound Nationals pitchers and he starts the Friday night game against Esteban Loaiza with a single. Like Hernandez on Thursday, Loaiza puts the first two runners on base. With no one out, Pujols comes to the plate arguably the most dangerous hitter in the game. He sends a ball high and deep into the dusk that appears headed over the center field wall. Whatever force has killed these high deep drives, this is just one more fly ball to the warning track and it settles into Jose Guillen's glove for the first out. Edmonds hits the ball well also, but the line drive is right at Nick Johnson, who gloves it and doubles Larry Walker off the bag to end the inning. Unlike Hernandez on Thursday, Loaiza slowly works himself into form in the second and third innings. By the fourth and fifth innings he is the dominating pitcher that Washington fans have seen on numerous occasions, striking out five of the six batters he faces.

The Nationals batters look much better against Jeff Suppan, the Cardinal pitcher. Brad Wilkerson starts the game by hitting a sharp line drive that carries over the bullpen wall in right field to give Washington a 1-0 lead. Suppan struggles in the inning but it is not until the fourth that the Nationals focus in and get three singles to lead off the inning. Though Castilla grounds into a double play, a run scores and the last run in the inning is batted in by Loaiza with the bases loaded and two out to give Washington a 3-0 lead.

Loaiza's hit ignites the RFK faithful. There are fans high fiving as the third run crosses the plate. The beautiful evening has brought out 36,000 fans, but the bright lights have attracted as many insects as there are fans. The moths are in some ritual ecstasy of their brief cycle and they are spinning and darting everywhere in the sky above the field. As the game progresses they begin landing in the hair and ears of the fans and distracting the hitters at the plate. One little girl dances from her seat in horror, shaking her leg loosely until a moth is dislodged from beneath her flip flop where it wedged against her foot.

Her theatrics are forgotten when Jose Guillen brings the faithful to their feet with another long shot into center field. The stadium holds this drive but Jim Edmonds cannot take it in over his shoulder on the warning track. It bounces against the wall and before Edmonds can run it down Guillen stands on third base. He scores when former Expo Larry Walker runs down Preston Wilson's long line drive in the gap.

Loaiza makes the 4-0 lead hold up, although he gives up a single run in the seventh after tiring. Chad Cordero comes in for what are becoming infrequent appearances, but he pitches a perfect ninth to close out the win. The fireworks above center field spew colored lights into the night to celebrate the win. It is a short game, well under three hours. There is plenty of weekend left for the Cardinal fans in town to watch their league leading team.

There is more to cheer them before the weekend is over. Washington's rotation is depleted by injury and several players are called up from New Orleans during the week. One is Marlon Byrd, who has played well in the minor leagues after his demotion. Another is Matt White, whose name cannot be remembered by Frank Robinson, but he is scheduled to start the second game against the Cardinals.

Both White, who starts the Saturday game, and John Halama, who pitches on Sunday, hold up well against the makeshift Cardinal lineup. Halama has to face Pujols only once after Pujols is ejected from the Sunday game, arguing doggedly with the second base umpire over a close call. Yet it matters very little. The Cardinals put on a clinic for how to score runs with little or no offense. On Saturday they manage only eight hits and only two extra base hits, but with patience at the plate and timely hitting they score six times.

The highlight of the lesson is on Sunday when Pujols—their cleanup hitter—is replaced with weak hitting Einar Diaz. The advantage swings to Washington. The Cardinals have been forced to pitch Cal Eldred much the way Washington is using John Halama. Both are now journeymen relievers being used as starters. Eldred's storied potential and persistence to return after a horrible injury are discussed in the LaRussa book. He puts in a performance that is worthy of Bissinger's praise, holding the Nationals in check until the fourth, when a crucial mistake cements the direction of the game.

Eldred gives up nothing until the fourth when singles by Jamey Carroll and Nick Johnson to start the inning are enough for LaRussa, who goes to his bullpen to bring in 23-year-old sinkerball reliever Brad Thompson. Thompson works out of the jam with some help from the Nationals, who are impatient and cannot keep the pressure on the Cardinals. With two on and no one out, Guillen, the cleanup hitter, tries to push a bunt out beyond the pitcher for a hit. He seems to catch his teammates by surprise and the bunt is fielded easily by the pitcher, who fires to second for the first out and barely misses doubling Guillen at first base. Wilson hits into a double play and the rally is over.

Conversely, in the sixth inning the Cardinals provide a primer on how to maintain an even approach and they use every trick they have to score runs. David Eckstein leads off the inning with a long double into the left field gap. During the series he is the most consistent source of offense for St. Louis. It is not Pujols or Edmonds who win the games so much as Eckstein. With Eckstein standing on second, Edmonds refuses to bite and Halama walks him rather than let the only strong hitter still in the Cardinal lineup beat him. It is the same situation the Nationals had. Runners on first and second with no outs. Frank Robinson brings in Hector Carrasco from the left field bullpen.

John Rodriguez is patient at the plate and forces Carrasco to throw strikes. He nibbles and cannot get Rodriguez to chase a pitch. Rodriguez walks to load the bases. The first run scores on a weak grounder to short that Guzman cannot convert into an inning ending double play. Then LaRussa forces the issue. It is not statistics, nor is it instinct. It is chess, a game of ancient strategy, and after Robinson allows LaRussa to seize the initiative, LaRussa does not give it back. LaRussa sends Molina, a catcher, though fleet footed, from first in a straight steal. Either Bennett has not done his homework or he is just napping. Whatever his reason, he throws through to second base without even looking at Edmonds on third. Edmonds is edging down the line as Bennett rises from his crouch and as soon as Bennett commits Edmonds charges for the plate. Bennett's throw to second is a poor one, and Edmonds scores easily before Jamey Carroll can throw back to home.

The game is a comedy of errors. It is a study in contrasts against the attentive and measured approach used by LaRussa. He is watching and waiting, and when the opportunity presents itself he seizes it. Robinson's team is impulsive and undisciplined and they waste their chances. The Sunday game ends with the final score once again 6-0, and the lack of a close score is truly indicative of the gulf between the two teams.

Whatever energy was generated by the Friday night win is long forgotten. Rather than having momentum in their favor as they had in May, now the Nationals' momentum is all going the wrong way as they head to Atlanta

## 17. Staying the Course

**The Cardinals always draw big crowds when they come to town.**

for a three game series against the team with the best home record in the National League. They are slipping further and further back, and the race is no longer for the wild card, it is for respect. They have a tenuous hold on that respect, fashioned by their two remaining aces, Esteban Loaiza and John Patterson. Brian Schneider is the only position player still playing a brand of baseball that warrants special attention. Jose Guillen and Preston Wilson are playing hard and getting hits, but their impatient approach at the plate wastes some of the excellent energy they generate. Even Nick Johnson is making mental errors and leaving runners in scoring position consistently.

While the team is sliding downhill, losing the hard fought heights, there are numerous issues being discussed around town that have important ramifications for the longer term directions baseball in Washington, D.C., will take. There is progress on contractual agreements surrounding construction of the new stadium, but more importantly, news reports discuss the lease for the new stadium. The terms of the lease are being negotiated between Major League Baseball, Inc., and the D.C. Sports Commission that oversees operations at RFK and will play the same role at the new stadium. MLB states that

**Bands for all the uniformed services played at RFK in 2005.**

the lease must be in place before they will announce new ownership. That announcement has been pushed back several times over the course of the summer. Most recently the date was pushed back while MLB looked for ways to drive up the price and bask in the revenues pouring in from Washington fans.

On Sunday morning there are two articles in the news discussing the *Moneyball* directions some in the game are moving toward. Dave Sheinin, in the *Washington Post*, discusses at length the sacrifice bunt and when, if ever, it is worth giving the other team the free out a sacrifice entails. In the *New York Times*, an article in the editorial section celebrates the pitched battle waged between the traditionalists and the stat heads. It is clear from everything said in the articles that Robinson and the rest of Washington's management team are firmly rooted in the traditionalist camp.

It matters not so much whether Frank Robinson is a traditionalist. It matters more that his team does not execute any strategy, new or old, particularly well. Frank Robinson is correct when he says that ultimately the players have to play the game. It is up to them. Tony LaRussa says as much in his book, and admits that he does little to influence the outcome of the games; his book is filled with his abiding frustration when his players fail to execute the most fundamental of plays. Yet in the end, it does not seem to be one philosophy that is so much better than the other, but rather that organizations

**The view from the highest part RFK stadium.**

like Oakland's are from top to bottom the best possible expression of Beane's philosophy. He has tailored his team to his specifications and it works.

Bobby Cox and the many excellent *traditionalist* baseball people in the Atlanta organization are on the other pole from Beane. The Braves are remarkably successful because they have an intelligent, if very traditional, plan, and they execute it well whether it is in Richmond where their Triple-A team plays or in Atlanta. They use great scouting and player development, while Beane discounts these same commodities for computer analysis. Both Beane and his counterpart in Atlanta, John Schuerholz, are successful because they do a good job with their chosen approach and they do it at all levels of their organization. Both Oakland and Atlanta are known for the strength of their organizations, so whether they are doing it with computers or Ouija boards, the end products are remarkably similar where it counts.

Washington cannot compete yet with such top to bottom excellence. Their minor league system is not able to produce the filler material that both St. Louis and Atlanta can. It will take many years to craft a minor league system that has the depth of Atlanta's or Oakland's. Yet teams like Florida and Arizona have been able to field excellent teams very quickly, to win the World

Series within years of entering the league. Washington can do as well, but they have yet to decide which path they will take because Major League Baseball is still pulling the strings, Like a mother who cannot cut the apron strings on her fair haired child, Bud Selig cannot give up control. He is still writing into the contracts with the new owners his own personal philosophy of baseball and its corporate character. Selig cannot let the city develop its own baseball personality, traditional or nouveau. It is Washinton's decision how it will play the game, not Bud Selig's. Yet it remains to be seen whether he will ever give up control. Washington fans have no choice but to stay the course.

# 18

# Cry Me a River

The month of August ends with a four game series in Atlanta at Ted Turner Field. There are several Washington sportswriters, Tom Boswell, Wilbon, and others, who are still holding forth publicly that the team can compete for the wild card play-off spot, but many fans suspect they know better. The Nationals *are* in a remarkably strong position strategically. If it were a horse race their position just behind the leaders nearing the stretch run might provoke hopeful yells for the jockey to step up the pace, ducats would be waved in the air along the rail and entreaties made, "You can do it big fella."

Yet the Nationals are not well positioned for the final move to the forefront; they are rather more like a broken horse that has managed to last this long only through heart and drive. The big fella is clearly laboring as he enters the stretch run, panting hard, and the jockey's face is lined with worry; the owners and bettors are wishing the track were shorter, wincing as they watch their prize thoroughbred falling further and further off the pace.

For Nationals fans the Atlanta series has the cruelty of a Christmas outing with Richie Rich to FAO Schwarz. The Braves have their organization shelves stocked with much of the best young talent in the major leagues. Washington has played wonderful veterans like Vinny Castilla a Braves castoff, all year. Even when injuries to their regulars were a clear impediment to their play on the field, they have gone out day after day because there was no help from the minors.

Contrast this with the Braves, whose veteran outfielder, Brian Jordan, was immediately put on the disabled list when nagging injuries affected his play. In his place and that of other poor-performing veterans like Raul Mondesi have come Kelly Johnson, Ryan Langerhans, and, most notably Jeff Francoeur. Washington's great thoroughbred, Livan Hernandez, should have been disabled several times so that his knee could rest for the stretch run, but there was no talented New Orleans minor league roster brimming with young talent waiting for a chance to spell him.

The Nationals' toy chest is bare. In Atlanta, when pitchers like Mike Hampton and Tim Hudson are beset by injuries, they call up pitchers from their minor league franchise hopefully, and give them a chance to mentor with Leo Mazzone. Young pitchers like Jorge Sosa, like so many others before him, have a unique opportunity to turn their careers around under his tutelage. Mazzone, like Dave Duncan in St. Louis, is just part of the organizational strength that it takes to endure the long season successfully, to find within the structure of the team the resources to keep going, to be ready when the final run stretches out before you and the finish line is in sight. You must have plenty in reserve and the Braves are living in the land of plenty.

Jorge Sosa is the starting pitcher in the first game of the series scheduled for Tuesday. Under Mazzone's watchful eye, Sosa leads the Braves in earned run average and has begun to realize a modicum of the promise in his strong right arm. The Tuesday game is rained out by a torrential downpower reaching up from the Gulf of Mexico as Hurricane Katrina makes its historic landfall. The storm lets loose along the Gulf a fury that will last far beyond the September stretch run and go down as one of the great natural disasters and human tragedies of the 21st century. Wednesday gives each team a welcome day of rest and Sosa starts the game against the Nationals looking fit and getting three quick outs in the first inning.

John Patterson pitches for the Nationals and is emerging as the ace of the Washington staff. Yet he is still a young man and, while Ron Darling has been charting his maturation as the season progresses, there is still work to be done, if only physically. In the third inning of a scoreless tie, Patterson is sweating profusely in the humid subtropical night and the sharp breaking curve and well-placed fastballs begin to wander in the strike zone. That becomes clear when he walks Jorge Sosa on four balls well out of the strike zone after giving up a leadoff double. He labors through three more batters, giving up a walk and a single that gives Atlanta a 1-0 lead. After a walk to Chipper Jones he motions and, as Brian Schneider is coming to the mound, Patterson motions to the dugout, beckoning the trainer to the mound. The collective hopes of the Nationals for the season turn to vapor and are fast headed for the open window.

As enigmatic as ever, Patterson seems to recover after talking with the trainer. He throws a few warm-up pitches and pronounces himself ready to go. He walks Andruw Jones, however, and Frank Robinson is willing to take no more chances with an important game and an important player like Patterson. He brings in rookie pitcher Jason Bergmann from the Washington bullpen. Bergmann is the Nationals answer to Jorge Sosa. The Rutgers star has never been charted anywhere as a promising pitcher but has risen quickly through the Nationals system to arrive in Atlanta at the end of August. He quickly dispatches Adam LaRoche to end the inning with Washington behind by only a 2-0 score.

Much is anticipated about Jose Guillen's first at bat against the Braves. His take-out slide in Washington against Chipper Jones has been replayed on all of the ESPN shows as well as Jones's indignant remarks about dirty play and retaliation in the future. Guillen does not back off an inch and when Sosa dusts him with a pitch he answers quickly with a solo home run into the left field stands of Turner Field. It is made more remarkable because the first pitch after the pitch at his head he hits long and foul. The intensity to take the very next inside pitch and drive it long, hard and fair is something difficult to imagine for the average person. It makes the score 2-1 and signals an end to Jorge Sosa. In the next inning, doubles by Jose Vidro and Nick Johnson follow a single by Jay Bergmann and two runs cross the plate for the Nationals to give them the lead 3-2. Bergmann makes it stand up and with help from the usual

**Guillen, after the brush back, drives the next one into the left field stands to bring the Nationals back against the Braves.**

bullpen suspects, Carrasco, Majewski, and Cordero, the Nationals record a surprising win in the opener of the series.

The series continues on Thursday with a double header. The rainout allows Washington to skip a turn in the rotation and to pitch Loaiza and Livan Hernandez for the two Thursday games. Loaiza goes against another young Atlanta pitcher Horacio Ramirez, who outpitches the Nationals veteran. Ramirez lost well-pitched games to the Nationals in April and June and the statistical probabilities catch up with Washington by a score of 5-3. The difference in the game, though, is Andruw Jones. His is the long and enduring magical season. His first inning home run against Loaiza makes the score 3-0 and it is his 43rd home run of the year. He is on a pace to reach the pre-steroid era mythic figure of 50 home runs in a season.

When the Nationals tie the score in the game 3-3 in the top of the fifth inning on a solo homer by Marlon Byrd, one of three hits by him on the day, Andruw Jones answers in the bottom of the inning. With one out and runners on first and second, he singles and both runners score. It chases Loaiza from the game. Though the Nationals bullpen is again perfect, Andruw Jones beats Washington 5-3. He is being mentioned as the Most Valuable Player of the Year and clearly no other player is more important to this Atlanta team. Albert Pujols and Andruw Jones will give the hot stove types something to argue over for many years to come. "Who do you think was better, Pujols or Jones?"

"Jones is the greatest defensive center fielder ever to play the game," opines Ron Darling, because, "He can go back on the ball as well as come in, everyone else it's either one or the other. Only Andruw Jones can do both."

With the offensive surge that he has shown during the 2005 season, the scales seem to be tipping toward Jones for the present.

The nighttime is the right time and Livan Hernandez is the one we love. His teammates show him some early love by getting him a one run lead in the first inning on a long double into the corner by Preston Wilson. Hernandez immediately gives the advantage back to the Braves when he allows a run on two singles and a sacrifice fly by Chipper Jones. But he does not allow Andruw Jones to hurt him, getting him on a double play to end the inning. John Thomson, the Braves pitcher, is clearly outclassed. He allows multiple base runners in every inning and the Nationals end the game with eleven hits. Yet their base-running blunders continue to hurt them in every game. They are thrown out stealing in poorly advised hit and runs; they venture too far off bases as Castilla does constantly in an attempt to play even on his gimpy legs. Andruw Jones fires behind him to cut him down, though, and the Braves' young catcher catches Washington runners napping as well.

Yet it is base running that wins the game eventually. To start the ninth inning Brad Wilkerson leads off with a single against Atlanta closer Chris

Reitsma. Vidro sacrifices him to second. Then when Reitsma takes him for granted, Wilkerson slips further from the second base bag until he has a walking lead and he takes off for third. Atlanta catcher Brian McCann, who is known for his defense, hurries to compensate for the great jump Wilkerson has gotten. His throw sails into left field and Wilkerson scores easily with the go ahead run. Jose Guillen makes it all possible with a great throw to the plate in the eighth to get Adam LaRoche trying to score the go-ahead run and keep the score in tact. The bullpen again is the winning pitcher, this time Mike Stanton picking up the win in relief of Livan Hernandez, who pitched well enough to cheer the Washington faithful as the team heads into September.

The team ends the month of August winning fewer games than they lose and playing inconsistently. Yet there are still spots of brilliance, like Jose Guillen's maturation as a hitter and an adult. His handling of the brush back pitch and his continued strength both as a defensive player and with the bat are making him the best imitation of Andruw Jones that Washington has to offer. It is no cheap comparison and Guillen is starting to earn that kind of consideration.

The final game of the series can provide only faint praise for the Braves. They must win to salvage a split against Washington, not only for the series but also for the year. For all of the vaunted youthful excellence of the Braves, the Nationals bullpen and Jose Guillen have been the best ticket in town. The final game offers a match-up that tilts heavily toward Atlanta, however. John Smoltz, still the ace of the Braves, goes against Tony Armas, who is still struggling to justify the buzz that he once generated as a young prospect.

The *Post* runs a beautiful photo above the masthead on page one of the sports pages the next morning that sums up much of the final game. Tony Armas is featured in the shot, wiping his brow in the third inning when he gives up five runs and dooms the Nationals' chances early on. The angle of his head thrusts his nose into his armpit and it is hard not to say in looking at the photo, "Yes, Tony, you stink." The Nationals show immense character in the game. They know how important the series is and how much it could do to give them a shot of momentum if they could win on the road against Atlanta. They scratch and claw back from the 7-1 hole that Armas digs for the Nationals, giving up home runs to Jeff Francoeur, the rookie sensation, and Chipper Jones.

A run scoring hit by Brian Schneider makes the score 7-3 in the fourth inning. Then after Jay Bergmann dispatches the Braves quietly again, the Nationals hitters take an approach in the seventh that has been missing since June. Marlon Byrd continues to hit the ball hard and starts the inning with a double into the corner through Chipper Jones. Jamey Carroll takes a pitch the other way for the same single he has gotten dozens of times during the season and Brad Wilkerson is hit by a pitch to put two runners aboard with two outs. Jose Guillen comes to the plate.

During the course of the season this situation has presented itself many, many times. Jose Guillen has forced the issue in almost every one of them even when he has been successful. He swings wildly, attempting to make something happen with his potent bat. It is an approach that makes sense for the thin offense, but National League pitchers began early in the season to pitch around him more and more. He is forced to swing more and more often at pitches well off the plate to have an impact and he has been both stubborn and impulsive enough to oblige the opposition by making key outs more often than he has gotten key hits. It is part of baseball. It is a tough game and one of inches. The difference between Andruw Jones and Jose Guillen is not fields apart but just inches. Guillen shows that, maybe, he can push the bar higher as he gets older as a player.

Guillen lays off the pitches and takes a walk. Even though there are two outs, he takes a pitch with the bases loaded and walks in a single run to make the score 7-4. Yet it leaves the door open for much more. Pressing many times during the season to do too much, he has swung at pitches far out of the strike zone for easy outs, but he keeps the rally going this time. Nick Johnson takes a walks to force in another run, which gives Vinny Castilla the chance to knock in two more runs with his second RBI single of the day. It is the best offensive showing by the team in two weeks.

Then it is the Atlanta youth movement's day in the sun again. Kyle Davies, called up from Richmond the previous day, comes in and shuts the door that Reitsma, Kolb and others had opened. Then, the sparkling jewel in the Atlanta crown, Andruw Jones, homers in the 10th inning to win the game. It is the first and only run the Washington bullpen surrenders to Atlanta, but it gives the Braves the split. It is a bad win for them, but a tougher loss for the Nationals.

## The Army Navy Surplus Store

After the game, a realization settles in that is captured well by Dave Sheinin in the *Washington Post* the next morning. Describing the outfielders walking in after Andruw Jones's final blow, he paints the picture as one of "near hopelessness" for the Nationals' situation in 2005. Sheinin's pronouncement is not as dire as it sounds, though he does note the emerging gravitas of Jose Guillen. The team still has four more victories on the season than losses, a mark that is many wins better than anyone imagined. That the team's record at this juncture in the season is even discussed in the same breath with the word "play-offs" is remarkable. Jose Guillen's longing last look at Ted Turner Field has meaning to him no one can know, but one suspects that he knows he reached an important watershed in his professional career during the series.

There are pictures taken from the series that can be downloaded into the computer and mulled as to their meaning more easily. One photo is that of Jim Bowden talking in the booth to Ron Darling and Mel Proctor and the accompanying shot of Bowden in the stands with a drop dead gorgeous blonde who gets none of the attribution provided for earlier shots of him with his children in Cincinnati and Washington. Bowden discusses in the on-air interview the moves that the team has made. They have traded for a new shortstop, Devi Cruz, and they have brought up first round draft pick Ryan Zimmerman, who strikes out during the game while the proud Bowden looks on.

During the discussion of Zimmerman, Bowden responds to Barry Larkin's role in the scouting of Zimmerman with words of praise. It is reminiscent of an earlier session when Hernandez was pitching on Wednesday.

"Did you know Hernandez was this good going into the season?" Ron Darling asks.

Bowden answers affirmatively, but on the field, as Hernandez breaks off a beautiful slow curve for a strike on the inside corner, he says, "Yes, he reminds me so much of Jose Rijo that I had in Cincinnati, who could throw that same slow curve."

Like a divorcee who cannot stop talking about his ex-wife in a singles bar Bowden keeps talking about Cincinnati. First it is Larkin and then it is Rijo—always about the connection to Cincinnati, to his first love. During the segments, Bowden discusses the future of the Nationals intelligently and openly, citing the need to develop a strong organization from top to bottom, the need for more players of Zimmerman's character. He acknowledges these tasks will need to be the immediate focus of whoever the general manager for the Nationals may be in the future.

Bowden is a talented man, but his ability to put his intellect into action is problematic. Devi Cruz is hardly an improvement over Cristian Guzman. He is another veteran on the down side of his career. It was injury to veteran second baseman Jose Vidro—whom Cruz will replace—that cost the team Tomo Ohka. Bowden has insisted on the presence of veterans like Castilla to buoy the hopes of the fans. Castilla, Vidro, and Livan Hernandez have provided thrilling play over the course of the season, but all three are beat up, and during the second half of the season the inability for them to take a break from play while they heal has cost the team. The immediate problem is the lack of quality reserves and a weak minor league system. Bowden knows it is a problem, but has done nothing to address it.

Bowden talks of Ryan Zimmerman like he is a whole minor league system. He may be as good as Bowden says, but he is no substitute for the draft pick compensation that MLB has refused the Nationals since taking over the team. The *Post* addresses the issue of MLB abuse of the Nationals/Expos for the first time in an article by Barry Svrluga. The team is limiting the number of young players who will be called up during the September roster expansion.

Each September, the roster limits are relaxed to allow teams to include their best minor league players for a few weeks. MLB has placed a ceiling on the call-ups. Svrluga writes:

> *The issue of call-ups is a sensitive one in the Nationals' clubhouse because the team still remembers the 2003 season, when MLB prohibited new additions even though the club, then the Montreal Expos, was in a pennant race.*
> *"It was frustrating," catcher Brian Schneider said.*
> *Told that additions to the roster were being delayed because of financial reasons, Schneider chose his words carefully.*
> *"The team is making a lot of money right now, "Schneider said." Just put it like that. Revenues are higher than predicted."*

The 2003 season was the first time that MLB betrayal of the Expos was overt and documented. The players remember it. It is not something anyone can do anything about, so none dwell on it. Yet, as the deadline for announcing new ownership is pushed back, as the opportunity for slipping the tight bonds of MLB, is lost, cracks are starting to show through the rich velvet curtain that Bud Selig and his court have pulled across the RFK stage. Resentment among players is surfacing that has been there for seasons. The players are savvy and hear all of the rumors. Schneider and others may worry that not only will Bud Selig postpone the announcement of new owners, but they also may be concerned about what ownership will bring when it comes. That story of how MLB, Inc., has played the team cheap is waiting to be written, and it looks more promising that local writers will finally cover it.

The Philadelphia series brings the Nationals back to RFK for a 10-game home stand. Vincente Padilla, the young Nicaraguan pitcher who dominated Washington in a game in mid-August, starts against John Halama for the Nationals. Halama is another example of Bowden's Annie Hall approach to managing the Washington roster. Halama was dropped by Boston after failing to fill the role of a left-handed reliever and spot starter. He drops into the slot vacated originally by Tomo Ohka, still pitching extremely well for Milwaukee, and replaced with Ryan Drese, who was released by Texas. Drese was the first Salvation Army pickup by Bowden that failed.

Halama has enduring value to the team because he can pitch as a left-handed reliever. However, he profiles remarkably like Matt White, who filled in as an emergency starter in August. The only real difference is that Halama makes $850,000 every year that he pitches, while White can be paid the major league minimum of $300,000. Bowden's economy from his days in Cincinnati is showing. The hundreds of thousands of dollars that he has wasted on Jeffrey Hammonds, Wil Cordero, Ryan Drese, and other "veterans," could be used for the weak scouting system and for recruiting Latin ballplayers—anything that would shore up the levees in New Orleans.

Halama matches Padilla in the early innings, but in the fourth he implodes, much the same way that Matt White could not survive the early innings. Frank Robinson brings in another Bowden veteran, Mike Stanton. Buying off the bargain racks really does not apply to Stanton since he is making a cool $4 million. His salary likely is twice what the rest of Washington's stellar bullpen corps is making for 2005 and is an excellent example of just how skewed the current salary structure of the game is toward teams that can find great young talent that earn only the major league minimum salary during their first few years in the league, and are not even eligible for salary arbitration. Teams like Oakland and Minnesota have thrived with their focus on youth that leverages their overall salary structure. Almost every team has bought into the economic inevitability of the numbers, only a few GMs like Jim Bowden believe they can afford to ignore it.

The core of excellence that has carried the Nationals all season is on display in the final two games against the Phillies. Pitching, pitching, and more pitching. John Patterson is as cool and crisp on the mound as the September weather that has made its way into RFK, seemingly to stay. Nationals fans are hoping they have a better chance to keep Patterson. He has talked about the stress of pitching in the many close games and said how much easier it is to pitch with a lead. The Nationals give him one in the first inning. Preston Wilson and Marlon Byrd follow a Devi Cruz double with run scoring hits to give Washington a 2-0 lead. Patterson gives a run back on a home run by Pat Burrell and has a 2-1 lead going into the eighth inning.

He maintains that lead and pitches with the same great stuff and determination that have marked almost every start in 2005, carrying the lead into the eighth inning. To start that inning he gets two quick outs, including his eighth strikeout. Yet he yields back-to-back singles to put the lead in jeopardy. Robinson goes to get him and brings in Joey Eischen, who gets Bobby Abreu swinging to end the threat. After the Nationals score two in the bottom of the eighth inning on clutch hits by Marlon Byrd and Gary Bennett the Nationals have a 4-1 lead. Chad Cordero comes into the game to pitch the ninth, and Patterson's win seems safe. Yet the "Chief" gives up back-to-back home runs to rookie Ryan Howard and veteran David Bell to tie the score at 4-4.

It is a dejected crowd that settles in for extra innings, some heading for the exits to sample more upbeat environs on a Saturday night. The Nationals have not won an extra-inning game since before the All-Star break and the odds on a win are long and the sun looks to have set on a good finish to the season. Even when Gary Majewski comes in and quiets the rambunctious Philly offense in the 10th and 11th innings, the mood is dark after the Nationals offense once again is on vacation. Hector Carrasco gets Washington through the 12th inning. In the bottom of the 12th, Preston Wilson redeems the offense

**Frank Robinson brings the hook.**

driving in the game-winning run. The mood rises as the believers who stayed for the game-ending rally leave satisfied that they may have seen a deciding moment in the Nationals' first season.

Esteban Loaiza had one of his best outings against Philadelphia in late April. He struck out 11 in that game and carried a shutout into the ninth inning before tiring. Then, stuck in a 0-0 tie, he gave up a three run homer to Jimmy Rollins that just cleared the left field bullpen wall. This time he is pitching in the series finale. The Sunday afternoon game will decide whether the prior evening's win will have any lasting value. Frank Robinson is determined that it will. His ban on music and frills in the clubhouse is featured in news stories and he puts down small rebellions, throws a wet blanket over ill will that has been simmering in some quarters, but most importantly, he sends Loaiza out to pitch on three days' rest. It is a gutsy decision and the game veteran Loaiza redeems his manager's confidence and keeps the mojo going for game two. This time when Esteban tires in the ninth, Frank Robinson takes him out still leading the game.

Loaiza's lead is a commanding one in the ninth. The offense reappears for the deciding game. In the second inning, Brian Schneider stands at the plate chewing a huge wad of gum and smacking off big bubbles, Vinny Castilla and Preston Wilson on base. Schneider hikes his sleeves, pumps his bat, and muscles a Gavin Floyd pitch out of the ballpark for a three run home run that is really all Loaiza needs. He strikes out Abreu twice; he strikes out Howard twice; he has complete command of the Phils lineup and it is September. His rep is that he is an April and May pitcher. It is September and he is pitching the best he has all season.

A highlight for the fans, the moment that decides the game and gets the fans back in the mood, occurs in the seventh inning. Preston Wilson catches a hanging curve, a flirt of a pitch that he hits as far as almost any other home run of the year. It carries into the upper deck in left field and lands in the first row of section 447. Three young fans grab the souvenir, celebrating their cheap seats with calls on their cell phones to describe to anyone who will listen what a great time they are having in $10 seats at RFK. Loaiza gives up a single run in the eighth, which ends the scoring. The two three-run homers give Washington a 6-1 win and the first series win against a NL East opponent since the All-Star break.

The July and August slide by Washington has produced losing records against every team in their division except Atlanta, with whom they have a single game advantage out of 15 games. Now the final month focuses play on all of these teams—Atlanta, Philadelphia, New York, and Florida—the NL East. The Monday Labor Day game brings Florida to town for a long four game series. Florida features Dontrelle Willis, who has won 18 games. He was once tied with Livan Hernandez for wins and innings. He has moved on, but Hernandez will have a chance to make the Fish remember him, as he will start the first game of the series. Willis will pitch in the third game on Wednesday and Josh Beckett will pitch against John Patterson on Thursday.

Livan Hernandez had his knee drained prior to his last start. It seems to be having a positive effect as he starts the game, getting ahead of hitters and spotting his fastball effectively.

"How about Livan Hernandez?" Mel Proctor says with the exuberance of a fan, in the end of the eighth inning, as Livan Hernandez pokes a ball to left field that falls into no-man's-land for a run scoring single to give the Nationals a 2-0 lead.

"How about Frank Robinson?" he asks in the next breath, acknowledging prescient manager Frank Robinson's insight for letting Hernandez bat in the pressure packed situation.

The game is near its conclusion after the usual tight contest, this one with the Nationals nursing a 1-0 lead since the first inning. Hernandez has made it stick until the eighth. Hernandez moves to second base after a walk to Wilkerson loads the bases. Then Marlon Byrd, whose bat has been smoldering since his recall from flood ravaged New Orleans, tags a ball that carries beyond the left fielder's outstretched glove and one-hops the wall for a three run double. The fans are jumping and everyone is celebrating a Labor Day victory over the Florida Marlins, who have spoiled so many moments for the Nationals.

Livan Hernandez pitches his best game of the year. There have been many Livan highlights for Washington, the great games where he bent but did not break in the first half when he won 12 games, when he was the very deserving All-Star who represented the team for its first mid-season classic. He is the most popular player on the team, but there is no bigger moment, no bigger win all season than the one on Labor Day. He gets two long-standing ovations during the game and he has had so many of them all year long it must seem common by now.

Hernandez gives up a two-run home run in the top of the ninth inning and departs with a 5-2 lead. Mike Stanton and Chad Cordero close out the game to give the Nationals their third straight win. Three wins in a row is the best streak the team has seen since August when Washington swept Colorado. They won four in a row then, but were unable to sustain the momentum. The problem was Hernandez. Whether it was his knee or his disposition, he was not right in August and his spot in the rotation hurt when it rolled around. With Hernandez back in top form, the three-man rotation that they could take into the play-offs is more intimidating.

# 19

# Just Another Turner Classic Movie

The Labor Day holiday marks the end of the summer holiday for children, and yellow school buses are back on the roads again. Like the fickle hearts of the young, the Nationals' fortunes in September run hot and cold. They win three in a row, including the first game of the Florida Marlins series. Yet no sooner do they begin to resemble the team that swept the Marlins during the June winning streak, than their bats go quiet as Sunday church. The excellent example Livan Hernandez sets in the opener of the Florida series is quickly lost on the rest of the staff, who collapse during the next three games.

The RFK crowd watches the season's hope begin to ebb away quietly. The crowd noise grows dimmer. The sounds are those of a great day in the park—people buzzing in their private conversations, smiling as they talk over the news of the day, thinking perhaps of the faces of the New Orleans evacuees, thinking of that specter haunting the great national conversation. There is much to talk about in Washington, not much to say about the Nationals as they slide toward October.

"You think Guzman is going to make .200?" asks the Methodist minister, disguised in a plaid shirt and Oklahoma Sooners hat.

"No way," says the sinner. "You think just because he's named Cristian, he can hit?"

The minister grins, "He could be the shortstop on my all-religious team. Let's see, I like Encarnacion, I could put him in center."

"I bet you a bag of peanuts Guzman never makes .200," says the sinner.

"You're on, my friend," says the minister.

Fans are settling into their own games as the Nationals game begins to slouch inexorably southward. The Florida series on the second day looks more like the early season series when the Marlins pitchers dominated and Miguel Cabrera tore it up. Even the early heroics by Brian Schneider are fast forgotten, as the top of the Florida lineup—Luis Castillo and Juan Pierre—are running the bases with abandon. In the second game Washington sends out Darrell Rasner, called up from Washington's Double A affiliate in Harrisburg, against Ismael Valdes. The untried rookie with nothing special going for him is at a huge disadvantage even against a journeyman put into the rotation in the place of Brian Moehler.

Rasner and the Nationals bullpen make it a fair fight, but after a two run home run by Wilkerson gets the Nationals within hailing distance at 3-2 the home team fails to mount a serious rally again in the game and loses 4-2. In the third game, the odds become more formidable as Dontrelle Willis goes for his 20th victory against John Halama. Like the Liston-Ali fight, it is over so fast that fans are left wondering how it happened. Frank Robinson takes Halama out in the first inning with two outs and only a single run in. It is another inexplicable Robinson move. He summons six relievers, and the bullpen, now on the verge of serious overuse, surrenders eleven runs over the course of the game. Every reliever is touched for runs as the game ends in a 12-1 embarrassment.

The final game of the series is notable only for Cristian Guzman's emergence from infamy. Mired the entire season below what is known as the "Mendoza Line," a batting average below .200, Guzman gets three hits in four at bats to push his average to .202. He and Jamey Carroll are the only hitters who manage multiple hits as young Josh Becket has another win against the Nationals. John Patterson fails to make it out of a very long fifth inning in what is his worst outing of the year. He surrenders seven runs in the 8-4 loss.

The Nationals are only three wins over .500. They are slipping once again, edging ever closer to the bottom of the NL East. Only the failures of the Mets and Phillies, who are on losing streaks of their own, keep the Nationals afloat. Houston and Florida are pulling ahead in the wild card race. Atlanta sits alone atop the NL East, like it is home, like baseball in the National League is nothing more than some Turner Classic Movie that everyone has seen before a dozen times.

The weekend series brings the Braves to town for three and it is more like a rowdy weekend at the drive-in than a classic movie. Before the first game is over, the Braves are trying to count how many Nationals snuck in without paying. The start of the games seems scripted enough. Esteban Loaiza gives up two runs in the first inning on three clutch two-out hits, one a double to Andruw Jones, who continues what will no doubt be the first of many notable career years. In the fourth inning Andruw Jones's three run home run pushes the lead to 6-1. The high fly ball carries just beyond the left field wall. Everyone knows the end of this movie.

Esteban Loaiza shows remarkable courage pitching into the sixth inning. He surrenders ten hits and six runs, but never seems to break a sweat. He delivers the game to the beleaguered bullpen and Jay Bergman again shows the promise that has marked most of his appearances in a Nationals uniform during the last part of the season. First he and then Gary Majewski keep the Braves in check. The Nationals add a run here, a run there; pretty soon it's a ballgame again. Marlon Byrd scratches out a single run, Cristian Guzman continues his torrid hitting and doubles in Devi Cruz, and Washington chases Atlanta's starting pitcher, Aramis Ramirez, after five innings, bringing the score back to 6-3. Vinny Castilla hits a solo home run in the seventh and the game is suddenly within reach, the score 6-4 going into the eighth inning.

The Atlanta bullpen has been inconsistent all year, but no more so than the Marlins and others that have easily held Washington's anemic offense in check. When Kyle Davies, another young player being groomed by the Braves organization, begins the eighth inning, the crowd at RFK stirs only slightly as they try to decide if there are more inviting places they need to be on a Saturday night other than under a cool night sky. Many decide to give the Nats just another few outs. They are not disappointed.

Ryan Church, who has not been healthy in weeks, pinch hits for Devi Cruz and does something Cruz would never have been able to pull off. He draws a four-pitch free pass to start the inning. Then, almost as startling, Cristian Guzman follows suit and forces Davies to throw the ball over the plate. Larry Young, the home plate umpire, is known to have a small strike zone and Washington exploits it. Atlanta lifts him and brings in the more seasoned pitcher, John Foster. Jamey Carroll, batting for Brandon Watson, sacrifices the two runners to second and third. Brad Wilkerson, who has begun to find his stroke in the last few weeks, gets his second hit of the evening, a double into the right field corner to score two runs. The score is tied and the fans are back in celebration mode, jumping and smiling.

Carlos Baerga pinch-hits and draws the third Washington walk in the inning to confound Bobby Cox, who shakes his head in the dugout. There are runners once again on first and second and Jose Guillen comes to the plate for the Nationals. He has failed to get runners in scoring position home in the first and third innings. He is a man who is hard on himself, so when he follows Wilkerson's lead and finds the right field corner with a line drive, he is dancing on second base as two runs cross the plate. Jose Guillen gestures to the dugout from second base like a kid who just learned to ride a two-wheeler, who wants his Dad to notice.

Everyone in the stands notices the 8-6 lead, and they can all spell C-h-i-e-f; that spells victory in the ninth inning and Chad Cordero. The loyal fans have been rewarded with a change in fortune as quirky as the difference between Guillen and Jones's fly balls. It is baseball. In the ninth inning the baseball gods continue to smile as Preston Wilson makes a beautiful running catch of a long drive against the left centerfield wall. Cordero strikes out the last two batters and suddenly the Nationals are alive again. The unlikely has happened; the offense has won a game on its own.

Washington's chances are thin, but it does not show on the faces of the team, who are chest butting and high fiving with the same broad grins that are visible when you are plucked from disaster, when you were grimly holding on with not much hope and suddenly the flood waters of bad luck recede and rescue seems possible.

Every time they manage a key win the Nationals talk in the postgame interviews about how they have recaptured a small piece of the June magic. Barry Svrluga of the *Washington Post* writes of the Friday night win against Atlanta as one that, "felt very much like the hot, sweltering days of June when these kinds of wins were nightly events." He quotes Frank Robinson as saying, "like old times."

There was the three-game sweep in Colorado, the series win against Philadelphia. They all brought the feeling back, and yet after each resurgence the team and the fans are left with some elusive ephemera, a beautiful mistress gone in the early morning light as though really just a dream, the mental picture of a loved one that fades memory. The stark reality is that the time is past. It is not June anymore. It is September and the teams that have been down this hot, difficult stretch so many times before have an advantage. They do not panic when they lose a game. When they waste an Andruw Jones three-run home run, they come back and get another. Success is no mistress for them; it is a possession and no one guards her like the Atlanta Braves.

Livan Hernandez, whose win on Monday against Florida, his 15th, marked the end of the last win streak. Fans are hoping he will start another on the beautiful afternoon with paid attendance of 44,000 at RFK. There are many empty red and orange seats showing through the crowd, but fans are congregated near the top of the stadium and, despite no-shows, it is a great gathering of the faithful. Some have brought radios on which they can follow college football games; some have just brought their kids for one of the last weekend games of the year. There are still great stories left to tell in the stands.

"Did you know that Carlos Baerga throws baseballs with his phone number to good looking girls near the dugout?" asks a fan bending around to talk to another fan in the row behind him.

"You're kidding," says the fan in response.

"A friend of mine's daughter knows someone that got one," he continues.

"Have you ever seen his hair up close on TV?" asks the fan in the back row.

"Pretty greased back, isn't it?"

"Hell, it looks like it's made out of plastic," says the second fan as they both laugh at Baerga, whose friendly face can still be seen peering out over the dugout roof as he sizes up the contingent there for the game.

Another fan is talking to his son about games he saw as a child at RFK. "See up there in section 469, just to left of the foul pole?" asks the Dad.

"Yeah," says his son, looking toward the right field corner still in shadow while the rest of the field is bathed in warm yellow sunlight.

"I saw Mike Epstein for the Senators hit one up there that was still rising when it hit one of the old wooden seats that were here when RFK first opened," adds the dad. "It hit that seat and busted the back slats. We went up and looked at the seat after the game."

"Mike Epstein, now that's an old name," says the fan next to him.

"Yeah, a long time ago, we used to come to Sunday doubleheaders and stay all day out here. No one cared or thought anything about it."

Livan Hernandez wasn't even born when the Senators left RFK, but he feels at home on that same mound now. As the high school band finishes the national anthem and scatters for the center field exit, Hernandez finishes his warm-ups and the game begins. He pitches well in the first three innings, getting rookie Langerhans swinging in the second inning and Furcal looking in the third. He is using that same 63-mph slow curve that amazed the fans on opening night, and looks just as good in September.

Andruw Jones is for Atlanta like a great tenor whose voice dwarfs the rest of the cast. In the second inning he follows Chipper Jones to the plate, and after his long time team mate is out on a weak grounder Andruw Jones hits a ball that Jose Guillen only turns and watches as it goes over his head for a solo home run that sails above the Atlanta bullpen. It is his 47th homer of the season and ties him with Eddie Mathews and Hank Aaron for most in a season by a Brave. He has three in his last six games and seems certain to stand alone in the Braves' record book before the season is done. Yet it is not Andruw Jones that breaks the backs of the Nats. With two outs in the same inning, rookie catcher McCann hits another home run to right, this one a three run affair that lands even further up in the right field mezzanine. It ends the scoring for the day as Atlanta wins 4-0.

Washington manages only six hits against Jorge Sosa, who is having a phenomenal year under the tutelage of Leo Mazzone, especially given that he was bullpen filler for the Tampa Bay Devil Rays in 2004. The win is his 11th of the year and his ERA of 2.55 moves him ahead of John Patterson to lead the National League in this category. Cristian Guzman gives the Nationals their only brief moment of hope in the fifth inning when Jeff Francoeur goes over the wall in right field to bring Guzman's long fly ball back into the park. A moment's caution to McCann and an extra foot for Guzman's fly ball are what the game turns on. The Nationals can still play with the best, but now they are just a foot shy of really being there at the end of the day.

That distance seems even greater for the Sunday game against the Braves. John Smoltz is pitching for Atlanta and Washington can offer only a patchwork of newly called up rookies and Army Navy Surplus players. Smoltz is headed for the Hall of Fame, and Jay Bergmann, who starts for Washington, is not in that league. Whereas Washington once could match Livan Hernandez against Smoltz, the rotation is thinner now, but the Braves' pitching is their Achilles' heel. For the Nationals, however, what was a thin organizational fabric to start the season is now moth-eaten from injury, with gaping holes like the fourth and fifth spots in the rotation.

Smoltz pitches effectively for seven innings and the Nationals look like a minor league team playing exhibition ball against the parent club. Then in the eighth inning Bobby Cox gives his bullpen a chance to redeem themselves and to prepare for the postseason theatrics where they will be tested severely. The game is suddenly one of equals. Blaine Boyer starts the inning by walking Cristian Guzman, who is more and more consistently showing patience at the plate. Then he walks Marlon Byrd and Bobby Cox brings in John Foster. Brad Wilkerson hits a long line drive off the base of the wall to bring Guzman in to score and Foster hits Rick Short with a pitch to load the bases. Nick Johnson has a single to score Byrd and Short and suddenly the game is 6-5 and the Nationals have no outs and runners on first and third. A sacrifice fly and a pressure packed single by rookie Ryan Zimmerman score two more runs to give Washington an amazing 7-6 lead going into the top of the ninth inning.

It is a replay of the first game and Chad Cordero comes on to close it out. Only half of the fans are still in attendance, but they are all standing and smiling. Julio Franco leads off for the Braves with a single and everyone in the stadium is looking toward the Braves dugout at Andruw Jones. He is standing on the steps with a bat and everyone wants Cordero to leave him there. He gets two fly ball outs against Furcal and Giles and the Nationals are one out away from a miraculous comeback win and a series win against the league leading Braves. It is not to be. Chipper Jones hits a monster home run off Cordero, which lands in the mezzanine level just to the right of dead center to give the Braves the lead. Then, Andruw Jones has a second home run and the final score is 9-7. It is a difficult loss, but the rally gives the team a sense of pride along with the frustration. They battled back, but could not pull it off. The pitching has begun to let them down.

The third week of September is the last road trip of any proportion, including a short run to New York for three games at Shea Stadium, and then a long trip to San Diego to play three weekend games against the Padres in front of the navy and the marines. The week provides the same ebb and flow as the team sweeps the Mets during the week, and almost pulls off a miracle in San Diego. The game on Saturday night in San Diego is the final blow to the season, and it comes only after three games won against the Mets and a great game won to begin the series in San Diego.

During the week, the pitching staff comes back against the Mets. In the opener, Hector Carrasco starts the game and, pitching against Tom Glavine, the deck seems stacked in New York's favor. Yet somehow, the bullpen wins the game as John Rauch, Joey Eischen, and Gary Majewski keep the Mets off the scoreboard and Chad Cordero finishes a 4-2 surprising victory. Then the Nationals bats come alive in the next two games. Vinny Castilla and Preston Wilson hit home runs and Nick Johnson has two doubles as the team scores six behind Esteban Loaiza to win 6-3. It is Loaiza's eleventh win and Cordero gets his league-leading 46th save. Livan Hernandez gives the Nationals six innings the following night as Preston Wilson and Vinny Castilla continue to power the offense as it scores a 6-5 victory. Cristian Guzman hits a solo home run that marks a turnaround in his fortunes. He is well over the Mendoza line and rising steadily.

Against the Padres, John Patterson pitches a game like he has not pitched in many weeks. He pitches in the same precarious position the team has put him most of the year, with no margin for error. He gives up a solo home run in the first inning and then shuts down the Padres for the rest of the game. Cristian Guzman continues his hot hitting with a fifth inning, two-out double that scores two runs and gives Patterson a lead he would not have had earlier in the year when Guzman was an automatic out. The Nationals score three more and Patterson allows only three hits over nine innings for only his ninth win. It is an important game for the overworked bullpen that can watch the parade of Nationals crossing the plate.

On Saturday night, the miracle seems to be building again. Hector Carrasco, the thirty-five-year-old veteran reliever who has not started two games in his long career, starts back-to-back games down the stretch for Washington. The unlikely hero pitches six innings and is never in trouble, departing with a 5-0 lead. What a gift is handed to the bullpen that has been the strength of the team through most of the season. But unfortunately the stress and strain of over-work show unfortunately on this night when the stars seem to be aligning once again in the Nationals' favor.

Frank Robinson starts the ninth with Jason Bergmann, who gets an out but walks a batter. Robinson brings in Joey Eischen to face the left-handed Brian Giles. Eischen gets Giles, but Xavier Nady singles to put two runners aboard with two outs. Robinson changes horses again and this time he chooses wrong. Travis Hughes gives up a run scoring single to Joe Randa. With the score 5-1 and two outs, Cordero comes in and walks the first batter before yielding a grand slam home run to Khalil Greene to tie the score. The Padres push across three more runs in the 12th to complete the undoing of the Washington season.

Just as the many wonderful wins by Livan Hernandez seemed to push the team higher and higher in June, the team was on the verge of winning five in a row on a gift from Carrasco. It would have moved the team closer into consideration for the wild card slot as they prepare to head home. But the momentum swing is palpable the next day as the journeyman Pedro Astacio beats the sleepwalking Nationals 2-1, wasting another fine outing by Loaiza.

Barry Bonds is back, and all his poisoned and prodigious talent is back with the ill wind that it blows for baseball. In May it could be hoped that he would fade graciously away, much the way that Palmiero now may be doing. Only that same very public humiliation that forced Palmiero out will make Bonds go away without the record he so badly, so perniciously desires. It may come. Before the first game of the Washington series at RFK that holds less and less promise for the season-long quest of the Nationals, Bonds opines loudly about the congressional investigation of steroids. "They are wasting their time," he offers.

The fans at RFK are less than polite in their greeting for Bonds. The media may be obliged to follow Barry's lead, to pretend not to see the steroid laced, puffy-faced persona that stares defiantly back from TV sets around the country as he returns from a knee injury that has miraculously healed. Less restrained, the crowd of thirty thousand at RFK boos him lustily and without remorse. When he sends a long and deep home run into the upper deck rows formerly reserved for Frank Howard's mammoth swats, the fans yell at the poor man who holds the precious souvenir aloft.

"Throw it back," they demand, "throw it back." The chant grows in vigor until the security guards escort the fan from the seating area to where he can hand the ball to security for safekeeping.

The ball might be worth enough to put his child through a year of college or more, especially if it is the last Bonds hits in his poisoned career. The fans demand it be exorcised from their midst because they know it is a tainted icon, a poisoned apple that represents the dangers to young athletes of steroids and also the mendacity that taints our public lives, seemingly without fear of contradiction from media starved for excitement, starved for any controversy to drive ratings up. Fans do not concern themselves with ratings but share with Bonds their belief that he is staining the game and its sacred history.

Livan Hernandez pitches a marvelous game and, despite giving up the home run to Bonds, pitches into the ninth inning ahead by a 2-1 margin provided by Brad Wilkerson, whose bat has shown growing strength in the waning weeks of the season. But Hernandez does not have the stamina to finish what he has started. His legs, like Castilla's, may have improved, but they are old nonetheless.

Chad Cordero has shown signs that the other Nationals All-Star is also running on empty. Frank Robinson does not bring him in to close out the ninth and lets Livan finish, even when it is apparent he cannot. Moises Alou hits a three run home run with two out in the top of the ninth inning to give San Francisco a 4-2 lead. Ryan Zimmerman gets a run home in the bottom of the inning on a sacrifice fly to make the final margin 4-3. The loss leaves the Nationals only three games over the break-even point of .500. The wild card race is over, but the race for respect is going strong.

**The crowd of 30,000 boos Barry Bonds lustily.**

Barry Bonds' stay in the nation's capital, just down East Capital Street from the hearing room where Palmiero lied, and where many want to see Bonds testify, continues something that many are beginning to understand is a distasteful distraction from the wonderful pennant fights in both leagues. The Cleveland Indians have matched up against the Chicago White Sox and they are locked in a head-to-head, mid-week series as they jockey for position going into the final week of the season. The Red Sox and the Yankees are dueling in a contest that has brought forward little gentlemanly conduct in recent years. In Washington, D.C., the Barry Bonds show is still playing. The RFK fans cannot say why they have been chosen to endure this indignity, but the close proximity of Congress may be one reason, as though Bonds is daring the Congress to investigate him further.

"He'll flip on the BALCO folks and walk away from the whole mess unscathed," says a former district attorney watching the game, commenting on the likely outcome of the mess playing out before them on the field.

"I saw in the *New York Times* today that Bonds is saying how much he respects Palmiero, how tight they are," says the other lawyer. "I suspect he is worried Palmiero is busy ratting folks out even as we speak."

Bonds answers with a long upper deck home run.

The comment proves prescient, as news surfaces the next day that Palmiero has identified Miguel Tejada, the heir to the Ripken legend. Everyone who has ever worn an orange and black Orioles cap can only shake their heads in disbelief and disgust

"He sure as hell looks like he is still on the juice," says the DA, looking toward Bonds as he climbs out of the dugout in the first inning and walks to the plate. "That home run he hit the other night, hell, he's forty-one frigging years old, and he is still competing in a league all by himself. No way he is not juiced."

Bonds, and Palmiero's attempts to drag baseball down a river of shame continues when, in the first inning, against John Patterson, Bonds pokes a long line drive over the right field wall that Guillen just turns and watches. It is Bonds' reply to the booing fans, but it does not stop them as he rounds the bases. In the third inning Patterson wins the battle, striking out Bonds. Bonds heads toward the dugout questioning the umpire's call and the fans cheer Patterson and boo Bonds in turn. Patterson gets Bonds again to end the fifth inning. With two strikes, Bonds tries to check his swing on a curve in the dirt, but the third base umpire has no mercy, signaling a strikeout with gusto. Yet the Giants are in command of the game, leading 5-1. There is no more scoring, as the Nationals can manage only five hits. Fans leaving the game cannot help but feel as if they have been part of something distasteful. The whole scene is an ugly one and leaves fans looking to wash up before they leave the stadium.

The last game of the series brings a quiet end to the noisy affair, as Bonds does not appear during the game. The afternoon game offers a beautiful view of September baseball. It is the rookies who will take their turns now. Rick Short and Ryan Zimmerman start the game and provide the spark behind Hector Carrasco's third start of the season. Washington wins 2-0 and is closing in on a winning season. Zimmerman's two hits push his September batting average toward .400. Rick Short has been no less impressive. He is not as important to the future of the organization, but to fans in September, who cares. He is a great story and everyone loves watching him confound the experts who say he has no position, that he is too old. His hot bat makes fans wonder what would have been possible back in April and May when Jeffrey Hammonds and Wil Cordero were getting paid a lot more money, were leaving runners stranded every time they came to bat and did a lot less to help the team win games.

The Mets open a three game weekend series with the Nationals on Friday night, with the heart of their rotation pitching against a team they swept in New York a week earlier. The Mets are in last place and are playing for pride; from the start look more game than the Nationals. Steve Trachsel dominates the listless Washington offense and Esteban Loaiza pitches as well as ever but gives up two runs on a Cliff Floyd single in the sixth inning and departs behind 2-0, which is where the game sits in the bottom of the ninth inning. Then a surprising development derails what seemed a scripted loss.

Ryan Zimmerman seems the only Washington hitter who is doing more than going through the motions. He collects his third hit of the game, but cannot be expecting Carlos Baerga's two-run home run any more than anyone else. It carries easily over the right field fence and suddenly the Nationals seem in business. The score is tied 2-2 and though there are two out Roberto Hernandez, the Mets pitcher, looks shaken by the home run. But Gary Majewski, who pitched the top of the ninth, comes out to bat for himself. Frank Robinson does not pinch-hit.

Something is not right. Frank Robinson announces during the weekend series that he will let his regulars rest. He sits Guillen, Castilla, and Schneider, and says he is "giving them the rest of the season off." Marlon Byrd, who came back from New Orleans hot as a Tennessee Williams tin roof, has played hardly at all. Ostensibly, Robinson is giving players like Zimmerman a chance to audition, but why is Baerga pinch-hitting? If youth is to be served, where are Church and Byrd? Why not send one of them up to take a hack at Roberto

Hernandez and let the team go down swinging? Instead, Majewski makes a quiet out and puts two runners on base and faces Carlos Beltran with two out in the top of the tenth inning. Beltran is a left handed hitter and Robinson has Mike Stanton and other lefties in the bullpen, but he stays with Majewski, who gives up a three run home run to Beltran that wins the game 5-2.

Robinson is going through the motions. If the Nationals are listless, their manager has set the tone with a surrender flag that all can see. Mets manager Willie Randolph speaks proudly of his team's comeback win and their ability to rise from the depths of the losing streak that sank their chances and pushed them to the bottom of the NL East. They are playing for pride. Frank Robinson is playing out the string.

The Saturday game is little better. Livan Hernandez pitches well in a match-up against Tom Glavine, but has a second string lineup playing behind him. Tony Blanco, the rule-5 pickup who has sat on the bench the entire season, is playing first base and misplays a routine ball into a run for New York. Brandon Watson bats leadoff and plays left field. The irony is that Robinson is forced to stretch his pitchers. Hernandez, Patterson, and Loaiza are pitching on three days' rest. Robinson has robbed one of his healthy arms from the bullpen in Hector Carrasco, who has ably filled in as a starter. His three starters are all that is left from the long list that auditioned in April and May—now appearing elsewhere.

Glavine gets better support from his teammates and wins by the same margin as the night before, 5-2. The Sunday crowd at RFK sees the first team bat in the field. They give it a game effort. The picture of Wilkerson climbing the centerfield wall in a fruitless effort to bring David Wright's deciding home run back into the ballpark is a fitting portrayal of the position Washington now finds itself in. The Mets bang out four home runs, two by Mike Piazza and, despite game performances by Nick Johnson and Brad Wilkerson, the Nationals lose 6-5. Wilkerson seems frozen in time, reaching for the ball just inches away, as though he is trying to bring back another time that seems a distant memory now—as if he is reaching for the drama that was once the Nationals' first season in Washington, for that time when possibility trumped defeat and enthusiastic fans left RFK with a smile and a song.

# 20

# Trojan Horse

Fans have not been raptly attentive to the dilemma of ownership, but as an issue it represents a milestone achievement that is akin to that of the nation's founders—independence. Washington is seeking a declaration of that independence and it will come when MLB, Inc., finally hands over the keys to the front office at RFK. MLB has published dates for announcing the new ownership of the Washington, D.C., baseball team through out the season. Yet, the season is in its last few days and it is hard to remember all of the promised dates when ownership was to be announced. The first target to slip by was Memorial Day, followed by July 4, and then Labor Day, and now it is anyone's guess whether it will be announced at all.

In midsummer the building drama had anticipation running high. Fans hoped that new owners might fund those July trades to keep the Nationals going, to keep the magic rolling. Fans were ready for someone with deep pockets to pitch in and help build on what was clearly a sound foundation. The time for a new owner to take a role in the 2005 season has come and gone. The ownership announcement will now be staged in the off-season and it is beginning to bear all the markings of a recess appointment by the president, when an unpopular or questionable selection sneaks past the formal confirmation process with less fanfare and no questions asked. What is Bud Selig hiding?

There has been much speculation about who the owner will be. Holding the announcement until after the season significantly raises the chance an owner will be selected from outside the Washington, D.C., area. A D.C. ownership group might have been paraded through the streets on July 4, confetti in their hair and waving to adoring crowds. The fact that MLB has deferred such fanfare suggests that something else is in store.

The long sale process looks more and more like it will end with the team being given to someone who means nothing to fans in Washington, who has no history in the very long war with MLB to bring baseball to D.C. Like the recent purchase of the Boston Red Sox by a Los Angeles entrepreneur, it seems more and more likely the new owner will be an absentee landlord whose purchase—like the one in Boston—has been eased through by Bud Selig. Using the Boston scenario as a model, the likely winner of the Nationals' bidding is Jeff Smulyan, who among all candidates is the closest to Selig.

Smulyan is the Indianapolis CEO and founder of EMMIS, the international communications giant. Smulyan's corporate interests are focused on radio traditionally, but he also has substantial investments in television, magazines, and other communication media. He lives in Indianapolis, where he started his company in 1980 with two Midwest radio stations. In 1989 he ventured into the world of baseball for the first time, purchasing the Seattle Mariners for a mere $77 million. His radio interests include the top rated stations in the country, and are especially strong in the lucrative markets of LA and New York City. He is a lawyer by training and got his legal degree from the University of Southern California, home of the Trojans.

What is missing from Jeff Smulyan's very interesting story is any connection to Washington, D.C. Of the ownership groups that are vying for the team, four have strong ties to the area and three have almost none. Two of the groups, one headed by Fred Malek and another by William Collins III and Albert Lord, are part of the decades long effort to relocate a team to Washington, either by buying an existing team or by participating in baseball expansion. The lead investors for other bid groups, like Jonathan Ledecky and Fred Haney, have strong ties to the area, although Haney's are more recent. Stan Kasten, who heads another bid group, has no link to the Washington area. He has been a sports executive in the Atlanta area, most often tied to Braves baseball. New to baseball and D.C. are the investment group headed by Jesse Jackson's son Yusef, who partnered with grocery billionaire Ron Burkle.

In many ways the choice of Smulyan is a great one. He is a savvy businessman who has everything necessary to be a successful baseball owner. There are many unique characteristics that can help him shape the team into a long-term contender, but certainly money and intellect are two of the most prominent. The first problem with Smulyan is one of fit—those Midwestern roots look nothing like Washington, D.C. The southern parts of the states of Indiana, Ohio, and Illinois—where Smulyan is from—are farm country and Washington, D.C., has not had an agrarian focus since the end of the "Dust Bowl." Whatever "D.C. Baseball" may become, it will never look like Jeff Smulyan. He is white bread in a whole wheat and rye town and there are some important reasons why Washington fans should be concerned about Smulyan's ownership.

The first variable that raises very serious questions is his link to Bud Selig.

## 20. Trojan Horse

Baseball writers in the last half of the season, expecting the sale announcement at any moment, have reported Selig's top concern that whoever buys the Nationals should retain the current management team, and be "compatible" with the current ownership group within Major League Baseball. It is the latter part of this statement that is troubling. Analysts within both the business and baseball communities have taken this statement as a signal that Smulyan, as a favorite of MLB, Inc., and Selig, is the front-runner. *USA Today* reported that, "Selig likes Smulyan ... and his media expertise." Smulyan responded to the charges that, as a friend of Bud, he had an inside track by saying, "I think that's overstated."

Smulyan's courtship of Selig began when Smulyan owned the Seattle Mariners between 1989 and 1992. He served on the Television Committee during that time, when broadcasting revenues were becoming more crucial to the overall financial success of the game and its ownership group. That importance has grown exponentially, as witnessed in the ongoing fight between Baltimore Oriole owner Peter Angelos and some as yet unnamed other for television rights within the mid-Atlantic region.

One positive outgrowth of Smulyan's ownership of the Nationals might be his stature in the communications industry, where he is recognized as "one of the 40 most influential people in radio." Both Angelos and Smulyan are lawyers, but Angelos was a personal injury attorney whom other attorneys characterize as an ambulance chaser who struck oil—or asbestos, more accurately—that provided the billion dollar settlements against Baltimore industrial interests. Smulyan's influence in the media industry may blunt the attempts by Angelos to milk the Washington area media market even as his fan base in Washington disappears, but that is not the reason Selig may put Smulyan's bid for the Nationals ahead of others.

According to a discussion thread on the *Nightly Business Report* entitled, "Field of Green," Smulyan was active in labor negotiations with the Major League Baseball Players Association in 2002. Oddly enough, Smulyan is a fraternity brother of MLBPA's executive director, Donald Fehr. Smulyan was involved on the periphery of the 2002 negotiations that led perilously close to another disastrous strike. Nothing Bud Selig has done to scar the game of baseball rivals his relationship with the players' union and his attempts to break the union during the strike of 1994. No event in the history of baseball more conclusively establishes that baseball's ownership group under Selig has as its first priority its own economic gain, and that the interests of the fans and the sanctity of the game are secondary to their ability to profit from it.

Smulyan was openly critical of Fehr and the players in a variety of media outlets. He said of Fehr's role in the pending strike that August, "I like Donald, but blame him and [Gene] Orza. They don't serve the game." By inference, Smulyan clearly believes that owners do serve the game rather than their own narrow economic interests. "I learned long ago, nobody loves the owner of a ball club," said Smulyan in 2002. Smulyan's inside track with the Nationals has much more to do with how he will behave in any future labor negotiations than with his ties to Washington or the fan base here.

"Baseball also wants potential owners to prove they won't roil the economic waters by paying too much for players," said Darren Gersh of the *Nightly Business Report* said in a March 2005 discussion with Smulyan, Kasten, and others on the pending sale of the Nationals.

"They are trying to get people who will go along," agreed Gary Gillette of ESPN in response to Gersh in that same discussion.

Selig and MLB are not evaluating the bids for the Washington Nationals so much from the perspective of who will serve the area and the fans, but who will serve *them*. It is why the negotiations have been so quiet, so protracted. It is not as though Malek's group are wild-eyed radicals, nor are the others. Selig will make the decision for a set of concerns that Selig alone can fathom. One thing is certain, though, Smulyan is Selig's friend, and Bud looks after his own.

While the local media are largely quiet, Washington fans should be wary. What long-term commitment to Washington does Smulyan have that recommends him over others? Why should Washington fans believe that Smulyan, during tough economic times, will roll up his sleeves and work with others in the community to make the future of D.C. baseball a success? Can he do that from Indianapolis as well as if he were here?

Looking back over Smulyan's history one discovers significant reason to doubt the tenacity of his commitment. It is important to note how short Smulyan's commitment was to Seattle baseball. He bailed out of Seattle after only three years, at the earliest signs of economic trouble. What has not been widely reported are his efforts to relocate *that* team. In the winter of 1991, shortly before he sold the Seattle Mariners, Smulyan explored the possibility of moving the team to the Tampa Bay area. In a long article on the origins of the Tampa Bay franchise, Bob Adelman discusses Smulyan's interests in the Tampa area as one of the early chances for baseball relocation to Tampa. He quotes Smulyan:

"It was a *remote* possibility, but it *was* discussed," said Smulyan, according to Adelman. "I am not the kind of guy who is going to move a team in the middle of the night."

Smulyan did admit that had the economic situation in Seattle continued to deteriorate, relocation was a legitimate option. So within three short years, with almost no effort to turn the franchise around, Smulyan was looking for another home, ready to move the team. Washington fans might ask Mr. Smulyan where his heart lies, what it might take for him to consider moving their team, and how long might it take him to jump ship this time. Smulyan's reference about leaving in the middle of the night is a reference to the departure of the Colts from Baltimore to Indianapolis. What are his thoughts on issues like this? Aren't they germane to the sale of the Nationals? The answer to those questions, if asked, remain hidden. In the game of baseball ownership, play is conducted in the dark and there are no bright lights.

"Potential owners must also navigate baseball's secretive ways," wrote the *Nightly Business Report's* Darren Gersh. "The rules could change at any minute. There's a reason they call it Inside Baseball."

Jeff Smulyan was initiated into the fraternity of MLB, Inc, long ago. That fraternity is "the most exclusive ... country club in the world," said Gary Gillette of ESPN. Smulyan clearly belongs in this world of wealth and power, but does he belong in Washington? His interests are in Indianapolis and in the recent past it was rumored he wanted to buy the Cincinnati Reds. His ownership there would make far more sense. Indianapolis is the site of the Reds' Triple A affiliate and less than a two hour drive from Cincinnati. However, Smulyan is a corporate CEO of an international corporate firm with interests in Belgium and Hungary, so having interests in distant areas is not foreign to him. It is not completely fair to assume that he will not be a good steward to the Nationals franchise.

"I would call it more like people who are trying to be the best stewards they can be," Smulyan said of his and other owner's interests in baseball.

But in light of his closeness with Bud Selig, whose overarching concern is not that of fans, and his solid base in the Midwest, why should ownership groups who have toiled for many decades to bring baseball to the Washington area be snubbed in favor of Jeff Smulyan? Because he is a friend of Bud Selig? Because he will help MLB, Inc., with its media interests? For Washington baseball fans, this is not about country club membership, but about keeping a baseball team in the nation's capital, where we have watched one twice before. We do not want to be set up to fail because the Washington franchise is just another wild card that Bud Selig wants to keep in his deck to deal off the bottom when the time is right.

Washington fans may be too giddy with their success to look a gift horse in the mouth. Yet the success of bringing baseball back to Washington needs to be considered from a more long-term perspective than just getting a baseball team for this year, in this pennant race, and with these players. The lessons of Montreal are there for everyone, and Washington fans should put aside the joys of the moment to remember how quickly the expansion Senators failed and left for Texas.

What Washington fans will not get in the selection of Jeff Smulyan is an independent franchise ownership group whose commitment to this area is unquestioned. Nor will they get an owner who can make his own decisions about whom he hires and fires. Rumors abound that Selig, who likes Nationals general manager Bowden enough to hire him to begin with, will obligate new owners to retain him; like Smulyan, Bowden is a friend of Bud and, like Smulyan, he is an asset in a labor dispute or any other gambit-like contraction that could benefit ownership. Are labor issues and being on Bud Selig's A-list all that define the essential interests of D.C. baseball and the game itself?

Hockey and football have expanded into places like Tampa, Nashville, and Jacksonville, Florida, providing fans in those cities with new civic pride and involvement in sport. MLB, Inc., in stark contrast, convinced everyone for more than a decade that what was once considered the National Pastime could not be moved into the nation's capital where it started more than a century ago. Yet if there really is no market for expansion of the game, why were there 2.7 million fans willing to pay to watch games at RFK this season? Are they not exhibit A in a hypothetical case that Bud Selig and his cronies are denying millions of potential fans a chance to be part of the game? Are he and the ownership of MLB unfairly controlling the baseball market like the Hunt brothers, who hoped to achieve such control of silver several decades ago in order to run up the price?

It may be naïve to think that anything can be done about the direction that baseball is headed. D.C. fans certainly cannot expect any say in control of baseball in their town. The current political climate in the country can be characterized at its kindest as laissez-faire. Yet the situation in baseball could be improved relatively easily. Since the owners terminated the Office of Commissioner as even a nominally independent voice in the affairs of the game, much has gone wrong. Steroids are just another symptom of the lack of effective oversight that has plagued the game in its recent history. Labor disputes that cannot be resolved without long disruptions in the game, the cancellation of the World Series, attempts to sell off successful clubs like Minnesota—those are the serious threats of which steroids is just the latest.

Baseball's ownership group are like drunks from the country club careening down the road on a Saturday night. The visible danger is the car swerving on the road, but the underlying problem is the substance abuse—in this instance abuse of unchecked economic power. Not until Congress mandates the return of an independent commissioner to serve as a countervailing force to that power will the many problems that have plagued the game during the last two decades be addressed. Steroids are just the latest mismanagement of what was once the commissioner's realm, namely, managing what was "in the best interest of the game."

D.C. baseball is going to have a busy off-season, and it is uncertain how the play will end. The D.C. politicians have their hands full with MLB, Inc., and their chief negotiator, Jerry Reinsdorf, no shrinking daisy he. Whether the owner is Jeff Smulyan or a local group they will soon fit into the jackets reserved for members of the club. They will all stand together for the benefit of the members, rather than for the game or its fans. Baseball fans in D.C. won one when they forced MLB to move the Montreal franchise rather than kill it. We can look forward to another year of sitting under the stars at RFK, of sharing magic moments with friends and family. The hard fought victory of bringing baseball back to Washington will give us that much and it is no small gift, regardless of whether MLB, Inc., has something else in mind down the road. D.C. baseball is a young seedling and the fans have done the watering; now corporate America needs to give it room to grow.

# 21

# Our Winning Season

"Though I learned some things from the games we won that year, I learned much, much more from loss." Pat Conroy, *My Losing Season*

Washington's place seems to have been predestined. Last place in the NL East is where everyone expected them to be at the end of the long season. As they start the final week, the Nationals march doggedly toward their fate like medieval prisoners returning to the keep cellar. Hope has been extinguished by losing seven of the last eight games and even the lowly Mets are pulling away, leaving Washington alone in the dank confines they have so skillfully avoided all season. The team goes on the road one last time—to the home of Livan Hernandez, Miami, Florida, and the Marlins' home turf. The three game series is a showcase for how fortunes in baseball can change overnight and provides insight into the further exploration of baseball management in the 21st century.

Ron Darling's comments during the Marlins series offer echo the theme of Pat Conroy's book on his senior year as a basketball player at the Citadel, *My Losing Season* (New York, Doubeday, 2002). Conroy contends that losing teaches the lessons of a lifetime, winning just the joys of the day. Darling says of the situations in both Miami and Washington that everyone looks good when a team is winning, but it is the character that a team shows when it is losing that counts, that establishes what kind of players they are, what kind of chemistry they have, and how effectively the leadership of the team can show the way. Darling's assessment offers hope for the seasons to come.

In the first game Hector Carrasco demonstrates how good coaching and conditioning can help players, even toward the end of their careers, to achieve remarkable turnarounds. Carrasco, 35 years of age, has used the advice of pitching coaches and other starters to refine his pitch assortment. Formerly a two-pitch pitcher only, he was best suited for relief, but by adding a very effective changeup and a running fastball he has become a very good starter. In the first game against the Fish, he shuts them down for six innings and leaves the game with a 1-0 lead, allowing only two hits. The bullpen, diminished by the loss of both Cordero and Ayala, holds the lead, with Jay Bergmann and Majewski getting the last outs.

Ryan Zimmerman and Cristian Guzman continue to provide much of the offensive punch for the final weeks and they drive home the 4-0 win. Washington is playing for nothing more than respect and the win earns them some momentum, but the second game will be against Dontrelle Willis. A-Train has beaten the Nationals three times and is battling Chris Carpenter for the Cy Young award in the National League. He starts the game in typical fashion, but the Marlins look more lackluster than Washington. The young players filling the void for Nationals regulars are enthusiastic at the chance to prove themselves and they give Willis no respite.

In the second inning of the game, John Rauch squibs a ball that Willis fails to field, which keeps the inning going and loads the bases. Then a ball goes between the legs of Carlos Delgado to give Washington the lead, and with the help of another error the Nationals cross home three more times and take a 4-0 lead. Florida has watched its own play-off chances evaporate during a disastrous run starting in mid-September. Their futility since then mirrors that of the Nationals and even Willis cannot right the ship. One of Florida's vaunted threesome of young pitchers, A. J. Burnett, has been dismissed from the team for stating that the negative atmosphere created by Jack McKeon in the clubhouse has hurt the team. Old time managers and old time methods get scrutiny from young ballplayers that was not allowed a generation ago.

For Washington the game is a laugher and an 11-1 win. Marlon Byrd gets four hits, including a clutch double. Jamey Carroll continues to play the same way he has all year, without any noticeable change of expression, no diminish in his enthusiasm or hustle. He drives in three runs while Zimmerman and Guzman continue to hit the ball hard as well. The win for Washington creates a three-way contest for last place between the Mets, Marlins and Nationals, all of whom are in essence tied.

The final game of the series is more remarkable still. Not since May has the team scored eleven runs. Like some storm tide, it is the high water mark for an offense that has reached the figure on only five occasions. During the first six weeks of the season, when Castilla and Vidro were still healthy, the team scored 11 runs three times, but after that the Nationals were able to score no more than seven or eight runs and that level was reached on only a handful of occasions. During June it was the pitching that carried the team, but now, with the team playing loose and easy, against a team that is dispirited and down, they score eleven runs on consecutive nights. Nick Johnson and

Preston Wilson hit long home runs to lead the offense, but Byrd, Zimmerman, and Guzman continue to hit as well. Byrd's fine running catch in right field in the early innings is just one of several outstanding defensive plays during the series that says the Nationals are back.

The sweep of the series against the demoralized Marlins assures that the Nationals will not finish with a losing record. They have climbed out of the cellar and when they return for the three game series against the Phillies, they have a chance to make sure that the first season in Washington is a winning one. It is a remarkable hope, one that has surprised everyone, except perhaps the players. Players always believe they can win each game, that the stars can converge even on the toughest of nights. They believe they can always hear that voice that Conroy identifies as coming from the heart of every athlete saying to them, "Play the game because you love it ... don't think. Play. Get into the rhythm of the game and let it flow through you." It was flowing in Miami and it will carry the team back home.

RFK stadium feels as comfortable as an old stuffed chair. The African American ushers in their green, park ranger-like shirts have first names now, family histories, grandchildren in college. It is a long, long season, but over its course the mysteries of the stadium have been peeled back, revealed like Toto tugging at the Wizard's curtain. A season of experience has revealed exactly where those Tofu Hot Dogs are hidden, how the hell to get in and out of the parking lots along Benning Road, and, of course, how the home run mystery resolves itself. As the final home stand against the Phillies begins, the fireworks in center field go off and the smoke spirals slowly downward in the prevailing winds that buffet fly balls hit to deep center.

The Friday night game sends Livan Hernandez out for one last time. The newspapers have announced the date for his knee surgery as the next week, but the game veteran says he will not quit until the season is over, and he ventures out to the same mound where he began the adventure back in the middle of April, many months ago. Like the smoke from the fireworks that still hangs in the air, Hernandez's first game in April can be remembered easily, and as he strands Utley on second in the first inning and strikes out Bobby Abreu with a slow curve that barely registers on the radar gun, the memory is still there.

Hernandez pitches remarkably well against one of the most potent offensive teams in the National League. But the Phillies are playing for this year. They are within reach of the postseason if they can outlast the Houston Astros; if they can come pounding down the stretch with more heart and resolve than the 'Stros, then their season will last into the cool nights of October, when the Nationals will watch from home. The resolve shows as they bang out eleven hits and refuse to let Livan wiggle off the hook, pushing four runs across the plate and taking a 4-2 lead into the bottom of the ninth inning.

In the bottom of the ninth, Phillies closer Billy Wagner takes the mound to close out the game. His fastball has been known to top out at 100 mph on radar guns and, as he pitches to Keith Osik taking the last swings of his career, Wagner's grim tenacity registers an unbelievable 102 mph before Osik manages a weak grounder for the first out. Marlon Byrd watches one go by that hits an even higher mark, 103 mph on the radar gun, and the announcers question whether they have ever seen anything as intimidating as Wagner on the mound.

Marlon Byrd, whose late season hitting gives the Nationals another reason to hope for next year, smacks a double to the center field gap. The next batter, Brad Wilkerson, is hit in the arm by a Wagner fastball; the pain of a 100 mph blow can be seen on his face, but he shakes it off and gives the Nationals one last chance for a winning season, runners on first and second with only one out, Wagner facing the gamer, Mr. Grit and Grime, Jamey Carroll. Announcing his determination to give the Phillies nothing cheap, Robinson sends Byrd and Wilkerson on a double steal. The throw to third is late and Carroll can tie the game with one of his punch-and-judy singles to left field.

Carroll gives it his best shot, but can manage only a grounder to the hole which does not make it through. Byrd scores from third to make it 4-3, and Nick Johnson is the Nationals' last best hope. Wagner's fast ball shatters Johnson's bat like *The Natural* in reverse, as though his fastball is some demon coming out of the dark that cannot be tamed by wood bats, and the ball carries meekly to Wagner on the fly. The Phillies run off the field with the win, hanging on 4-3.

The Phillies inch closer as the Astros lose a heartbreaker to the Cubs on Friday night. The Astros are sending out their incredible threesome of pitchers for the Cubs series. Andy Pettite is beaten on Friday, but Roger Clemens and Roy Oswalt give Houston reason to believe that, no matter what heroics the Phillies can manage, Houston will be there for the first play-off series against the Atlanta Braves. But the Phillies are game and they give no quarter to the Nationals on Saturday afternoon. While college football teams are playing serious games across the country, the Phillies offense is focused on one task; they dismantle John Patterson systematically and take back to the hotel an 8-4 win. Roger Clemens is even better and pushes Philadelphia to the brink.

It is the last game of the year at RFK. There are 36,000 fans on hand to turn the final page on the season and put away the record book that is this renewal of hope in the nation's capital. The Irish beer kiosk ladies are there just like opening day, the Smithwicks, Guinness and Harp flowing like rare wines.

"So, will you be back next year?" asks a fan of the middle aged woman who is wrestling one last keg of suds over to the makeshift bar.

"We hope so," she says with a smile. "We are supposed to get a bigger bar for next year, but we'll have to wait and see."

"I'll look forward to it," says the fan as he carries his plastic cup full of brown beer toward the seats.

The field can be seen behind the Irish beer kiosk. Where it was once new and green with the possibilities of spring, it has become as worn and faded as the hopes for a winning team that now can be put aside with the short sleeved shirts and summer bathing suits. The soccer team punished the field and the drought killed off the new sod that replaced the old. Yet from somewhere, somehow, for the final game of the season, the team has brought in new sod and there is a green sparkle to the field that reminds the fans of the beginning of the season—memories that, along with unspoken hopes for next year, will be put away like toys in the closet.

The team owners—whoever that may be—give away gifts or all kinds during the last game, including one trip to spring training. There are free golf bags, game shirts, and gift certificates held aloft in the hands of smiling fans between each half inning of the game. The largesse is flowing like beer in October and the fans are smiling on the Jumbotron all day long.

The focus on the game is dimmed but the newspaper reporters lay out the hope that the Nationals can finish with a winning record and, with some luck, avoid sole ownership of last place in the NL East. Washington's starting pitcher for the last game is a most unlikely candidate. Hector Carrasco did not start the season with the Nationals and has never started a major league game until this season, but he has had a great run of starts in September, especially for a thirty-five year old journeyman who seems to have learned more new tricks than anyone would have believed possible.

The Phillies hitters cannot get traction against Carrasco, and do not get their first hit until the third inning when Jimmy Rollins extends his incredible 36 game hitting streak with a single through the left side to start the inning. The Phillies bring him around to score without another hit and take a 1-0 lead into the fifth inning. In the fifth, with two out on a hot shot through Ryan Zimmerman that the scorekeeper generously accorded a hit, Carrasco walks Jon Lieber on five pitches to put two runners aboard. The pitches to Lieber are all high and seem to suggest that Carrasco is tiring. He will no doubt come out at the end of the inning for a pinch hitter because he has thrown more than eighty pitches, too many for a relief pitcher who has never started and never pitched this many innings in his career. He is well past his point of endurance.

Frank Robinson looks on unconcerned, his arms, folded under his his chin, propped on the top rail of the dugout as he stares out at Carrasco coming apart at the seams. There is no one warming in the bullpen.

"Wake up, Frank," yells a foghorn behind home plate.

Others yell their assent, wondering if they are watching yet another game that Robinson lets get out of hand. A Phillies fan looks over in the direction of the loud fan continuing to ride Robinson.

"Man, that guy's carries, doesn't it?" asks the Nationals fan.

"Did I tell you about my trip to Milwaukee?" asks the Phillies fan, ignoring the rude comments directed at Robinson.

"I was at Miller Park when they had a big celebration for Bob Uecker's 50th year in baseball," says the fan to his friend, painfully watching Carrasco get hammered for three runs that might have been prevented.

"Yeah, they had clips on the big screen in center field of him appearing on the Johnny Carson show when he started his comedy career," he continues.

"What's the Astros score?" asks the Nationals fan, needling his friend.

As they both look at the scoreboard, and with the Phillies winning in Washington, the Cubs accommodate the Philadelphia faithful who have traveled to D.C. The Cubbies take the lead 4-3 against Roy Oswalt, the last of the formidable Houston pitching trio. The Phillies fans roar as the score is posted and D.C. fans are hard pressed to understand what the cheering is about. It has been many months since they were watching the scoreboard to see if they could slide into first place ahead of the Braves.

The Nationals are mired in last place now in the NL East and even a win will not really dig them out. Every team in the NL East has a winning record, but at the end of the day the Nationals will be the only ones proud of their 81 wins. The last game against the Phillies is slipping away and with it the last hope for the Nationals' winning season. Between innings the juke box cranks up and the fans stand to sing the Neil Diamond hit, "Sweet Caroline," one last time in 2005.

The team's record is far from the minds of most fans. The scoreboard posts the final attendance figures for the season: 2,731,993. A huge cheer for themselves goes up from the crowd as the number flashes repeatedly from the center field screen. When Ryan Church launches a Jon Lieber pitch into the left center field upper deck in the sixth inning, the fans are back into the game for an inning. But when the team cannot put a dent in Lieber in the seventh and Ugueth Urbina gets himself in a jam in the eighth, Billy Wagner ends the inning as Charlie Manuel brings him in early and now there is only one last ninth inning appointment with Billy Wagner and his 100 mph fastball left in the season.

In the Philly half of the ninth inning, the hitters are having their way with Gary Majewski, pitching his second inning of the day and just one more inning the overworked reliever should not pitch. The Philly fans watch the scoreboard hopefully as Abreu doubles in a run and their offense puts four more runs on the board to put the game out of reach at 9-3. When Majewski comes out of the game in the middle of the ninth, the 20,000 fans that have stayed for the final outs rise and give him a stirring ovation. He takes his hat off and

The Nationals draw 2.7 million fans in their return 2005 season.

holds it aloft in thanks until he exits. Robinson brings in Chad Cordero to finish the game and the fans likewise stand for their great closer, though he cannot record a single out on the final afternoon of the season. Joey Eischen gets the final out. The pitching staff that has carried the team for the 2005 season is done.

The out-of-town scoreboard announces that Houston has pulled ahead to stay at 6-4. The Phillies wait through the final inning, hoping that somehow the Cubs can rally again. Billy Wagner comes in to close out the win for the Phils, knowing that his counterpart, Brad Lidge, is probably putting the finishing touches to the Houston win many miles to the west. When Wagner gets the final out of the final game, the Philly players scamper off the field, a 9-3 win in their pockets as they run to watch the last of the Houston game. They watch in the clubhouse as Lidge records the final out of the game and nails the coffin lid for the Phillies' season as well.

Charlie Manuel comes out on the field and Frank Robinson embraces him near home plate. They are two old timers, both of them saluting another season, embracing not only one another, but also their long season of joy in a game they love. As Robinson walks back toward the Nationals dugout, the fans begin a loud, noisy ovation. Robinson stops in his tracks and takes off his hat and waves toward the stands in recognition of the contribution the fans have made to the season.

"He walks awful slow," notes a Philly fan of Robinson. "Is he okay?"

"He's just old," answers the Nationals fan as Robinson's slow strides take him back to the dugout. The ovation grows and the Nationals players join Robinson on the field en mass. They begin to throw baseballs into the stands and the joyful throng lingers, holding onto the last dying moments of the season. The fans and the players look at one another until both begin to move off toward the rest of the fall season, to watch football, to play golf, to wait for what will become of the Nationals.

The season's end marks a remarkable journey and a part of Washington's history that will always stand apart. In the same way that no run of historic feats by the Yankees will ever wipe from the memory of New Yorkers that one season in 1969 by the Amazing Mets, 2005 will be a season to remember in this town for a very long time. Its closing marks a sad end. The stretch of games that ends leaves a sad mark in the hearts of the fans. And like a child packed off to college, the players also will be sorely missed in the off-season months. The team may announce awards, but the fans have settled on some clear favorites, the faces that will, hopefully, be back next year, like favorite uncles, who appear at Christmas. Livan Hernandez is the most beloved of all players, though his tired knees may be older than his birth certificate.

As the players perform their last acts of generosity, John Rauch gives his hat to a fan, and other players give away bats and balls that cannot help but remind fans of Livan Hernandez's irascible personality that exploded one evening as he heaved his glove into the stands. Several nights later on TV he was giving his bats away after renouncing his statements that he would not pitch again in 2005. The long run of great games, as well as the theatrics, have won Hernandez a huge spot in the hearts of the fans in this first Washington Nationals season, a spot that should be retired when he leaves.

Finding a most valuable offensive player would be difficult since the offense has been so inconsistent and such a weak spot on the team. The Phillies' great offense is in stark contrast to Washington's middle of the lineup hitters, Utley, Abreu, Burrell, all with at least 20 home runs. Then they are followed by the young slugger Howard, and there is Jimmy Rollins, who gets them started. Jose Guillen, who does not let the fans in, but who cares so much about the game and winning, would be the first choice as Nationals MVP, perhaps. He swings hard at everything, and not just the pitches thrown by the opposition. He connects often as a hitter, but less often with the fans as a player.

There is the team's very talented young pitcher, John Patterson, and the bubble gum blowing pair of young stars, Nick Johnson and Brian Schneider.

**Robinson's slow strides take him back to the dugout during the last game of the season.**

Guillen, Patterson and the many other talented young players, like Brad Wilkerson and Zimmerman, give the Nationals and their fans much to look forward to in 2006. There are many who may not return. Baseball players move constantly, seeking new opportunities much the way many other Americans do. Esteban Loaiza and his countryman, Vinny Castilla, are veterans whose salaries are always subject to scrutiny by their clubs, though press writers have all put in their vote of confidence in bringing Loaiza back, whatever it takes.

Bullpen pitchers shuttle between teams with regularity. The young bullpen of Cordero, Majewski and Ayala should be back but there are no sure things during off-season. In December the management of each major league team will meet to discuss trades and free agents, and thus will begin the hot stove discussions that warm the fan's heart, until that last week in February when pitchers and catchers report to Florida and Arizona for spring training. Then the light is truly at the end of the long winter tunnel.

Washington fans have not fully digested this first season. It is difficult to sort through all that has happened, the many great surprises and realizations that have made up this very special year.

"Did you know Hernandez was this good?" Ron Darling asks Mel Proctor half way through the season.

No, Mel Proctor did not and neither did anyone else in D.C. He was our first all-star and very few except the most determined baseball fans knew anything about him, nor did they realize that the round-faced relief pitcher, who was not named the closer until late in spring training, would dominate his peers and earn an All-Star selection in his second full season.

"I did not realize that Vinny Castilla was such a great fielder," says a fan in April, watching him shorthop the ball short of the bag and just inside the foul line. It is an athletic play that he makes look so easy and then he fires across the diamond, effortlessly beating the runner to first base with his throw.

We did not realize the strength of Jose Guillen's right arm in right field, Wilkerson's grit and hustle wherever he played on the field, Johnson's sweet swing, or Brian Schneider's astute defensive play in all facets of his game. It was all a surprise, a learning process that settled over the fans at RFK as happily as a wedding ceremony joining all that were gathered here together. At times it has seemed an arranged marriage, the RFK fans staring across at their new team and wondering "Who is this strange person playing shortstop?"

"You know, I loved going to minor league games in Bowie, but it's not the same," says a Methodist minister returning to a major league game for the first time in years.

"It's not the same as having a real major league team and I had forgotten what that was about," he adds.

"Whadya mean?" asks his friend.

"Well, it's great to sit out under an open sky, eat some peanuts, shoot the breeze, and drink some beer," he says. "You can do that at Bowie and it was fun, but this is different. I'm really into the game again."

"Yeah, I hear that attendance is really down in Bowie," says his friend a bit sadly. "I wonder if they are going to have Little Elvis this year at Bowie?" He continues, mentioning one of the many promotional nights held annually in Bowie.

"When I first moved to Washington in the seventies," says the minister, "we used to drive up to Baltimore and you could buy a ticket at Memorial Stadium minutes before the game. You could get good seats cheap and we watched some great teams play ball up there."

"The Nationals play some pretty damn good baseball," says his irreverent friend defensively.

"Well, I'm just saying I forgot what it was like. Are you listening to me?" says the minister, reaching across into his friend's bag of peanuts, wondering if his flock has strayed.

"You know I am," says the irreverent fan, smiling.
Who knew it was going to be this much fun?

## A Change Is Gonna Come

There is one thing that fans have not taken to. With all the zeal of a smelly dog staring at a washtub full of soapy water and bath time, Nationals fans have balked at the continuing influence of Bud Selig and Major League Baseball. The September papers, local ones like the *Washington Post*, and national dailies like *USA Today*, all have cataloged the lethargy of MLB, Inc., in handing over the reins of D.C. baseball to local ownership. Selig has dallied, holding the process hostage to the lease he ostensibly desires between MLB, Inc., and the Washington Sports and Entertainment Commission to govern the investment in the new stadium.

Peter Gammons of ESPN states that the city and MLB have dug in their heels on two very difficult and unyielding issues. The city fathers, who control the fate of the new stadium, want ownership from the Washington area. Gammons does not speculate on their reasons, but local politicians do not want to cede control of something that will cost local taxpayers so much. Selig wants to give ownership to Smulyan from Indianapolis, wants to hang onto his control of the franchise through third party loyalties, and D.C. will have none of it. There they stand like prize fighters slugging it out until one falls.

Before Selig, teams built their own stadiums, and owners like Clark Griffith used them for whatever they liked to make money, including hosting Negro League baseball in a segregated town. Then owners began the game of holding teams hostage, like Walter O'Malley as he tried to entice the great master builder himself, Robert Moses, into building a stadium for the old Brooklyn Dodgers. That game has been played now in many cities by Selig, and the only difference is that most of the fans who lost their teams during the westward march during the sixties got new teams and everyone benefited from the process. Baseball grew in new places, grew back in old ones. The Dodgers' relocation to California was part of a great expansion of the game, and within a relatively short time a second team was reestablished in New York, the Mets.

It was not an efficient process, but it had a positive outcome ultimately— millions of new fans across the country were welcomed to Baseball. D.C. fans hope the same can eventually be said of this prolonged process of resolving the Washington Nationals ownership and new ballpark. The dynamic of baseball as a local enterprise may disappear and it may not matter whether ownership is in LA or Hong Kong. It may not be worth the shouting to fans who will always be pawns in the game. Once, fans had representation in the process. Once, local elected officials had more leverage over the wealthy interests that owned the teams. That equation long ago melted into a pot of larger player salaries, TV revenues, and advertising dollars that has been stirred until anyone who grew watching was dizzy.

Perhaps that confusion is part of a shell game, perhaps not. One thing is certain, however; until fairly recently baseball was a growing sport, being played in new places and bringing in new fans. D.C. baseball should be viewed as part of restoring that trend. Yet while there are millions of happy new fans in the D.C. metropolitan area, just as many have lost out in Canada. Now fans can be taken out of the game completely, like those in Montreal, by corporate interests who move teams with all the fanfare of closing an auto plant.

For all its flaws, baseball was once more a part of the community. In August, in a game in Cincinnati, a six-year-old boy comes to a game with his grandfather. It is hot and muggy, and fans are drawn to Tony Perez bobblehead night, when each attendee can carry a prize home, a little something to remember. Before the first pitch is thrown, the grandfather slumps over in the seat next to the child, stricken with a massive heart attack. He dies in his seat, never revived by the doctors and EMTs that are summoned to treat him. The little boy does not comprehend exactly, but senses that he is alone. He has no one to turn to, no one to translate the tragedy for him about his deathly still grandfather.

A stadium security person leads the little boy away, promising to help him. Many people might see an element of worry there, about the security guard and who he is. But this is baseball; the stadium personnel are no different there than those wonderful green-shirted retirees who man each section at RFK. The man walks the young boy down to the bullpen away from the stands where his grandfather is dying and sits him among the coaches and players on the bench. He assures the little boy that his parents are coming to get him and for the remainder of the game and afterwards, the child is entertained by the Cincinnati players and coaches, Ken Griffey playing a key role.

The relationship between players and fans is a human one and one that has always been separated by artifice—by owners to begin with and now increasingly by corporate intrusion. The connection between the fans and players has always been troubled, starting with the Black Sox scandal when Charlie Commiskey was too cheap and malevolent to pay his players a decent wage. More recent history has featured the arrogance of George Steinbrenner, who treats his players like children, requiring them to conform to codes for dress and appearance. Then, of course, there is Bud Selig and Peter Angelos, who have sought to limit the access of millions of fans in major American cities because doing so may enhance their bottom line.

Baseball is but a tiny mirror reflecting back at us whatever we like of American culture. In the baseball mirror there is human drama of every type at a very personal level; then there is a touch of political and economic dispute, at times more than just a touch. Baseball, in moving toward large cor-

Fans heading to their cars for the last time in 2005.

porate ownership and larger corporate control of the media that bring the games to the fans, may be losing a bit of the intrinsic connection between baseball and the individual communities where it is played. That disconnect has been happening as players become corporate entities of their own, and it is worth considering what these corporate trends may ultimately mean to fans.

The first and best lesson of the game is to take what it gives and make the most of it. Whether it is a low inside pitch that you can turn on and drive out of the park, a high tight pitch that tests your mettle, or a pitch away that you have to take the other way, the game presents a situation, an opportunity to learn and grow, something to take away that makes you richer than when you started. As Pat Conroy opines, the losses teach as much as the wins. But this season for Nationals fans has been all about winning despite the many losses. We have won baseball back and there is no losing it in the cards. This is our winning season; everyone on both sides of the chalk lines can walk away a winner in 2005.

Washington fans have made the most of what the game has given them this year. They have proven their love of the game and formed a bond with a team that has it all—firebrands, unendurable slumps, and irascible old veterans. We have been there through the wonderful winning streak, that magic ride to first place. We were there for the losing, the close calls and the long frustrating nights. We have taken whatever the game has given us each night of the season and it has been a great ride throughout. Now we can watch the postseason knowing that the game will give us another season next year, and that is enough for now.

"You know, sometimes I still have a hard time believing this is all real, that we are arguing about a *D.C.* baseball team." says the gray-haired former Dodgers fan, an incredulous smile spreading across her face as she walks beside another fan on the way out of the stadium toward the parking lot.

"I know, it's hard to remember we didn't even have a team a year ago," says the gray-haired former Cardinals fan. "Here we are, complaining about the owners, like any other fans."

"Geez, what a long strange season it's been."

"Wouldn't change a thing though, would you?"

"No, I guess not. I would have been happy with anything to be honest, but playing great baseball right up 'til the end, who would have believed it?"

"Wait 'til next year," says the former Cardinals fan, and they both smile at the old baseball cliché, knowing that there will *be* a next year for the first time in a long, long time.

"It's a cliché, I know. But it's a great one to hear and have it mean something, you know?" says the ex–Dodgers fan, shaking her head and smiling.

"I'll see you next year," says the old Cardinals fan, waving as they both head for their cars and the traffic that leads away from RFK.

# Epilogue

More than a month after the start of the 2006 season, Major League Baseball, Inc., announced the result of the sale of the Washington Nationals. The Lerner family, developers who own extensive real estate in the metropolitan D.C. area, including some of the largest and most successful shopping centers, was awarded rights to the team. The Lerners, Ted and Mark, are local businessmen with strong ties to the community. Ted Lerner once worked selling programs at old Griffith Stadium. More important, they have pockets deep enough to develop a winning team for the nation's capital, something that was missing from every ownership group that owned the old Senators, from Clark Griffith to Bob Short.

Bud Selig deserves hearty thanks from D.C. area fans. Down to the wire there were many voices, allegedly speaking for Jerry Reinsdorf and others, who continued to lobby for out-of-town ownership. Mayor Anthony Williams deserves more praise than he will ever get for making the deal work. Others such as Mark Tuohey at the D.C. Sports and Entertainment Commission put in many long hours talking the deal through numerous D.C. council votes.

As the council debated the terms of the sale during the winter, there were many harrowing moments. There were nervous times when it seemed the Nationals would pull up stakes and move once again. The players, like the fans, may have been discouraged by the push and pull of politics, but it was part of a process as baseball sank its roots deeper into the soil along the Anacostia River—where the new stadium will rise sooner than we think. The 2006 Washington Nationals are having far less success than in their first season. Much of the magic is gone as are many of the wonderful players from that first team. We miss Vinny Castilla, Esteban Loaiza, Jamey Carroll, and now Livan Hernandez. But it is great to have a team and to see talented stars like Alphonso

Soriano take the field wearing the Nationals uniform and to see young stars of the future like Ryan Zimmerman. The team is building for the future, management says, and it is great to *have* a future, to think about the seasons to come. But for Nationals fans there will never be another inaugural season, season, never another season like 2005.

# Appendix: The Washington Nationals 2005 Season Recap

## 2005 National League Standings
## July 4, 2005

### East

| Team | Wins | Losses | Pct. | Games Behind |
|---|---|---|---|---|
| Washington | 50 | 32 | .610 | - |
| Atlanta | 46 | 37 | .554 | 4.5 |
| Florida | 42 | 38 | .525 | 7 |
| Philadelphia | 42 | 41 | .506 | 8.5 |
| New York | 41 | 41 | .500 | 9 |

### Central

| Team | Wins | Losses | Pct. | Games Behind |
|---|---|---|---|---|
| St. Louis | 52 | 30 | .654 | - |
| Chicago | 40 | 41 | .494 | 11.5 |
| Houston | 39 | 42 | .482 | 12.5 |
| Milwaukee | 39 | 43 | .476 | 13 |
| Pittsburgh | 35 | 46 | .432 | 16.5 |
| Cincinnati | 32 | 50 | .392 | 20 |

### West

| Team | Wins | Losses | Pct. | Games Behind |
|---|---|---|---|---|
| San Diego | 45 | 38 | .542 | - |
| Arizona | 41 | 43 | .488 | 4.5 |
| Los Angeles | 39 | 43 | .477 | 5.5 |
| San Francisco | 34 | 47 | .420 | 10 |
| Colorado | 28 | 53 | .346 | 16 |

## 2005 National League Standings
## October 3, 2005

### East

| Team | Wins | Losses | Pct. | Games Behind |
|---|---|---|---|---|
| Atlanta | 90 | 72 | .556 | - |
| Philadelphia | 88 | 74 | .543 | 2 |
| New York | 83 | 79 | .512 | 7 |
| Florida | 83 | 79 | .512 | 7 |
| Washington | 81 | 81 | .500 | 9 |

### Central

| St. Louis | 100 | 62 | .617 | - |
|---|---|---|---|---|
| Houston | 89 | 73 | .549 | 11 |
| Milwaukee | 81 | 81 | .500 | 19 |
| Chicago | 79 | 83 | .488 | 21 |
| Cincinnati | 73 | 89 | .451 | 27 |
| Pittsburgh | 67 | 95 | .414 | 33 |

### West

| San Diego | 82 | 80 | .506 | - |
|---|---|---|---|---|
| Arizona | 77 | 85 | .475 | 5 |
| San Francisco | 75 | 87 | .463 | 7 |
| Los Angeles | 71 | 91 | .438 | 11 |
| Colorado | 67 | 95 | .414 | 15 |

## 2005 Washington Nationals
## Opening Day Roster

### Position Players

| No. | Pos. | Name |
|---|---|---|
| 29 | c | Gary Bennett |
| 2 | inf | Jamey Carroll |
| 9 | 3b | Vinny Castilla |

### Pitchers

| No. | Name |
|---|---|
| 36 | Tony Armas |
| 56 | Luis Ayala |
| 53 | Francis Beltran |

## Position Players

| No. | Pos. | Name |
|---|---|---|
| 47 | of | Endy Chavez |
| 26 | of | JJ Davis |
| 6 | of | Jose Guillen |
| 15 | ss | Cristian Guzman |
| 24 | 1b | Nick Johnson |
| 23 | c | Brian Schneider |
| 18 | of | Termel Sledge |
| 32 | b | Jose Vidro |
| 7 | of | Brad Wilkerson |
| 28 | of | Tony Blanco |

## Pitchers

| No. | Name |
|---|---|
| 32 | Chad Cordero |
| 54 | Zach Day |
| 61 | Livan Hernandez |
| 39 | Joe Horgan |
| 21 | Esteban Loaiza |
| 34 | Tomo Ohka |
| 13 | Antonio Osuna |
| 22 | John Patterson |
| 52 | T.J. Tucker |

# 2005 Washington Nationals Final Roster

## Position Players

| No. | Pos. | Name |
|---|---|---|
| 29 | c | Gary Bennett |
| 26 | of | Marlon Byrd |
| 2 | inf | Jamey Carroll |
| 9 | 3b | Vinny Castilla |
| 19 | of | Ryan Church |
| 6 | of | Jose Guillen |
| 15 | ss | Cristian Guzman |
| 24 | 1b | Nick Johnson |
| 23 | c | Brian Schneider |
| 3 | 2b | Jose Vidro |
| 11 | 2b | Junior Spivey |
| 7 | of | Brad Wilkerson |
| 44 | of | Preston Wilson |
| 26 | 3b | Ryan Zimmerman |

## Pitchers

| No. | Name |
|---|---|
| 36 | Tony Armas |
| 56 | Luis Ayala |
| 48 | Hector Carrasco |
| 32 | Chad Cordero |
| 58 | Joey Eischen |
| 61 | Livan Hernandez |
| 21 | Esteban Loaiza |
| 38 | Gary Majewski |
| 51 | John Rauch |
| 22 | John Patterson |
| 30 | Mike Stanton |

# Index

Aaron, Henry "Hank" 229
Abreu, Bobby 41, 43, 127, 189–192, 194, 221, 249, 251
Accardo, Jeremy 59
Acevedo, Juan 189
Adelman, Bob 240
All Star ballots 90
All Star Game 149–152
Alou, Felipe 28, 56, 59–60
Alou, Moises 59, 232
Anaheim (Los Angeles) Angels 53, 95, 135–140
Angell, Roger 5, 130
Angelos, Peter 4, 47, 79, 115, 117, 132, 196, 239, 255
Arizona Diamondbacks 13–16, 17, 61, 211
Armas, Tony 61, 71, 80, 92, 102, 121, 132, 145, 148, 158, 164, 165, 170, 178–179, 187–188, 192–193, 200, 203, 217
Arquette, Rosanna 182
Astacio, Pedro 231
Atlanta Braves 17, 19–26, 35, 49, 56, 89, 96–106, 127, 147, 149, 163, 167–174, 185, 191, 211, 213–218, 223, 226–228
attendance figures for RFK (2005) 68, 102, 199, 228; final 2005 attendance 249–250; attendance in Montreal 135, 200
Ayala, Luis 15, 20, 37, 44, 51, 66, 70, 74, 101, 103, 105, 109, 113, 122, 132, 145, 147, 154, 169, 179, 183, 193, 203, 252

*Baby It's You* (Sayles) 182
Backe, Brandon 164
Baerga, Carlos 37, 53, 59, 61, 86, 88, 103, 105–106, 113, 119, 123, 125, 128, 130, 132, 135, 146, 155, 163–164, 170, 177–178, 193, 228, 235–236

Baez, Edgardo 120, 126
Baker, Dusty 151
Bako, Paul 176
BALCO 233
Balester, Colin 120
Baltimore Orioles 21, 28, 45–47, 79, 93
Barrett, Michael 65, 68, 69
Barry, Marion 4
Bartosh, Cliff 67, 69
*Baseball America Magazine* 118–120
Baseball Hall of Fame 27, 47, 76, 90, 230–231, 233
Beane, Billy 27, 29, 31, 84, 121, 201, 211
Beckett, Josh 106–109, 131, 170
Bell, David 221
Bell, James "Cool Papa" 47, 86
Beloit College 7
Beltran, Carlos 37, 43, 48, 50–51, 194
Bennett, Gary 38, 50, 64, 66, 71, 80, 105, 114, 148, 165, 172, 180, 183, 208
Benson, Kris 195
Bergmann, Jason 214–215, 230, 245
Berkman, Lance 165
Bernero, Adam 100
Betemit, Wilson 103, 105–106
Bissinger, Buzz 29, 57, 92, 118, 148, 149, 208
Black Sox scandal 255
Blanco, Tony 66–67, 72, 106, 111, 117, 132–133, 236
Blanton, Joe 121, 124
Blyleven, Bert 21
Bonds, Barry 56–58, 91, 190, 232–234
Boone, Bob 83
Boone, Bret 132
Boston Red Sox 4, 45, 63, 71, 111, 127, 233
Boswell, Tom 213
Bowa, Larry 91

265

Bowden, Jim 61, 67, 81–87, 89–90, 93, 100, 103, 121, 128, 138, 140, 153, 157, 163, 178, 219–221, 241; record with Cincinnati 83–84
Boyer, Blaine 230
Boyer, Ken 6
Bradley, Milton 52, 179
Bray, Bill 120
Brazoban, Yhency 178
Brinkman, Joe 111
Broadway, Larry 120
Brock, Lou 6, 27, 31
Brooks, David 72
Brower, Jim 60
Brown, Dana 119
Brown, Kwame 119
Bryant, Howard 57
Bump, Nate 109
Burkle, Ron 238
Burnett, A.J. 110, 112–113, 132, 245
Burnitz, Jeremy 66
Burrell, Pat 189, 191, 194, 221
Byrd, Marlon 67, 70, 71, 88, 94, 97–98, 100, 105, 107, 111, 113, 130, 132, 165–166, 207, 216, 224, 224, 235, 245–247
Byrnes, Eric 122, 157, 159

Cabrera, Daniel 136
Cabrera, Miguel 18, 108, 110, 112, 172
Cabrera, Orlando 26, 134, 137
Calero, Kiko 122
Camden Yards 2–3, 17, 87
can of corn 99
Canseco, Jose 27, 57
Capuano, Chris 73
Carpenter, Chris 94–95, 171, 206, 245
Carrasco, Hector 25, 37, 49, 51, 52, 69, 74, 101, 103, 154, 216, 221, 230–231, 236, 244, 248–249
Carrera, Miriam 150
Carroll, Jamey 21, 60, 66, 72, 73, 80, 89, 90, 95, 98, 103, 105, 107, 109–111, 122, 129, 133–134, 147, 154, 158–160, 193, 201–202, 204, 208, 216, 227, 245, 247
Carter, Gary 76
Cassidy, Jack 134–135
Castilla, Vinny 14, 18, 31, 36–39, 43–44, 48–49, 54, 58–60, 64–65, 69, 72–74, 80, 82, 91, 94–95, 98, 100–101, 106–107, 109–110, 113–114, 120, 122–124, 158, 162–163, 170, 180, 185–188, 191, 193, 201, 206, 213, 216, 232, 245, 252–253
Castillo, Luis 109, 112–113, 226
Chacon, Shawn 159–160
Chavez, Endy 31, 52, 54, 67, 70, 93, 192
Chavez, Eric 122
Chicago Bulls 46
Chicago Cubs 62–70, 110, 147–148, 180, 247, 249
Church, Ryan 15, 32, 41, 49, 59–60, 64, 67, 70, 71, 80, 88–89, 98, 101–103, 107, 109–110, 112, 114, 124, 145–145, 155, 162, 170–171, 179–180, 195–196, 202, 227, 235, 249
Cincinnati Reds 83–89, 162, 198–205, 241
The Citadel 244
Citizens Bank Park 190
Clark, Brady 72
Claussen, Brandon 88
Clayton, Royce 15
Clemens, Roger 90, 164, 186, 194, 247
Cleveland Indians 27
College of William and Mary 120
Collins, William III, 238
Colon, Bartolo 30, 139
Colorado Rockies 85, 157–162, 168, 179, 187
Comerica Field 149
Comiskey, Charles 255
Commissioner of Baseball 242; see also Selig, Bud
Conine, Jeff 170
Conroy, Pat 244, 255
Cordero, Chad 14, 15, 25, 44, 59–60, 66–67, 70, 74, 96, 99, 101–102, 104, 109, 120, 122, 125–126, 132–133, 139, 147–149, 152, 154, 164, 173, 179, 183, 193–194, 206–207, 216, 221, 223, 227, 230–232, 250, 252; as All-Star selection 150
Cordero, Wil 86, 146, 163, 220, 235
Cormier, Lance 14
Cormier, Rheal 42
Cousins, Derryl 108
Cox, Bobby 23, 28, 99, 101, 103–104, 211, 227, 230
Cronin, Joe 2, 149
Crosby, Bobby 124–126
Cruz, Devi 59, 219, 221, 227
Cy Young Award 121

Damon, Johnny 147
Darling, Ron 5, 87, 167–168, 170, 181, 187–189, 194–195, 203, 214, 216, 219, 244, 123
Davies, Kyle 218, 227
Davis, Doug 155
Dawson, Andre 76
Day, Zach 20, 32, 36, 53, 84, 93, 99, 153, 156–157
D.C. Sports and Entertainment Commission 209
DC United soccer team 120
Delgado, Carlos 19, 107, 112, 245
Desmond, Ian 120
Dewey, George (Admiral) 1
Diamond, Neil 249
Diaz, Einar 206–207
Diaz, Victor 39
DiMaggio, Joe 58
Disney Corporation 115
Dombrowski, Dave 151

## Index

Donelly, Brendan 136–137
draft, first year player 118–120
Drese, Ryan 137–138, 140, 147–148, 155–156, 164, 186, 191–192, 203, 220
Drew, J.D. 53, 118, 176
Dubois, Jason 66
Duncan, Dave 214
Dunn, Adam 199–200, 204
Dupuy, Bob 83
Durham Bulls 117
Duscherer, Justin 122

Easley, Damion 108, 113
Eckstein, David 93, 95, 206, 208
Edmonds, Jim 91–92, 94–95, 206–207
Eischen, Joey 39, 42, 51, 52, 90, 147–148, 154, 158, 183, 221, 231, 250
Eisenhower, Dwight D. 2
Eldred, Cal 207–208
Ellis, Mark 125
*Elysian Fields Quarterly* 7
Encarnacion, Edwin 200
Encarnacion, Juan 19, 111
Ensberg, Morgan 166, 186
Epstein, Mike 229
Epstein, Theo 29, 83, 85
Erickson, Scout 52
Erstad, Darin 135
ESPN 56, 86–88, 93, 118, 120, 122, 158, 162, 254; Sunday Night Baseball 34, 128
Estrada, Johnny 100–101
Eyre, Scott 59–60

Fehr, Don 239
Feliz, Pedro 59
Fillmore West 55–56
Flood, Curt 6
Florida Marlins 17–19, 49, 54, 70, 73, 96, 106–113, 121, 124, 167, 188, 223–226, 245–246
Floyd, Cliff 43, 49, 51, 235
Floyd, Gavin 223
Fox, Vicente 36
Franco, Julio 100–101, 103
Francoeur, Jeff 213, 217, 229
Furcal, Rafael 99

Gagne, Eric 176, 178
Gammons, Peter 56, 85, 118–120, 254
Gehrig, Lou 3
Gersh, Darren 240
Giambi, Jason 84
Gibson, Bob 6
Gibson, Josh 47
Giles, Brian 231
Giles, Marcus 24–25, 98–100, 103, 169
Gillette, Gary 241
Glaus, Troy 13, 61
Glavine, Tom 22, 36–37, 230, 236
Gleason, Jackie 70

Glenn, Ryan 71, 123
Goldstein, Tom 7
Gooden, Doc 36
Goslin, Leon "Goose" 2, 149
Le Grand Orange 76
Graves, Danny 87
Great American Ballpark 86
Green, Shawn 13, 58
Greene, Khalil 231
Griffey, Ken, Jr. 84, 87, 199–201, 204, 255
Griffith, Calvin 2
Griffith, Clark 1–2, 254
Griffith Stadium 46
Grudzielanek, Mark 95
Gryboski, Kevin 101
Guerrero, Vladimir 30, 76, 120, 134–135
Guillen, Jose 15, 18, 24–25, 32, 38, 41, 43, 44, 48, 58, 60, 67–69, 80, 82, 87, 89–91, 94–95, 100–101, 103, 105–107, 109, 111, 122, 130, 132, 137–138, 140, 147–149, 154–156, 158–159, 166, 170–171, 177–178, 189–190, 195, 199–202, 206–207, 215, 217–218, 235, 251–152
Gullett, Don 87
Guzman, Cristian 19, 23, 25–26, 31–32, 37, 44, 49, 50, 53, 59, 66–68, 72, 80, 98, 101–102, 106, 111, 121, 126, 129, 132, 134, 147–149, 158, 167, 170, 176, 186, 191, 193, 195, 201, 219, 225–226, 229–231, 245–246

Hairston, Jerry 65–66, 69
Halama, John 193, 105, 206–207, 220, 226
Halladay, Roy 80
Hallion, Tom 98
Halsey, Brad 15–16
Hammonds, Jeffrey 52, 59, 64, 73, 80, 88, 119, 220, 235
Hampton, Mike 22, 99–100, 163, 214
Haney, Fred 238
Harden, Rich 121, 123
Hargrove, Mike 130, 133
Harris, Brendan 86, 88
Harris, Lenny 113
Harris, Stanley "Bucky" 2
Harrisburg, PA, Nationals' Double-A affiliate 119–120, 226
Hatteberg, Scott 121, 125
Hayes, Rutherford B. 161
Heilman, Aaron 50–51
Helton, Todd 157
Helyar, John 116
Henderson, Ricky 27
Herges, Matt 60
Hernandez, Livan 13, 19, 38–39, 43–44, 53–54, 58, 61, 63, 67, 73–74, 88, 90, 91, 94–95, 106–108, 110, 123–125, 131, 135–136, 140–141, 145, 149–152, 154, 158, 161–162, 167–169, 171–173, 183–184, 186, 189–191, 195, 203–204, 206, 213, 216–217, 223–225, 228, 232, 236, 246, 251; as All-

Star selection 150; as World Series pitcher 150–151
Hernandez, Orlando 150
Hernandez, Roberto 235
Hershiser, Orel 54, 139
Hill, Aaron 80
Hillenbrand, Shea 80
hockey, in Canada 77–78
Hoffman, Trevor 183
HOK Architects 86–87, 117
Hollingsworth, Todd 66
home field advantage 97
home run distance at RFK 166
Homestead Grays 47–48, 62
Horgan, Joe 18, 37–38, 99
Houlton, D.J. 178
Houston Astros 163–166, 185–186, 226, 246, 249–250
Howard, Frank 4
Howard, Ryan 194, 221
Hudson, Luke 201–202
Hudson, Tim 22, 121, 214
Huppert, Dave 38
Hurricane Katrina 214

injuries, impact on Nationals 90, 145–147, 187
Ivany, Devin 120
Izturis, Cesar 176

Jackson, Jesse 238
Jackson, Yusef 238
James, Bill 29
Jenkins, Geoff 72, 74, 154
Jennings, Jason 161–162
Jeter, Derek 41
Jim Crow era 47
Johnson, Ban 7
Johnson, Dan 125
Johnson, Davey 83
Johnson, Kelly 101
Johnson, Michael 174
Johnson, Nick 14, 16, 18, 21, 31, 37, 40, 43, 49, 50, 53–54, 59, 64, 66–69, 71–72, 89, 91–92, 94, 98, 100, 102–104, 107–109, 112, 121–122, 124, 126, 128, 132–133, 146, 148–149, 153, 155, 159, 162, 171–172, 177–180, 187–189, 195, 202, 206, 209; NL Player of the Week Award 128
Johnson, Randy 15
Johnson, Walter 1–2
Jones, Andruw 98–101, 103, 105, 168, 214, 216–218, 226, 228, 230; as Braves home-run leader 229; as MVP contender 216
Jones, Chipper 25, 101, 105, 163, 168, 214, 216–217, 230
Jordan, Brian 98, 101, 105, 136, 191, 213
Jordan, Michael 78
Justice, David 54
Kansas City Monarchs 47, 62

karma, bad 162
Karp, Josh 120
Kasten, Stan 238, 240
Kearns, Austin 88, 204
Kelly, Kenny 163
Kendall, Jason 121, 125
Kent, Jeff 58, 167–168
Kim, Byung-Hyun 158, 187
Kim, Sun Woo 84, 89, 111, 119, 129, 135, 140, 155, 164
Kittell, Ron 130
KMOX Radio 6
Kolb, Danny 26, 106, 218
Koplove, Mike 126
Koskie, Cory 80
Kotsay, Mark 80
Kramden, Ralph 139
Kristol, William 175

LaBatts Breweries 78, 115
Landis, Kenesaw Mountain 7
Langerhans, Ryan 24, 103, 213
Larkin, Barry 84, 219
LaRoche, Adam 24, 102, 105, 168, 217
LaRussa, Tony 28, 29, 64, 92–94, 96, 101, 118, 138, 159, 207–208, 210, 215
Layne, Jerry 97–98
Ledecky, Jonathan 238
Lee, Bill "Spaceman" 183
Lee, Derrick 63–65
Leiter, Al 110–111
Leonard, Buck 63
Lewis, Michael 27–29, 31
Lidge, Brad 186, 250
Lidle, Cory 148, 193
Lieber, Jon 189, 191, 248–249
Lieberthal, Mike 41–42
Lilly, Ted 79, 145
lineup variations used by Nationals 30–32, 53
Loaiza, Esteban 15–16, 36–38, 40–43, 48, 52, 60, 63–66, 73, 82, 87, 94, 104, 123–124, 135, 145, 154–155, 163–164, 170, 176, 184, 187, 191, 195, 203, 206–207, 209, 216, 222–223, 226–227, 235, 252
LoDuca, Paul 110, 112, 170, 172
Lofton, Kenny 41, 43, 190–191
LOOGY 93–95, 113, 122
Looper, Brandon
Lord, Albert 238
Loria, Jeffrey 120, 135
Los Angeles Dodgers 43, 52–54, 176–180, 257
Lowell, Mike 109, 113, 170, 172
Lowry, Noah 58–59

Mabry, John 94
Maddux, Greg 22, 36, 63, 68–69
Madson, Ryan 192
Majewski, Gary 49, 52, 74, 95, 101, 105, 122,

147, 154, 178, 183, 195, 216, 221, 231, 235–236, 245, 249, 252
Major League Baseball Players Association 116, 239
Malek, Fred 82, 238, 240
Manuel, Charlie 190, 249–250
Manush, Hienie 149
Martinez, Pedro 37, 48, 120, 127, 134, 194
Mateo, Henry 64
Mathews, Eddie 229
Maxvill, Dal 90
Mazzone, Leo 19, 37, 68, 213, 229
McCann, Brian 217, 229
McGwire, Mark 4, 92, 206
McKeon, Jack 28, 109, 113–114, 245
McNamara, John 87
Mecir, Jim 113
Metro, as access to RFK Stadium 15, 20, 26, 43, 124, 198–199
Michaels, Jason 42, 192
Mientkeiwicz, Doug 37, 44, 51
Mile High Stadium 187–188
Miller, Jon 128
Miller Park 154, 249
Milton, Eric 87
Milwaukee Brewers 62, 70–74, 155–156
Minaya, Oscar 120, 167
Minneapolis Metrodome 31
Minnesota Twins 167, 221
Minor, Ryan 118
MLB, Inc. 26, 30, 57, 83, 119–121, 209, 219–220, 254; influence on ownership selection 237–242; negative influence on Expos 76–77, 138, 220, 241
Moehler, Brian 19, 171–172
Molina, Yadier 208
Molitor, Paul 70
Mondesi, Raul 24–25, 213
*Moneyball* (Lewis) 28–31, 73, 77, 119, 121, 210
Montague, Ed 97–99
Montreal, Canada 75–79, 86, 145, 151
Montreal Expos 11, 16, 20 25, 28, 35–36, 61, 75–79, 88–89, 119–120, 137, 153, 167, 219–220; economic demise of 76–79; minor league system 119–120
*Montreal Gazette* 76, 145
Morgan, Joe 33–34, 128
Morris, Matt 92–93
Moses, Robert 254
Mostel, Zero 34
Moyer, Jaimie 131–132
Mulder, Mark 121
Museum of Architecture, Montreal 76
Myers, Brett 40–41, 189

Nady, Xavier 231
NASCAR 58
Navarro, Dioner 176
Negro Leagues 27, 47, 62

Nelson, Joe 111
New Orleans, LA, Nationals' Triple-A affiliate 52, 54, 68, 70, 88–89, 93, 119–120, 214, 220, 235
New York Mets 5, 17, 36–39, 43, 48–51, 68, 127–128, 147, 149, 164, 167, 188, 194–197, 223, 226, 245, 251
*New York Times* 57, 114, 134, 169, 210, 233
New York Yankees 6, 56, 61–62, 84, 89, 233, 251
*The NewsHour with Jim Lehrer* 175
*Nightly Business Report* 239–241
Nitkowski, C.J. 93–95, 100, 112
Nunez, Abraham 95

Oakland Athletics 27, 71, 115, 121–126, 211, 220
Obermuller, Wes 71–72
Ohka, Tomo 18, 37–38, 43, 48–49, 58–59, 80, 84–85, 98, 110–111, 113, 129, 138, 140–141, 153, 155–156, 194, 220
Ohman, Will 66
Oklahoma Sooners 225
Olympic Stadium 76, 145
Omaha, NE, Royals' Triple-A affiliate 69
O'Malley, Walter 254
Ontario, Canada 75
Orr, Pete 103
Ortiz, Russ 15
Orza, Gene 239
Osik, Keith 247
Oswalt, Roy 163–164, 186, 249
Ottawa, Canada (minor league team) 129
Overbay, Lyle 72

Padilla, Vicente 192–193, 196, 220–221
Paige, Satchel 62
Palmiero, Rafael 174, 232–234
Patrick, Danica 95
Patterson, Cory 67–68
Patterson, John 15, 21 24, 49–51, 59–60, 63, 68, 89, 99–100, 102, 112, 131, 148, 154, 159–165, 165–166, 171, 179–181, 184, 188–189, 195, 202–203, 209, 213, 221, 231, 234, 238, 247, 251; as ERA leader in NL 189; pitching to Barry Bonds 234–235
Peavy, Jake 184
Pena, Brayan 102
Penny, Brad 179–180
Perez, Nefi 68–70
Perez, Tony 255
Pettite, Andy 186
Philadephia Phillies 17, 127, 134, 138, 149, 159, 189–194, 221–223, 226, 246–250
Piazza, Mike 37–39, 194, 236
Pierre, Juan 19, 109–110, 112
Piniero, Joel 128–129
Pittsburgh Pirates 83, 112
Players Association 83, 116
Ponson, Sidney 49

Potomac, VA, Nationals' Single-A affiliate 120
Pratt, Todd 194
Prior, Mark 63
Proctor, Mel 93, 123, 147, 167–168, 189–190, 194, 196, 219, 223, 253
Pujols, Albert 91–92, 102, 118, 138, 206–207, 216
Putz, J.J. 132
Pynchon, Thomas 21

Quebec, Canada 75
Quebec Nordiques 78

Raines, Tim 76
Ramirez, Horacio 19, 104, 216
Ramirez, Manny 54
Randa, Joe 183, 231
Randolph, Willie 49, 236
Rasner, Darrell 120
Ratcliffe, Theodore "Double Duty" 62–63
Rauch, Jon 52, 59, 89, 93, 231, 245, 251
Reidling, John 109, 113
Reinsdorf, Jerry 115, 242, 244–245
Reitsma, Chris 103, 216–218
Repko, Jason 177
Reyes, Jose 43, 195
Reynolds, Harold 56
RFK (Robert F. Kennedy) Stadium 4–6, 11, 13, 17, 20, 21, 31, 44, 47, 62, 67, 82, 89–90, 90, 96–97, 102–103, 112, 116, 121, 123, 127–128, 131, 134–135, 149, 157, 166, 170, 173, 175, 177, 180–183, 185, 187, 195, 198–199, 202, 204, 207, 209, 220–221, 223, 227, 229, 232, 246–247, 253, 255–257
Rijo, Jose 84
Ripken, Cal 3–5, 12, 45, 56, 79, 90, 118
Ripken, Cal, Sr. 28
Robinson, Brooks 118
Robinson, Frank 13, 26, 27–34, 37–38, 41–43, 49, 53, 56, 59–60, 63–64, 66–68, 70, 72, 80, 89, 94, 96–98, 103–105, 109, 111–113, 122, 124, 129, 132–138, 149, 151, 154–155, 169, 178, 183, 187, 191–193, 202–204, 206–208, 210, 214, 222–223, 225–226, 228, 235, 248–252; incident with Mike Scioscia 136–138; managerial style contrasted to others 210–211; record as manager 30
Robinson, Jackie 48
Robles, Oscar 176, 180
Rodríguez, John 208
Rogers, Kenny 140
Rogosin, Donn 47
Rolen, Scott 91–92, 206
Rollins, Jimmy 41–42, 190–191, 222, 248, 251
Rusch, Glendon 63–65
Russert, Tim 175
Ryan, Nolan 164

St. Claire, Randy 129, 139, 190
St. Johns University 5
St. Louis Cardinals 28, 70, 89, 91–96, 173, 205–209, 257
sale of Nationals 115, 238–240
San Diego Padres 182, 230–231
San Francisco Giants 15, 53, 56–61, 231
Sanchez, Duaner 180
Sanders, Reggie 206
Santana, Ervin 136
Savannah, GA, Nationals' Single-A affiliate 120
SBC Park 56, 58
Schmidt, Jason 59
Schmoll, Steve 177
Schnieder, Brian 18, 38, 44, 61, 64, 68, 97, 102, 105, 123, 129–130, 139, 147, 162, 165–166, 168–170, 176, 180, 187–188, 191–192, 195, 203, 209, 214, 217, 220, 226, 251
Schuerholz, John 211
Scioscia, Mike 137–140
Scott, Dale 136
Seattle Mariners 115, 128–134, 238–239
Selig, Bud 4–7, 28, 76, 82, 86, 115–116, 212, 220, 237, 254–255
Senators, Washington 1–3, 46
Seo, Jae 37, 195
September roster expansion 219–220
Sexson, Richie 129, 131, 133–134
Shay, Dave 180
Shea Stadium 195
Sheffield, Gary 156
Sheinin, Dave 130, 134, 210, 218
Shields, Mark 175
Shields, Scott 137
Shilling, Curt 15
Short, Rick 129–131, 230, 235
Sisler, George (hits record) 128
Sledge, Termel 23, 32, 38–39, 43, 52, 90
Sloes, Charlie 180
Smith, Ozzie 206
Smoltz, John 22, 36, 102, 229–230
Smulyan, Jeff 238–241
Snyder, Brad 48
Society of American Baseball Research 8
Soros, George 82, 116–117
Sosa, Jorge 214, 229
Sosa, Sammy 4, 91
Spivey, Junior 84, 129, 134, 148, 156
Stanton, Mike 169, 179, 194, 217, 220, 223, 236
statistics, strategic use of 28–32
Staub, Rusty 76
Steinbrenner, George 115, 255
steroids controversy 56–57, 174–175, 232
Strawberry, Daryl 36
Street, Houston 125
Sullivan, Cory 158–160
Suppan, Jeff 94, 206

# Index

Suzuki, Ichiro 128, 130–133
Svrgula, Barry 203, 219, 228
*Sweet Caroline* (Diamond) 249
Swisher, Nick 32, 121, 125

Tampa Bay Devil Rays 229, 240
Tavares, Willy 164
Tejada, Miguel 45, 91, 120, 234
television broadcast rights 26, 196
Texas Chainsaw Massacre 101
Thome, Jim 43, 54, 101
Thompson, Brad 208
Thornton, Matt 130
Tofu Dogs 178, 246
Toronto, Canada 75
Toronto Blue Jays 78–81, 145
Toronto Mapleleafs 78
Toronto Skydome 80
Torre, Joe 28
Towers, Josh 80
Trachsel, Steve 235
Tucker, T.J. 90, 103, 112, 130, 135
Turnbow, Derrick 155
Turner, Ted 103, 115
Turner Field 167, 215, 218

UCLA 120
Uecker, Bob 249
University of Miami 118
University of Southern California 238
University of Virginia 118–119
Urbina, Ugueth 193
*USA Today* 239, 254
Utley, Chase 42, 189–191, 194, 246, 251

Valdes, Ismael 231
Vargas, Claudio 37, 61, 71–72, 79, 84–85, 89, 93, 98, 140, 157
Varitek, Jason 140
Vasquez, Javier 30, 61
*Vegetarian Guide to DC* 178
Vidro, Jose 16, 18, 20, 24, 31, 38–39, 84, 90, 129, 156, 162, 167, 177, 179, 189, 191, 193, 215, 219, 245
Villone, Ron 130
Viola, Frank 5

Wagner, Billy 43, 193, 247, 249–250
Walker, Larry 207
Walker, Pete 80
*Washington Post* 114, 116, 120, 129, 166, 203–204, 210, 218–219, 228, 254

Washington Senators 1–3, 48
*Washington Star* 1
Washington Wizards 46, 53
Watson, Brandon 186–187, 227
Weaver, Jeff 52
*Weekly Standard Magazine* 175
WFED Radio 5–6
White, Matt 206–207, 220
Wilbon, Michael 203, 213
Wild Card race 185–186, 204–205, 213, 218
Wile E. Coyote 136
Wilkerson, Brad 5, 11, 16, 23–24, 32, 38–40, 43, 53, 59–61, 67–68, 72–73, 80, 91, 94–95, 99, 101, 105–107, 111, 128, 132, 134, 148, 153–154, 162, 167–168, 176–177, 180, 186, 189, 195, 205–206, 216–217, 226–227, 232, 236, 247, 252
Williams, Anthony 4
Williams, Ted 4
Williams, Tennessee 235
Williams, Woody 183
Willis, Dontrelle "D-Train" 18, 54, 70, 73, 90, 106, 110, 131, 223, 226, 245
Wills, Maury 27, 31
Wilson, Preston 84, 153, 154–156, 160, 170, 177–178, 180, 183, 189–190, 192, 195–196, 201, 209, 216, 221, 223, 227, 246; trade of 153
Winn, Randy 129, 132
Wise, Matt 154
Woods, Kerry 63
World Series 54, 106; Livan Hernandez in 150–151
Wright, David 39, 51
Wright, Jamey 187
Wrigley Corporation 115
Wrigley Field 147
Wynn, Early 139

Yabu, Keichi 124
Yazstremski, Carl 58
Young, Eric 183
Young, Larry 227
Yount, Robin 70

Zambrano, Carlos 63, 67
Zambrano, Victor 38, 49
Zimmerman, Ryan 118–120, 219, 230, 232, 235, 245, 248
Zito, Barry 121–122

www.ingramcontent.com/pod-product-compliance
Ingram Content Group UK Ltd.
Pitfield, Milton Keynes, MK11 3LW, UK
UKHW041931140426
5217IPUK00014B/413